WE SHALL SEE HIM
AS HE IS
(1 John 3:2)

Ἀριθμ.Πρωτ.823/1987.

Ὁσιολογιώτατε Ἀρχιμανδρῖτα κύριε Κύριλλε, Ἡγούμενε, καὶ οἱ λοιποὶ Πατέρες τῆς καθ' ἡμᾶς ἐν ESSEX Ἀγγλίας, Ἱερᾶς Πατριαρχικῆς καὶ Σταυροπηγιακῆς Μονῆς τοῦ Τιμίου Προδρόμου, τέκνα ἐν Κυρίῳ ἀγαπητὰ τῆς ἡμῶν Μετριότητος, χάρις εἴη ὑμῖν καὶ εἰρήνη παρὰ Θεοῦ.

Διὰ τῶν παρόντων Πατριαρχικῶν ἡμῶν Γραμμάτων εὐχαρίστως γνωρίζομεν καὶ ὑμῖν, διὰ τά καθ' ὑμᾶς, ὅτι εἰσηγήσει τῆς Κανονικῆς Ἐπιτροπῆς ὁ Γέρων Σιλουανὸς ὁ Ἀθωνίτης, ὁ καὶ πνευματικὸς πατὴρ τοῦ κτίτορος καὶ πρώτου Ἡγουμένου τῆς Ἱερᾶς ὑμῶν Μονῆς Ὁσιολογιωτάτου Ἀρχιμανδρίτου κυρίου Σωφρονίου, συγκατηριθμήθη τοῖς ἁγίοις τῆς Ἐκκλησίας, ἀντίγραφον δὲ τῆς ἐν τῷ Ἱερῷ Κώδικι τῆς καθ' ἡμᾶς Ἁγίας τοῦ Χριστοῦ Μεγάλης Ἐκκλησίας καταστρωθείσης καὶ ὑπογραφείσης σχετικῆς Πατριαρχικῆς καὶ Συνοδικῆς Πράξεως συναποστέλλεται τῇ καθ' ὑμᾶς Ἱερᾷ Μονῇ, μετά τῆς διαπύρου εὐχῆς ὅπως ὁ νέος οὗτος Ἅγιος τῆς Ἐκκλησίας πρεσβεύῃ ἀδιαλείπτως ὑπὲρ τοῦ Ἁγίου Ὄρους, οὗτινος μέγα τέκνον ἀναδέδεικται, ὑπὲρ τῆς Ἱερᾶς ὑμῶν Μονῆς καὶ ἑνὸς ἑκάστου ἐξ ὑμῶν τῶν ἐν αὐτῇ ἀσκουμένων καὶ ὑπὲρ τῆς Ἐκκλησίας ἁπάσης καὶ τῆς εἰρήνης τοῦ σύμπαντος κόσμου.

Ἡ δὲ τοῦ Θεοῦ χάρις καὶ τό ἄπειρον ἔλεος εἴη μετὰ τῆς ἀγαπητῆς ἡμῖν Ὁσιότητος ὑμῶν.

ϛαϡπη Ἀπριλίου α΄.

διάπυρα πρὸς Θεὸν εὐχέτης

Ἀριθμ.Πρωτ. 823.

Τοὺς ἐν τῷ μετὰ σώματος βίῳ κατορθώμασιν ἀρετῆς διαπρέψαν-
τας, καὶ μετὰ τὴν ἀποβίωσιν εὐλαβεῖσθαι καὶ τιμᾶν, ἐτησίοις τε
τελεταῖς καὶ ἐγκωμίων ὕμνοις γεραίρειν, ὅσιον καὶ τῷ τῆς Ἐκκλησίας πληρώματι λυσιτελέστατον πέφυκεν· ἐκεῖνο μέν, ὅτι ὁ τοῖς
κατ'ἀρετὴν βεβιωκόσιν ἀπονεμόμενος ἔπαινος εἰς αὐτόν τόν θεόν
ἀναφέρεται, παρ'Οὗ πᾶσα ἀρετή εἰς ἀνθρώπους, ὥς που θεολογῶν ὁ
τῆς θεολογίας ἐπώνυμος ἀποφαίνεται Γρηγόριος, τοῦτο δ'ἐπειδή ὁ
περί τά καλά ἔπαινος τούς μέν ραθύμους καί ὀκνηρούς πρός τήν
τῆς ἀρετῆς κατόρθωσιν παραζηλοῖ καί προτρέπεται, τούς δέ φιλο-
πόνως πρός αὐτήν φερομένους ἀκμαιοτέρους ἐργάζεται.

Ἐπειδή τοίνυν τοιούτοις ἐξόχοις ἀρετῆς κατορθώμασι διακέ-
κριται καὶ ὁ ἐκ Ρωσσίας καταγόμενος καὶ ἐν Ἁγίῳ Ὄρει, ἐν τῇ
Ἱερᾷ Πατριαρχικῇ καὶ Σταυροπηγιακῇ Μονῇ τοῦ Ἁγίου Ἐνδόξου
Μεγαλομάρτυρος καὶ Ἰαματικοῦ Παντελεήμονος, ἐπὶ ἥμισύν που
αἰῶνα βιώσας μοναχός Σιλουανός, ὁσιότητι μέν καὶ ἁγιότητι βίου
τύπον τοῦ κατά Χριστόν πολιτεύματος καὶ ζῶσαν ἀρετῆς εἰκόνα,
ποικίλοις δ'Ὀρθοδόξοις καὶ ψυχωφελέσι συγγράμμασι ἀποστολικόν
καὶ προφητικόν διδάσκαλον τῆς Ἐκκλησίας καὶ τοῦ χριστωνύμου
πληρώματος ἑαυτόν παραστήσας καὶ ἀναδείξας, φθάσας εἰς ὑψηλά
πνευματικά μέτρα καὶ γενόμενος σκεῦος τοῦ Ἁγίου Πνεύματος, ἀσκή-
σας ὅσον ὀλίγοι τήν ἀγάπην, καὶ διά πάντα ταῦτα τιμηθείς ὑπό τοῦ
θεοῦ διά τῶν χαρισμάτων ἰάσεώς τε ἀσθενῶν καί πασχόντων καί ἐκ-
πληκτικῆς διορατικότητος, ἡ Μετριότης ἡμῶν μετά τῶν περί ἡμᾶς
Ἱερωτάτων Μητροπολιτῶν καί ὑπερτίμων, τῶν ἐν Ἁγίῳ Πνεύματι
ἀγαπητῶν ἡμῖν ἀδελφῶν καί συλλειτουργῶν, πρός τήν θεάρεστον

./.

πολιτείαν καί τάς πράξεις καί τά κατορθώματα αύτοῦ ἀπιδόντες,
καί τῆς κοινῆς τῶν πιστῶν ὠφελείας προνοούμενοι, ἔγνωμεν, συνῳδά
τοῖς πρό ἡμῶν θείοις πατράσι τῷ κοινῷ τῆς Ἐκκλησίας ἔθει κατα-
κολουθοῦντες, τήν προσήκουσαν τοῖς θείοις ἀνδράσιν ἀπονεῖμαι αὐτῷ
τιμήν.

Διό καί θεσπίζομεν συνοδικῶς καί διοριζόμεθα καί ἐν Ἁγίῳ
διακελευόμεθα Πνεύματι, ὅπως ἀπό τοῦ νῦν καί εἰς τό ἐξῆς εἰς αἰῶνα
τόν ἄπαντα ὁ Γέρων Σιλουανός ὁ Ἁγιορείτης συναριθμῆται τοῖς ὁ-
σίοις καί ἁγίοις τῆς Ἐκκλησίας ἀνδράσιν, ἐτησίοις ἱεροτελεστίαις
καί ἁγιστείαις τιμώμενος καί ὕμνοις ἐγκωμίων γεραιρόμενος τῇ κδ΄
Σεπτεμβρίου, ἐν ᾗ μακαρίως πρός τόν Κύριον ἐξεδήμησεν.

Εἰς ἔνδειξιν δέ τούτου καί βεβαίωσιν ἐγένετο καί η παροῦσα
Πατριαρχική ἡμῶν καί Συνοδική Πρᾶξις, καταστρωθεῖσα μέν καί ὑπο-
γραφεῖσα ἐν τῷδε τῷ ἱερῷ Κώδικι τῆς καθ'ἡμᾶς Ἁγίας τοῦ Χριστοῦ
Μεγάλης Ἐκκλησίας, ἐν ἴσῳ δέ καί ἀπαραλλάκτῳ ἀποσταλεῖσα τῇ Ἱε-
ρᾷ τοῦ Ἁγίου Ὄρους Κοινότητι, πρός κατάθεσιν ἐν τοῖς οἰκείοις
Ἀρχείοις.

Ἐν ἔτει σωτηρίῳ ᾳϡπς΄, κατά μῆνα Νοέμβριον (κς΄),
Ἐπινεμήσεως ΙΑ΄.

ὁ Δημητουπόλεως Διονύσιος   ὁ Κασσανδρείας Γαβριὴλ

                             ὁ Λιτῆς καὶ Ρεντίνης

ὁ Δέρκων Κωνσταντῖνος   ὁ Ξανθουπόλεως Ἀθανάσιος

ὁ Ἡρακλείας Διονύσιος   ὁ Φιλαδελφείας Βαρθολομαῖος

+ DEMETRIUS, by the grace of God Archbishop
of Constantinople, New Rome and Oecumenical Patriarch,

To the Very Reverend Archimandrite Kyrill, Abbot, and to the Brethren
of our Holy, Patriarchal and Stavropegic Monastery of St John the
Baptist in the County of Essex in Great Britain –

Beloved children in Christ that are in my care — Grace be with
you, and peace from God. By this our Patriarchal deed with joy we
would inform you in so far as you may be concerned that in accordance
with the proposal of the Canonical Commission STARETZ
SILOUAN of Mt. Athos — spiritual father of the Very Reverend
Archimandrite Sophrony, Founder and first Abbot of your Holy
Monastery — is now numbered with the saints of the Church. A
transcript of the relevant Patriarchal and Synodal Act, duly constituted
and subscribed in the sacred Codex of our Great and Holy Church
of Christ, is herewith dispatched to your Holy Monastery, with the
fervent prayer that this new Saint of the Church may constantly
intercede in the behalf of the Holy Mountain, of the which he
manifested himself a goodly son; For your Holy Monastery and each
of you who strive therein; For all the Church; And for the peace of
the whole world.

The grace of God and His infinite mercy be with your beloved
Reverence.

In this Month of April 1988

+ Archbishop of Constantinople Demetrius
Fervent intercessor before God.

+ DEMETRIUS, by the grace of God Archbishop
of Constantinople, New Rome and Oecumenical Patriarch,

PROTOCOL No. 823

Right is it and exceeding profitable for the fulfilment of the Church
that they who excelled in virtuous deeds while in the flesh, and are
now departed this life, be venerated and honoured and glorified and
celebrated yearly, in that the praise accorded to them that lived
virtuously is directed to God Himself, Who is the source of every
human virtue, as we are told by Gregory the Theologian. And in as
much as the praise of good deeds inclines and exhorts the slothful and
idle to acquire virtue, while the lovers of virtue are made even the more
inspired.

In so much therefore as the monk Silouan, a son of Russia, who
for nigh half a century lived on Mount Athos in the hallowed
Patriarchal and Stavropegic Monastery of the holy and all-glorious
Martyr and Physician Panteleimon, did excel in such goodly feats of
virtue, and by sanctity and holiness of life did make himself to be a
pattern of life in Christ, and a living ikon of virtue; and in his divers
Orthodox and edifying works manifest himself to be an apostolic and
prophetic teacher of the Church and the faithful who bear Christ's
name; Who attained to high spiritual measure, and became a vessel
of the Holy Spirit, practising a rare love; and for all these things was
honoured by God with the gifts of healing of the sick and suffering,
and with an amazing intuition –

WE humbly, together with our most holy and right honourable
Metropolitans, our beloved brothers and Concelebrants in the Holy
Spirit — Mindful of his godly conversation, his works, and his conduct;
and careful of the general good of the faithful, DECREE, in accord
with the customary practice of the Church and our fathers before
us, to bestow upon him the honour due to holy men.

Wherefore we decree synodically, and do ordain, and in the Holy
Spirit direct that from this day forth and for ever more Staretz Silouan

of Mount Athos be reckoned with the holy men and saints of the Church; that he be entered in the Calendar of Saints, and venerated with hymns of praise, on the twenty-fourth day of September, on the which day he departed gloriously to the Lord.

In witness thereto, and confirmation, this our present Patriarchal and Synodical Act is made, drawn up and signed in the Sacred Codex of our Holy and Great Church of Christ, and transmitted without change or alteration to the Sacred Congregation of the Holy Mountain that it be laid in their Archive.

ANNO DOMINI 1987, on the 26th day of the month of November, Indiction XI.

+ Archbishop of Constantinople Demetrius

+ Jerome of Rodopolis	+ Photius of Imbros and Tenedos
+ Maximus of Stravroupolis	+ Chrysostom of Myra
+ Symeon of the Prince Isles	+ Gabriel of Colonia
+ Evangelos of Perga	+ Callinicus of Lystra
+ Constantine of Dercos	+ Athanasius of Helenoupolis
+ Joachim of Melitine	+ Bartholomew of Philadelphia

WE SHALL SEE HIM
AS HE IS

By

ARCHIMANDRITE SOPHRONY (Sakharov)

Translated from the Russian by Rosemary Edmonds

ST. HERMAN OF ALASKA BROTHERHOOD

2012

Originally published in 1988 by the Patriarchal Stavropegic
Monastery of St. John the Baptist,
Tolleshunt Knights by Maldon, Essex, England.
Reprinted with minor corrections in 2004.

American edition published in 2006 and reprinted in 2012
by the St. Herman of Alaska Brotherhood,
P. O. Box 70, Platina, California 96076 U.S.A.

www.sainthermanpress.com

Printed in the United States of America.

Front cover: Icon of the Transfiguration of Christ
by Theophanes the Greek, ca. 1403 (detail).

Publishers Cataloging-in-Publication

Sofroniĭ, Archimandrite, 1896–1993.
    We shall see him as he is / by Archimandrite Sophrony (Sakha-
rov); translated from the Russian by Rosemary Edmonds.—1st
American ed.—Platina, Calif.: St. Herman of Alaska Brotherhood, 2006.—2nd printing, 2012.
    p. cm.
    ISBN: 978-1-887904-13-1
    Originally published as: Videt' Boga kak on est', by the Patriarchal
Stavropegic Monastery of St. John the Baptist, Tolleshunt Knights by
Maldon, Essex, England, 1988.
    1. Sofroniĭ, Archimandrite, 1896–1993. 2. Spiritual life—Ortho-
dox Eastern authors. I. Edmonds, Rosemary. II. Title.
BX597.S65 S64 2006
248.4/819/092—dc22 0612   2006935797

Contents

Prologue

The Lord bade us take heed that neither our prayers, our alms-giving, our fasting, nor any good deed, be seen of men, lest we be like hypocrites seeking glory – which is not pleasing to our heavenly Father 'which seeth in secret' [cf. Matt. 6:1–18]. And not only Divine commandment tells us to conceal our inner life from casual eyes but natural instinct, like a 'categorical imperative', prohibits one from violating the sacred recesses of the soul. Prayer of repentance to the All-Highest is the intimate action of our spirit. Hence the wish to hide away out of sight, out of earshot, leaving the soul alone with God. This was how I lived the first decades of my repentance before the Lord. By the same token, bitter experience has more than once demonstrated how vital it is to avoid self-centredness if we are not to fall victim to the spirit of vainglory which bereaves us of God.

However, since becoming a spiritual confessor on Mt. Athos – over forty years ago – I have slipped into disclosing the gifts come to me from on High. And with the continuation of my mission as a confessor I find myself more and more often baring my soul before my brothers.

Now, old in years and approaching my end, wearied by physical infirmity and day to day cares, I notice that I am less sensitive to criticism. My path through life, my experiences may be somewhat out of the ordinary but their essential content I share with millions of souls worldwide. So perhaps this my confession – or, more accurately, maybe, my spiritual autobiography – will help others to interpret their own ordeals.

Of a certainty no initiative of mine provoked the happenings in my inner life. But God of His providence, which is known only to Him, vouchsafed to visit me and, as it were, communicate His eternal Being. His holy hand mercilessly cast me, His creation, into indescribable depths, where, stunned and appalled, I contemplated realities that transcended my understanding. This is what I shall attempt to write of now.

My mind did not immediately assimilate my experiences and long years went by before they were transmuted into dogmatic perception. It was not my habit to study the Scriptures or the works of the holy Fathers of the Church, or the writings of contemporary theologians and the theology taught at theological academies, for the sake of erudition. Before my visitation from God I would peruse the Gospels or the Epistles without understanding them. Life itself showed me that, without real experience of God or cosmic spiritual phenomena, possession of intellectual information does not reveal the meaning of religion – does not lead to experimental knowledge of Primal Being – of God, that is. By 'knowledge' I mean ingress into the very Act of Eternity: 'This is life eternal, that they might know thee the only true God' [John 17:3].

In the hours when Divine Love touched me I 'recognised' the approach of God. 'God is love; and he that dwelleth in love dwelleth in God, and God in him' [I John 4:16]. After my visitation from on High I read the Gospel with a different awareness – profoundly and gratefully rejoiced at finding confirmation of my own experience. This wondrous congruity between the most vital elements of my consciousness of God and the data of the New Testament Revelation is incalculably dear to my soul – a gift from above, God Himself praying in me. I believe this. Yet at the time I lived it all as if it were my personal state.

I was baptised almost as soon as I was born. According to the rites of our Orthodox Church all the members of my body received 'the seal of the gift of the Holy Ghost'. Was it not this 'seal' that rescued me from straying along alien paths? May I not attribute to it the many marvellous coincidences between my experience and the spirit of the Gospel revelation?

In this book I concentrate mainly on some of the happenings

8

which were vouchsafed to me. But at the same time I think it important to stress how the whole course of my life in God convinces me that every lapse from right understanding of Revelation inevitably reflects on the manifestations of our spirit in daily life. In other words – truly upright life depends on a proper understanding of God the Holy Trinity, as revealed to us firstly on Mt. Sinai, then through the incarnation of the Logos of the Father, and, lastly, the descent of the Holy Spirit on the day of Pentecost. These three phases of revelation concerning the Triune Divinity our Church sees as the only truth. And they are the foundation on which I structured my life from the first days of my return to Christ.

So then I entrust myself confidently to my reader, in the hope that he will include me also in his prayers.

The Grace of Mindfulness of Death

I find it impossible now to chronicle events of over half a century ago as I experienced them in my inner world. There is no keeping track of the soul's flight in the spiritual sphere, as the Lord Himself pointed out to Nicodemus – 'The wind bloweth where it listeth, and thou hearest the sound thereof, but canst not tell whence it cometh, and whither it goeth: so is every one that is born of the Spirit' [John 3:8]. At the present moment I find myself reliving various desperately painful passages which were ultimately to afford me precious knowledge and be a source of strength for the spiritual effort required of each one of us. What I went through is incised, as it were by a sculptor's chisel, on the body of my life, and it is this that enables me to speak of what the right hand of God has done with me.

As a child I would ponder on eternity. The interest came naturally as the consequence of childhood prayers to the Living God to Whom my grandfathers and ancestors had gone – and also because other children who were my friends liked to speculate, naïvely but in all seriousness, about this mystery. As I grew up I found myself reflecting more and more often on the infinite – on what goes on for ever. With the outbreak of the First World War the problem of eternity began to predominate in my mind. The news of thousands of innocent victims being killed at the front placed me squarely before a vision of tragic reality. It was impossible to come to terms with the fact of vast numbers of young lives being brought to a senseless, cruel end. And I might find myself drafted into their ranks, with the object of slaughtering people I did not know, who in their turn would be trying to annihilate me as quickly as possible. And if the will of evil powers could create such a state of affairs, where was the sense of our presence in this world? And I . . . why was I born? I had only just begun to perceive myself as a human being: my heart was aglow with good intentions, seeking perfection like all young people, aspiring to the light of universal knowledge. Must all this be abandoned? And in such a fashion? And abandoned to whom, and why? For what good?

The prayers that I had repeated as a child declared that those who had gone before me had died in the hope of God; but now, no longer a child, I had not a child's faith. Was I eternal, was everyone else, or were we all destined for the black night of non-being? At first I mused peacefully but soon the question spread like a mass of molten metal, and a strange feeling took abode in my heart – *of the futility of any and every acquisition on earth.*

Outwardly, however, I continued tranquil, often laughing and behaving like everyone else. Something was quietly happening inside me, and my mind, stripped of all other interests, concentrated its attention within. A gigantic plough crossed and re-crossed the vast expanses of my country, tearing up the roots of the past. Everyone felt goaded into action. There was unbearable tension on all sides. Furthermore, the world over, incidents were occurring which presaged the beginning of a new era in the history of mankind. But I was not particularly concerned. Life was crumbling around me but my personal cataclysm was more intense – not to say, more important – for me.

Why was this? At the time I could not reflect logically. My thoughts sprang from the state of my spirit. If I really die – that is, sink into non-being – it means that like me everyone else will also disappear without trace. So then, vanity of vanities . . . authentic life is not for us. All happenings in the world are naught but a wicked mockery of man.

My spirit's suffering had been provoked by the current catastrophic situation of the world outside and I naturally identified the general disaster with my personal fate: my extinction would mean the disappearance of all that I had learned, of everything with which I was existentially linked. And this, independently of the war. My inevitable death was not just mine, someone of no account, 'one of these little ones'. No. In me, with me, all that had formed part of my consciousness would die: people close to me, their sufferings and love, the whole historical progress, the universe in general, the sun, the stars, endless space; even the Creator of the world Himself – He, too, would die in me. In short, all life would be engulfed in the darkness of oblivion. That was how I then saw my own death. The spirit that held me in thrall detached me from the earth and I was cast into a sombre realm where *time* did not exist.

Perpetual oblivion, as the extinguishing of the light of consciousness, filled me with horror. This state of spirit settled in me, against my will. Everything that was happening in the world reminded me forcibly of the inevitability of an end to human history. A vision of the abyss was always there, only occasionally allowing me a moment's peace. My ever-increasing consciousness of death attained such force that the world, this whole world of ours, seemed like a mirage liable at any moment to vanish into an everlasting void.

The reality of this non-earthly, incomprehensible, 'other' order took hold of me, despite my efforts to evade it. I can remember myself as I was then, behaving in everyday life like any of my contemporaries though there were moments when I could not feel the earth under my feet. I could see it with my eyes in the ordinary way but in spirit I was moving over a bottomless abyss. To this was added another, no less painful occurrence – a barrier rose up in front of me which felt like a solid wall, heavy as lead. Not one ray of light – mental light, not physical – could pierce this wall which was not a material one. It stood there, oppressing me for a long time.

Apart from all that was taking place in the outside world – war, disease and like calamities – the feeling that sooner or later I was doomed to die caused me unbearable suffering. And then, without reflection on my part, the thought suddenly occurred to me that if man is capable of such profound suffering, he is by his nature a noble creature. The fact that with his death the whole world, even God, dies is possible only if he himself, of himself, is in a certain sense the centre of all creation. And in the eyes of God, of course, he is more precious than all other created things.

The Lord knows my thankfulness to Him that He showed no mercy on me and did not 'end his work which he had made' [Gen. 2:2] until He had lifted me to a vision of the Kingdom, be it only still 'in part' [I Cor. 13:12]. Oh, the terrors of that blessed period! No one could have the stamina voluntarily to subject himself to such an ordeal. It makes me think of the cosmonaut who pleaded frantically with those below to save him from death in space. The radio registered his groans but there was no way of going to his aid. Perhaps I may be allowed to draw a certain parallel between what that poor cosmonaut went through and my own experience when I felt myself sinking into the black pit. But my spirit appealed not to the earth below but to Him Whom I did not yet know but of whose Being I was convinced. I did not know Him but somehow He was with me, possessed of all the means for my salvation. He fills all things with Himself but from me He hid Himself, and I contemplated death not only in the body, in death's terrestrial forms, but in eternity.

So it was, passively, as it were, that profound being was uncovered in me. The material world lost its consistency, time its duration. I grew weary, not understanding what was happening within me. At that stage I was still entirely ignorant of the teaching of the Fathers of the Church, and of their experience. Consequent on such a vital lacuna in my cognition I got carried away by the mystical philosophy of the non-Christian East. In my folly I supposed that this would show me the way out of the snare into which I had fallen. I wasted a lot of valuable time. Incidentally, much later on, having more than once experienced loss of grace because of my vanity, I sometimes reflected what grief spiritual ignorance entails. But in my case it was precisely this unawareness that made it possible for me to carry for long years God's rich gift to me – the grace of *keeping death ever in mind*, a grace which the early Fathers prize so highly. Indeed, when I met with the writings of the holy Ascetics, praising the greatness of this gift, I fell into the danger of losing the awareness that I had acquired of my own vacuity.

In that unforgettable but far from simple or easy period of my life I was more than once tempted into fearful wrath against my Creator. Tormented because I did not understand what was happening to me, I wrestled with God, thinking of Him as a hostile Potentate – 'the bitter adversary who had summoned me from nothingness' [Pushkin]. All of us have the one natural root, and so I applied my personal circumstances to everyone else. My little mind rebelled in the name of all who were saddled with the superfluous gift of this life, and I regretted that I had no fiery sword with which to destroy the 'cursed ground' [cf. Gen. 3:17] and thus put an end to the whole preposterous farce. Quite a few other imbecile ideas occurred to me but these two were probably the most extreme. Fortunately, the bile never penetrated into my heart, which was otherwise occupied. Somewhere in my spirit hope lived on – more powerful than all the paroxysms of despair – that the Almighty could not be other than *good*. Were it not so, how could I have got the idea of a Good Being? And my inner attention concentrated on something intangible, yet real.

I shall never be able to express in words the peculiar 'riches and wealth' [Eccles. 5:19] of those days when the Lord, heedless of my protests, took me in His strong hands and wrathfully, so to speak, hurled me into the immensity of the world He had created. How can I put it? He was stern and severe but He opened out before me the horizons of another being. My peregrinations really did take me along the road to martyrdom.

The war with Germany was approaching its sorrowful conclusion for Russia. A few months before the end another conflict broke out – this time civil war, in many ways more grievous than hostilities against a foreign country. The vision of the tragicality of human existence became engraved, as it were, on my soul, and wherever I happened to be the thought of death clung to me. In a strange fashion I was split – my spirit dwelt in the mysterious sphere which I cannot describe, while my mind and affections continued as usual, like those of everyone else.

I was in a hurry to live. I did not want to waste a single hour, anxious to acquire as much knowledge as possible, not just in my own sphere of painting. I worked hard in my studio, which was spacious and quiet, and travelled about Russia, then in Europe. I lived for several months in Italy and Germany before settling in France, where I made many acquaintances, for the most part concerned with the arts. But I never said a word to anyone about my 'parallel' life in the spirit – nothing prompted me to such self-revelation. What was taking place in me proceeded from some superior source, independent of my will or any initiative on my part. I did not understand what was happening in me and yet I held it sacred.

The beauty of the world around combined with the miracle of the dawning vision enthralled me. But in my art I tried to sense, beyond visible reality, the invisible, timeless essence which afforded me moments of exquisite delight. However, the hour came when increasing mindfulness of death entered into outright conflict with my passion for painting. The struggle was neither brief nor easy. I became a sort of two-dimensional battleground: the grace of mindfulness of death did not descend to earth level but summoned me to higher spheres. Art began to define itself as something lofty, transcending the material plane, in its finest achievements touching on eternity. All this travail was in vain: the disparity was too obvious, and in the end *prayer* won. I felt myself caught between the temporal form of existence and eternity. At the time eternity presented me with its 'negative' aspect – death enveloped all things.

It is impossible here to relate the various ways in which extinction of all life that I contemplated manifested itself in my spirit. I can remember vividly one of the most typical of those days: I am reading, sitting at the table. I take my head in my hands, and suddenly I feel that I am holding a skull, which I ponder, as it were, from outside. (Physically, I was still young and normally healthy.) Puzzled as to the nature of what was happening to me, I tried to rid myself of the sensations that were interrupting the peaceful progress of my work. Quietly I told myself: I still have a whole life-time before me – forty or more years full of energy . . . And what happened? Suddenly there came the instinctive, involuntary reply, 'And suppose you have a thousand years – what then?' And the thousand years in my consciousness were over before I could frame the idea in words.

Everything subject to decay lost its value for me. When I looked at people, without thinking further I saw them in the power of death, dying, and my heart was flooded with fellow-suffering. I wanted neither fame from those 'dead mortals' nor power over them. I did not look to people to like me. I despised material wealth and did not think much of intellectual assets which afforded no answer to what I was seeking. Had I been offered centuries of happy life, I would have refused them. My spirit required eternal life, and *eternity*, as I realised later, stood before me, effectively regenerating me. I was blind, I had no understanding. Eternity was knocking at my door and my soul was locked tight in fear [cf. Rev. 3:18–20].

How I suffered! But there was no solution anywhere save in prayer that had been engendered in me: prayer to the still Unknown – or, rather, to Him Whom I had forgotten. Ardent prayer snatched me to its bosom, and for many years never left me, waking or sleeping. My torment continued for a long time, until my whole strength was exhausted. Then, quite unexpectedly, it seemed as if a fine needle pierced the thick wall, and a ray of Light gleamed through the hairline crack.

Someone who is ill often does not know what is the matter with him and recounts his subjective feelings to his doctor, expecting an objective diagnosis. In the same way I am now simply recording the 'subjective' history of what I experienced.

★

I discovered that the Fathers of the Church taught of this form of grace – *mindfulness of death* – which is an especial spiritual state, quite unlike just knowing that one day we shall die. It draws the spirit away from worldly attractions. As a force descending from on High it sets us above earthly passions, delivers us from the power of fleshly desires and attachments, and so naturally makes us live righteously. Though perhaps not in a positive form it nevertheless clasps us close to the Eternal.

Mindfulness of death affords us the experience of being free from the passions – though not yet the unqualified freedom manifest when Divine love is sovereign. Neither does this mindfulness of death have an altogether negative aspect – which would be the antithesis of love. It arrests the action of the passions and thus initiates a radical change in the whole of our life activity and way of looking at things. The fact that this mindfulness of death makes us see our death as the end of the entire universe confirms the revelation given to us that man is the image of God and as such able to contain in himself both God and the created cosmos. And this, too, is the first step towards the concretion in us of the hypostatic principle. The experience prepares our spirit for a more real perception of the Christian revelation and the theology based on acquaintance with another level of being.

When this constant mindfulness of death translated my spirit on to the eternal plane it naturally meant the end of my puerile preoccupation with painting, to which I had become a slave. Strait is the gate and narrow the way of our faith: the whole body of our life is covered with wounds, and our sickness reaches the point where the tormented mind falls silent, somewhere beyond time. When we drop out of this existential contemplation we discover in the depths of our heart new thoughts not of our devising – notions which anticipate future revelations of God. This blessed gift cannot be described in everyday words. Experience shows that it is assimilated only after a prolonged process of *self-emptying*. Then, beyond all expectation as it were, comes the uncreated Light to heal our wounds. In the radiance of this Light the 'narrow way' that we have traversed appears like the Self-emptying of Christ through which even such as we are granted sonship to God the Father.

To the degree that Absolute Being is revealed to us, so do we become more acutely aware of our nothingness and squalor. And this is terrifying. Nevertheless, I regret that in my old age the intensity of this blessed state has relaxed in me. The Lord gave me to dwell in the flow of His mercy though I did not begin to understand. 'God moves in a mysterious way . . .' But He did not leave me altogether in darkness – He brought me to the feet of Blessed Saint Silouan, and I saw that all my previous experience had prepared me to fathom his teachings.

Blessed be the Name of the Lord world without end.

2

On the Fear of God

Fear of God comes with spiritual enlightenment. Its nature is not to be explained by psychology. There is nothing animalistic about it. It has many degrees and forms, of which just now let us consider the one most effective for our salvation: fear of proving unworthy of God made manifest to us in Light that never sets. This righteous apprehension liberates us from all earthly terrors. Our Fathers, dauntless servants of the Spirit, withdrew into the desert to live among wild beasts and poisonous snakes, in conditions of utmost poverty such as people of our day cannot imagine. And they did this to be free to weep over their remoteness from their beloved God. Not everyone can conceive how it is that spiritual men who scorn all the things of this world can lament no less, and even more, than mothers over the graves of their sons. Hermits weep when they contemplate the black abyss within themselves: the roots of the 'knowledge of evil' grow deep and are not to be torn up of one's own strength. Those who are ignorant of this state of the spirit will never understand. Because this mystery is hidden from casual eyes it does not mean that God is a 'respecter of persons' [cf. Acts 10:34] but that grace is entrusted only to those who entrust themselves to Christ-God. And this grace is also the gift of God's love, without which tears will not flow.

Divine love begets reverent audaciousness. Thus a handful of Apostles, hitherto faint-hearted, after the descent of the Holy Ghost were filled with courage and took on the whole of the rest of the world in spiritual struggle. Nearly all of them suffered martyrdom. When the governor of Patras threatened St. Andrew with crucifixion the latter made the marvellous reply,

'If I feared the cross, I would not be preaching it'. And he was crucified, and hanging on the cross extolled the death on the cross of his Master, Christ.

Inestimable are the gifts of the Holy Spirit. Every true gift is none other than a flame of love. But for our hearts to become capable of receiving the love of Christ in its glowing manifestations we must all, every one of us, endure many trials. People who live lives of ease atrophy spiritually and remain impervious to divinely universal, Christ-like love. They live and die without their spirit rising upward to heaven. Gifts from on High are commensurate to our ascetic struggle. All who walk the way of Christ's commandments are regenerated in their very following of Him – some more, some less, depending on the ardour manifested. Through being crucified together with God the Word-made-flesh, grace descends on the believer, likening him to God made man. This great gift also embraces in itself life-giving theology through a real dwelling in the Light of love.

The grace of repentance is given to him who in full faith accepts Christ's *dictum* that if we do not believe in His Divinity and the absolute truth of all that He commanded of us, the mystery of sin will not be unmasked to us in its ontological profundity, and we shall 'die in our sins' [cf. John 8:21, 24].

The very conception of sin obtains only where the relation between Absolute God and created man assumes a purely personal character. Otherwise, we are left with nothing but some intellectual assessment of the perfection of forms of existence. Sin is always a crime against the Father's love. Sin occurs when we distance ourselves from God and incline towards the passions. Repentance is always bound up with abstinence from sinful leanings. Humanism, too, involves overcoming various vices. But in so far as ignorance of the deep-rooted essence of sin – pride – persists, this evil source remains entrenched and the tragicalness of history continues to increase.

The holy Fathers tell us that humility alone can save mankind, and pride alone is enough to bring us to the darkness of hell. But victory over the whole complex of the passions indicates the attainment of God-like being. All the passions find some sort of expression, be it figurative, psychological, fanciful. Fervent prayer of repentance ignores extraneous impressions and rational concepts. Other ascetic cultures likewise practise this detaching of the mind from visual and intellectual forms. But in the darkness of divestiture the soul does not encounter the Living God if prayer lacks due recognition of sin, and genuine repentance. It is possible, however, to experience a certain sense of release from the kaleidoscopic process of everyday life.

In profound grief at having lost God the soul naturally strips herself of material and mental images, and the mind-spirit approaches the border beyond which Light can appear. But this border, too, can remain impassable if the mind turns in on itself. Where the mind is so fixated, it can even see itself as light. It is important to know that this light is natural to our mind since the mind was created in the likeness of God, revealed to us as Light, in which there is 'no darkness at all' [I John 1:5]. Thus the transition is effected to another mode of thinking, to another and superior kind of understanding compared with scientific knowledge. Divested in a surge of repentance of all that is transient, our spirit, as from a high peak, sees the relativity and conditional character of all empiric cognition. And again and again I repeat, God is truly experienced either as purifying fire or as Light that illumines.

'The fear of the Lord is the beginning of wisdom' [Ps. 111:10]. This fear descends on us from on High. It is a spiritual feeling, firstly of God and then of us ourselves. We live in a state of awe by virtue of the presence of the Living God together with awareness of our own impurity. This fear places us before the Face of God to be judged by Him. We have fallen *so* low that our distress over ourselves turns into profound suffering, more painful than the torment of seeing ourselves in the darkness of ignorance, in the paralysis of non-feeling, in slavery to the passions. The dread is our awakening from the age-old sleep in sin. It brings us the light of perception – on the one hand, of our fatal condition and, on the other, of the holiness of God. It is an astonishing phenomenon – without its naturally purificative action the way to perfect love of God will not be opened to us. It is not only 'the beginning of wisdom' but of love, too. It will also alarm our soul with a revelation of ourselves, as we are, and bind us to God in longing to be with Him. Reverence before the God revealed to us is accompanied by dread. To realise oneself unworthy of *such* a God – there is the horror. To continue perpetually in hellish darkness, the nature of which we discover through the uncreated Light, invisible still but which lets us see, begets a vehement wish to break out of the chains of our fall, to enter into the sphere of eternal Light, to go to the God of holy love. Only through faith in God-Christ do we arrive at the true criterion of the realities of the uncreated and created worlds. But for this it is essential that all our being, both temporal and eternal, be founded on the steadfast rock of the commandments of Christ. A great many of us frequent churches erected by man but relatively few find the 'narrow way' which leads to the heavenly tabernacle not made by hands [cf. Matt. 7:14].

At the outset of our repentance we see nothing, so it seems, except our inner hell but in a strange fashion the Light still invisible to us now penetrates like a vital sensation of the presence of God within us. If we cling tightly to the hem of the Lord's garment, the miracle of our growth in God will expand continually and the wondrous countenance of Jesus will begin to show itself to us, and with Him we shall see how we men were projected by the Creator before the creation of the world. Lest the heart of man grow conceited by reason of 'the abundance of the revelations', Providence causes him to travel a steep path up to this knowledge that exhausts mind and soul and body. Sometimes God removes His hand from the ascetic and an alien spirit snatches the opportunity to disturb our heart and thinking. So we are never quite secure and even when the beloved God pours out great mercies on us we do not become 'puffed up'. St. Paul writes about this in his Epistle to the Corinthians: 'And lest I should be exalted above measure through the abundance of the revelations, there was given to me a thorn in the flesh, the messenger of Satan to buffet me, lest I should be exalted above measure' [Second Epistle 12:7]. Thus it was at the beginning of Christianity, thus will it be to the end of the history of this world. Indescribable are the gifts of our God. And how can we avoid being puffed up? Only with the help of that same Divine strength, for God Himself is Humility.

3

Concerning Repentance

I.

Our Father dwells 'in the light which no man can approach' [I Tim. 6:16]. Invariably He remains a great mystery to us, even when we are filled with a sense of His nearness. But man, too, created in the image of the All-Highest, is also a precious enigma and we must never cease trying to learn more and more about him and the loftiness of his calling 'before the foundation of the world' [John 17:24].

God is Absolute Being, the Principle of all principles. He revealed Himself to us as 'I AM', as Person – Hypostasis. Now we know Him through the Son, Who is of one substance with the Father, Who revealed the Father to us. 'No man hath seen God at any time; the only begotten Son, which is in the bosom of the Father, he hath *declared him*' [John 1:18]. We know the Father likewise through the Holy Spirit: 'the Comforter, which is the Holy Ghost, whom the Father will send in my name, he shall teach you' [John 14:26]. And this living knowledge has delivered us from all the absurdity of intellectual aspiring to some Supra-Personal Absolute, to Pure Being transcending all that is – in fact, to *non*-being.

The Logos – the Word that was in the beginning with the Father and the Spirit – started His mission by calling the fallen to 'Repent: for the kingdom of heaven is at hand' [Matt. 4:17]. He taught knowledge both of the Father and of the Holy Spirit. And They bore witness to Him. It was the Logos Who showed us the surest way to the Father – repentance.

Now at the close of my life I would sing praises to this grace of repentance, echoing the Psalmist of old:

My God, my God, great and wondrous are Thy works.
Thou art holy, O Thou that inhabitest Light inaccessible.
My fathers trusted in Thee, and Thou didst deliver them.
They cried unto Thee, and were delivered.
But I am a worm, and no man;
A reproach of men, and despised of the people.
But Thou art He that took me out of the womb;
Thou art my God from my mother's belly.
Be not far from me, and I will declare Thy name unto my
    brethren.

'Ye that fear the Lord, praise him,
For he hath not despised my affliction;
Neither hath he refused my prayer.
I sought him, and he hid not his face from me.
And now my praise shall be of him in the great
    congregation'.
                                                          [cf. Psalm 22]

'Whether in the body, I cannot tell; or whether out of the body, I cannot tell' [II Cor. 12:2]. That is just how it is when there is burning repentance. The contrite spirit in fatal longing after God the Saviour is totally drawn to Him. And man himself does not know when and how the change in him occurred: he forgets the material world and his own body. At the same time he continues to be himself as *persona*, to be aware of himself more firmly and clearly than he ever was in his customary everyday state. He experiences himself as incorporeal spirit, so to speak. In such moments of blessing from on High he receives knowledge of another form of being – indestructible being.

It could happen that my spirit would find itself in a kind of illimitable space which in strange fashion is transparent though there is no light as such. I do not know how to define that fathomless sphere. My spirit would be completely absorbed in prayer: I saw naught, knew naught, save God.

Paul the Apostle wrote to the Corinthians that he was 'caught up into paradise, and heard unspeakable words, which it is not lawful for a man to utter' [II Cor. 12:1–4]. What did he have in mind when he spoke of the knowledge given to him from on High as 'words'? Were they really words – our human words – or facts of the spiritual heaven whither he was 'caught up'? His account only partially explains what happened.

It is presumptuous of me but I think that St. Paul never forgot how he had 'persecuted the church of God' [I Cor. 15:9] and been blasphemous and a wrong-doer, and in his agony of repentance he was 'caught up to the third heaven'. I remember that I felt my apostasy from Christ to have been a vile crime against His love. I had known this love in my early childhood: He had vouchsafed me to live it. When I repented of my madness prayer swept me into another world. So it is when we recognise our benightedness – when the infernal essence of our sin is revealed to us, then we become receptive to the action of grace, be it as illumination by uncreated Light or some other form of being 'caught up', of knowledge or revelation.

The Fathers tell us that to be aware of our sin is a gift from heaven greater than a vision of angels. And I over a long period was spiritually blind: I did not see any sin in my break with the God of my childhood. I acted ignorantly [cf. I Tim. 1:13]. I supposed that I was improving on the Gospel, which I abandoned without antagonism, merely telling myself that it did not afford higher knowledge. We can only comprehend the essence of sin by faith in Christ-God, as the action in us of uncreated Light [cf. John 8:24].

It is a fact that man as non-determined *persona*, as spirit endowed with the freedom of self-determination, is able to perceive in himself a certain absoluteness, a 'divine nature', which, so to speak, does not require any other God. He can regard himself as related to and even of one substance with Primordial Being; decide on an act of self-divinization; return to his immemorial being. I was given to this delusion in my youth, swayed by books on far-eastern mysticism and encounters with people from lands that have cultivated such esoteric doctrines for thousands of years. It is no simple matter to rid oneself of aberrations of this kind – you are persistently haunted by the suspicion that the experiment was a failure because you were unable to strip yourself of all the transitory phenomena of cosmical existence. You ought to have 'put off' your personality, considering it merely a temporary form of existence that restricts at every level. In a word – willingly accept the disintegration of human personality in the nameless ocean of Pure Being – of the Supra-personal Absolute.

I could not help asking – who is it that perceives? Who is self-determining? And again – If I proceeded from the principle without beginning, how could such a profound degradation of my being have occurred? Why do I now seek so strenuously to be separated from the flesh in order to return to what I always was and, according to abstract thinking, have not ceased to be?

Meditation released me from the distractions and cares of everyday life, afforded me hours of intellectual delectation, swept me up into imaginary spiritual spheres, lifted me into loftier circles. Philosophically, my mind could not conceive of the Absolute Principle as personal. This was partly because I was under a delusion common in the society in which I moved – I was confusing the notion of the person with the notion of the individual, whereas theologically they are diametrically opposed. As a child I had been taught to pray to the Immortal Heavenly Father, to Whom my fathers and forefathers had gone. In my childish faith [cf. Matt. 18:3; Luke 18:17] Person and Eternity easily combined into one. Thus from an early age the question of Christian personalism, as I perceived it, came to be one of vital importance – could Being, Absolute Being, be personal? My straightforward 'eastern' experiment was on the whole an intellectual one – the asceticism of the mental divestment of all that is relative. Gradually I became convinced that I was on the wrong road – that I was abandoning true, real

Being for non-being. Authentic knowledge was not yet on my spirit's horizon.

This was a period of extreme tension. I felt like a tiny boat that is buffeted by the waves in the stormy dark, now riding high, now angrily hurled down. But He Whom I had discarded as 'unnecessary' did not turn away from me altogether, and Himself sought an occasion to appear to me – suddenly He put before me the Bible text, the revelation on Mt. Sinai: 'I AM THAT I AM' [Exod. 3:14]. BEING is I. God, the absolute Master of all the celestial worlds is PERSONAL – I AM.

With this Name distant prospects were revealed to me which stretched into the unattainable. Not in the form of abstract thinking but existentially this Personal God became over-whelmingly evident to me. The whole structure of my spiritual life was transformed. My spirit now knew, though not alto-gether, which direction to take: the light of the pole-star reached me and my mind rose to it. Yes, this God was dreadfully far away but not out of reach of our spirit. To be a god apart from this True and Only God was folly, worse than any other folly. And I gave myself over to desperate weeping, to bitter, scalding tears, as I realised the horror of my fall. The Lord granted me blessed despair. And when I wept over myself with profound weeping, not daring to lift my thoughts to Him, the Light appeared to me. Thus did He lay the foundation of my new life, having begotten in me tears of repentance. Everything that had hitherto attracted me in this world now lost its fascination, and thinking of naught else I plunged deep into prayer. I cannot say that the struggle to free myself of all that I had pursued so passionately was easy, or even brief. (Tearing myself away from my painting was particularly painful.)

By the grace of repentance the soul is lifted up to God, enraptured by the manifestation of Light. At first this Light is in no way visible but its warmth softens the heart. The soul is torn in two – torn between the horror of seeing oneself as one is and the surge of hitherto unknown strength through beholding the Living God. In a curious fashion despair over myself prevailed to such an extent that even when He was with me and in me I could not stop weeping for my sin, which appeared to me in its metaphysical essence to surpass all patent transgressions. A powerful desire to break with all that had gone before took the form of detestation of myself as I had been in the past. The positive side of my repulsion of my passions lay in the fact that at the same time it presented itself as an act whereby I placed myself in God made manifest to me.

In the intensity of hallowed self-hatred prayer finds powerful energy and becomes like a hungry flame. The spirit then lives at one and the same time both its own death and benightedness, and hope in God the Saviour. I have no doubt that the strength of my prayer was not my own – it came from God. It exhausted me, physically and mentally. Then a marvellous peace would invade my soul. The atmosphere of another life would embrace me tenderly, bringing a feeling of the presence of God, Who loved His creature man.

The struggle to 'cast off the works of darkness, and . . . put on the armour of light' [Rom. 13:12] is a painful one. The age-old experience of holy ascetics demonstrates irrefutably that pride is the principle obstacle to enlightenment by the Holy Spirit. In the prayer that the Lord gave me when I felt worn out, as it were, on every level, it seemed to me that I began to sense something of the humility enjoined by the commandments [cf. Matt. 11:29], for then the radiant sphere would reveal itself to my spirit. And there would be no incompatibility between my spiritual state and the action of God in me. The humility of God is searchless, unconditioned, without parallel: it is an attribute of Divine Love, giving of itself without measure.

Generation after generation of those who have prayed before us – and, indeed, the Holy Scriptures also – have addressed God after His theophany, in respect of His relations to us, His manifestations: God is Light, God is Truth, Love, Mercy, and much else. I would make bold to add: God is *humility*. Nothing that is unclean – which means proud – can draw near Him. Pride is abomination, the opposite of Divine goodness. Pride is the principle of evil, the root of all tragedy, the sower of enmity, the destroyer of peace, the adversary of divinely-established order. In pride lies the essence of hell.

Pride is the 'outer darkness' where man loses contact with the God of love. 'Men loved darkness' [John 3:19]. Repentance alone can deliver us from this hell.

Repentance is a priceless gift to mankind. Repentance is the God-given miracle that restores us after the Fall – the outpouring of divine inspiration that stimulates us to rise to God, to our Father, for eternal life in the Light of His love. Through repentance is our divinization accomplished – an indescribably momentous event. And this gift is born of Christ's prayer of Gethsemane, of His death on Golgotha and His resurrection [cf. Luke 24:45–47].

Pride is the dark abyss into which man plunged when he fell. Heeding his own will, he became spiritually blind and unable to discern the presence of pride in the impulses of his heart and mind. It is only when the uncreated Light descends on us through our belief in the Divinity of Jesus Christ that we can perceive the metaphysical essence of pride. The grace of the Holy Spirit enlightens man's heart and discloses the malignant, fatal tumour within him. He who has experienced divine love finds himself revolted by the poisonous fumes emanating from the passion of pride. Pride separates man from God and shuts him up in himself. However gifted he may be intellectually, the proud man will ever be outside the all-embracing love of Christ. Intoxicated in paradise by the sweet poison of Luciferian self-divinization, man went mad and became the prisoner of hell. Turned in, centred on himself, sooner or later he will end up in a tedious void – the void from which the Creator had called him into this life. Resorting for compensation to the world outside, he submits to perversions of all kinds and finds himself capable of every sort of crime.

The manifestations of pride are innumerable but they all distort the divine image in man. Outside Christ, without Christ, there is no resolving the tragedy of the earthly history of mankind. The atmosphere reeks with the smell of blood. Day after day the universe is fed with news of the slaying or torture of the vanquished in fratricidal conflicts. Black clouds of hate screen the heavenly Light from our eyes. People make their own hell for themselves. Unless and until we allow repentance to change us totally there will be no deliverance for the world – deliverance from the most terrible of all curses, war. Better be killed than kill is the attitude of the humble man of love [cf. Matt. 10:28; 5:21–22].

Our spirit dwells in a state of grateful delight when the Holy Mystery, which transcends the created mind, is revealed to us: the Living God with Whom we may converse. His greatness intimidates us. His humility startles us. And however high we may ascend in our reaching for Him with the whole strength of our being, we continue joyfully aware of the process of ascending, yet at the same time He appears to us more and more unattainable. And sometimes we grow faint. A kind of despair seizes us, we see ourselves about to fall – and suddenly He, unexpected now, is with us and embraces us with His love.

God is wondrous strange. The soul would like to ask Him, Where wast Thou when my heart was so heavy? but cannot find words, seeing Him with her. The point of being abandoned by God is to show us that we are not yet ready; that the path has not yet been followed to the end; that we must face still more exhaustive self-emptying, drink of the cup that He drank of [cf. Matt. 20:22]. And so, in reverent awe and in the light of growing hope the soul resigns herself, and the heart rejoices over the increase in her knowledge of the ways of God our Saviour.

The imaginative mind is not suited to theology. Aware of the harm of dwelling in the sphere of the imagination, Blessed Saint Silouan strove to stand before God with a *pure mind*. Man can acquire this condition by straining with his whole being for the repentance which the risen Christ gave to the world. There is no explaining this state of our spirit, nor can any description enable one to live it. To many it seems inconceivable. Indeed, 'with men this is impossible; but with God all things are possible' [Matt. 19:26]. Prayer with a *pure mind* is a rare phenomenon. The approach to it is, first and foremost, through profound grief of the spirit as it recognises the deprivation which nothing can make up for – separation from God. This grief is an agony, the pain of it worse than a knife. If not accompanied by repentance, it seems to me that the suffering can assume a disastrous nature and, maybe, lead to death. But where there is prayer, it is a wondrous gift of divine love. The agonising struggle rouses in the soul the hitherto unknown energy of prayer that throbs day and night. And unexpectedly, not by design, prayer becomes *pure*. Then does man really live in the radiant reality of the Holy Spirit. And for God and for himself he will appear in the full nakedness of his being.

In such prayer as this our spirit is freed from the spells of phantom truth, of the many obscure attractions in the darkness of ignorance.

To pray was natural for me from childhood. But a day came – one morning as I was walking along a street in Moscow – when the thought forced itself into my mind: the Absolute cannot be 'personal', eternity cannot lie in the 'psyche' of Gospel love . . . It was a curious business. The idea hit me like a hammer. I shall always remember the spot . . . I then began – it required a certain amount of effort – to make myself stop praying and go in for meditation of a non-Christian character. One night soon afterwards I was awakened in a way that I did not understand. I saw my whole room flooded with patches of vibrating light. My soul was troubled. The vision repelled me – I felt something like the aversion mixed with fear that one feels if a snake gets into the house. I left my room and went into the sitting-room, where I stayed a while before returning to bed. The light had gone and I fell asleep again.

Soon after this, while I was engaged in my meditations, which had developed a certain degree of intensity, I saw my thinking-energy like a faint light inside and all round my skull.

My heart, meanwhile, continued to live separately from my brain.

Years later, after the mercy of the High God had visited me, I noticed that the uncreated Light is tranquil, integral, steady, acting on the mind, the heart, and the body, too. In contemplating it one's whole being is in a state unknown to the 'earth'. The Light is the light of love, the light of wisdom, the light of immortality and wondrous peace.

After my new discovery of Christ my 'eastern' phase, which had lasted some seven or eight years, appeared to my spirit like the most abominable crime against the love of God, Whom my soul had known from early childhood. I was overcome by a sort of pious horror at the thought that I, faithless and a renegade, would for ever remain unworthy of *such* a God. It is not without pain that I recall now that terrible and withal wonderful period of my life. I would pray like one demented, weeping copious tears, afflicted to my very bones. As I prayed I would feel fire within me burning up everything. I do not know how I survived. I shall never be able to find words for that fire which I experienced, and the despair; and at the same time the strength that held me in ceaseless prayer of extreme tension for years on end. At the moment I understood nothing. But now I cannot find ways to show God my gratitude for His 'mighty hand' of the Holy Sculptor. I suffered in every fibre of my being. I marvel at Him: He converted my diabolical loathsomeness into something different, less remote from His ineffable Light.

I was granted long hours of such prayer, from which I never wanted to come back to this world. I have lost it. I live in dread: what will happen to me – shall I ever find what I let slip?

God showed His providence for me when He granted me the *grace of repentance* [cf. Luke 24:47]. At first this fearful yet blessed spell in my life was all hopeless grief in prayer often accompanied by a sense of *fire*. I did not recognise the nature of this fire – I did not even try to account for it, since my mind was wrapt in Him, in my God. The fiery flame burned something in me, not without causing me pain. Many years later, when I was on Mt. Athos and my spirit at peace, I would remember what I had gone through like a circumstance which had given me new birth and launched me into a new orbit, in another sphere of being. And I would give thanks to God.

The period of desperate repentance that I have just described, I am inclined to see as an *event*, perhaps not only for me. How is it possible not to marvel – in my 'putting off' of the temporary form of existence I travelled somewhere far from ordinary life. And lo, His hand reached me *there*. It was the moment of the second creation of myself by His will: I was called anew from 'non-being' into the light of life. How strangely it all happened, and went on happening.

In the impulses and actions which our reason justifies, we cannot see 'sin'. The real vision of sin belongs to the spiritual plane from which we plunged at the time of the Fall. Sin is recognised by the gift of the Holy Spirit combined with faith in the Personal Absolute, our Creator and Father. It is a question of our personal relations with Him, and of nothing else.

Marvellous is the moment of our living encounter with Him. Yes, I am a criminal offender against His love. I did not know Him as one should. But I cannot say that I was innocent in my ignorance. The soul in every one of us is intuitively aware of a certain conflict with our conscience before we perform the inner act of inclining our will to something that cuts us off from God. So it was with me in my youthful years when I accepted the idea suggested to me by Satan, as I have related above.

When I try to investigate the inner workings of my conversion to God after my fall, I picture it like this: The Divine Light, the Light of the Holy Spirit, is somewhere unseen and behind me, and from far away enlightens me, shows me the spiritual 'place' where I am. And the name of this place is – hell. I do not see the Light as such but it opens my eyes so that I behold the darkness in which I live. I cannot understand the darkness without the contrast of light. The invisible presence of this light creates a situation in which I gradually begin to contemplate the idea of my Creator 'before the foundation of the world' [John 17:24]. My new, still only incipient knowledge of the Living God leads me to perceive in Christ the very image in which we are made [cf. Gen. 1:26–27]. And my heart is filled with sadness: 'That's how we ought to be, each one of us, in order to live our one-ness, inviolate throughout the ages, with the Father of all that is. Oh grief, to be bereft of that! The idea of eternity was granted to me in my childhood: I was given a certain intimation of, or approach to, that experience of uncreated being. But I am dying in the senseless darkness of my ignorance on every plane'.

This darkness stood before me like a solid wall separating me from God, insuperable by myself. St. Paul called this wall 'the law of sin' [Rom. 8:2]. Our God is 'light in which there is no darkness' [cf. I John 1:5]. In other words, He refuses to be associated with our darkness. We must cleanse ourselves from the pollution that has hold of us. Otherwise, we shall not enter into the Kingdom of Truth and Light [cf. Rev. 21:27].

The moment I was given the grace of repentance I realised that I was in hell. However painful the route may sometimes be, there is no other gateway to Divine Eternity for the fallen sons of Adam. Profound grief over myself – but there, beyond, I see Light. The ecstasy of my joy in God torments me when I try to find expression for it. I was brought up to avoid high-flown language.* And now all language seems dull and lifeless, incapable of expressing my gratitude to God.

When God's touch, having first illumined us with light, sets us on a new, hitherto unknown and lofty path, we meet with two hells – one of repentance, the other of love. Repentance is

* As a young man my set despised superficial eloquence. 'Fancy talk' was 'indecent', as Turgenev's Bazarov protested to Arkady in *Fathers and Sons*.

tied up with the two commandments, the more important of which is, 'Thou shalt love the Lord thy God with all thy heart, and with all thy soul, and with all thy strength, and with all thy mind' [Luke 10:27]. We do not have this love, and it costs a mighty struggle to acquire it. The second, no less afflicting step is bound up with the other commandment, 'Thou shalt love thy neighbour as thyself' [Matt. 22:39]. The Lord never sinned [cf. John 8:46; Luke 23:41] and therefore had no need of repentance. But having taken upon Himself 'the sin of the world' [cf. John 1:29] He descended into the hell of love for our neighbour and went to the last extreme – that is, to the final limits of the second commandment. Not many know this hell because there is little love in us for our neighbour, which means every fellow human being, the whole vast multitude of mankind that has ever lived. Christ's divine love expends itself in the service of the entire human race, from Adam to the last man to be born of a woman. He gave His soul for His friends and His enemies. Could we perceive the real significance of the second commandment we should see that we are not yet started on our repentance. But if it were given to us to live the commandment to our utmost, then we should know the One God in Three Persons and our own immortality [cf. Matt. 16:28].

Our existence in the flesh makes it extremely difficult clearly to appreciate and live the absoluteness of the task before us. The flesh always imposes a certain veil of imperfection and ignorance. However, where there is complete faith, unwavering and free from doubt, the grace of the Holy Spirit gives to the burningly repentant sinner the experience of descending into hell, together with the experience of the hell of love and the resurrection of the soul while still in this life and this body.

One of the most difficult problems for the landscape painter is the constantly vibrating blue sky. Coloured photographs show the blue solid like paintwork on a car body. My description of my spiritual life with the constant repetitions may seem just as tedious, though actually it has been full of dynamic contrasts. But I take the risk and continue the task embarked on – to confess what I have lived through.

It was given to me to know the Living God from my earliest childhood. There were occasions when coming out of church I would see the city, then the whole world for me, lit by two kinds of light. Sunlight could not eclipse the presence of another Light. To think of it brings back the feeling of quiet happiness that filled my soul at the time. I have forgotten almost all that happened in that period of my life but the Light I have not forgotten.

When I was about eighteen I turned my back on the God of my childhood. I did not commit any crime punishable by law but my mind and heart were open to every sort of evil.

Our God is intangible, invisible, searchless. Inscrutable, too, are the workings of His providence for us. How did His gentle but powerful hand catch hold of me when with the stubbornness of youthful folly I rushed headlong into the dark abyss of non-being? The heavenly fire burned into me and its heat melted my heart. Bitterly repentant, I prayed prostrate on the floor. Oh, the shame I felt in those years! My arrogant attempt to surpass God, in Whose Name I had been baptised, confronted me like the nightmare it was. My sin felt like a suicide – not suicide of corrupt mortal flesh but a defection from the eternity of my Creator, Who of His immense love wished to give me His radiant infinity. But I had knocked on the doors of death, not in time but beyond its boundaries. I detested myself and for long years wept out of sorrow and shame.

I wept bitter tears [cf. Matt. 26:75]. I do not know – yet perhaps I do to some extent – how Peter wept after his denial of Christ, and how, according to tradition, he never forgot and so at the end of his life sought to be crucified upside down. Certainly, I do not remember having harboured any feeling of hostility towards Christianity when the idea of transcendental contemplation took hold of me. It merely seemed to me that I was abandoning the lower plane – the psychic, emotional 'Love God and love thy neighbour'. But when I realised the spiritual

37

significance of my aspirations – to repeat Adam's fall – I was horror-stricken and my prayer was marked by self-loathing. In that prayer of repentance my mind was not turned on myself. I did not analyse my condition. I trembled with fear, counting myself unworthy of forgiveness. I stood as it were before the dread judgment-seat of the Supreme Tribunal. My attention was entirely concentrated on my Judge. I had no words and I prayed dumbly, with no self-justification. There was no hope in me. Yet maybe it would be truer to say that I prayed with the hope that lies beyond all despair. Praying thus, I sometimes lost awareness of my body. (I would discover this only after I returned to my usual consciousness of the outside world.) At the same time my spirit would enter some mental sphere, the boundaries of which it is impossible to reach – perhaps because there are no boundaries. In this spiritual abyss I sought only God. I was entirely alone. Somehow I knew that if the Lord so willed He would come to me without difficulty, wherever I was. And He did so will.

Is this form of prayer called 'pure' because my spirit was divested of all creature things? I do not know how to describe what happened to me but in it, in this prayer, only God existed for me. In all creation there was only God and myself, a pitiful monster.

II.

Concerning Repentance and Spiritual Warfare

The whole of our earthly life, from birth to our last breath, in its final conclusion will appear as a single act without duration in time. Its content and quality will be seen at a glance. Imagine an absolutely clear glass filled with water. One look will tell whether the water is clean or not, and if dirty, how dirty. So will it be with us when we cross into the other world. Every impulse, however transient, of our heart, every thought, leaves its mark on the general sum of our life. Suppose that just once during the whole course of my earthly existence an evil thought crossed my mind – murder, for instance [cf. Matt. 15:19]. This single thought will leave a black spot on the body of my life, unless it be wiped out by repentant self-condemnation. Nothing can be hidden: 'There is nothing covered, that shall not be revealed; neither hid, that shall not be known' [Luke 12:2–3]. We often reassure ourselves with the thought that nobody saw us, no one knows what we think or do. But when we begin to strive our utmost to prepare for eternity, everything is different and we yearn to be rid of all that is soiled within us.

'If we say that we have no sin, we deceive ourselves, and the truth is not in us. If we confess our sins, he is faithful and just to forgive us our sins, and to cleanse us from all unrighteousness' [I John 1:8–9]. Through sincere repentance and vigorous self-conviction before God and our fellows the inner man is cleansed – the water in the glass, passed through the spiritual filter of repentance, becomes pure again. Hence, when I confess, I charge myself with every evil, since I cannot find any sin in the whole world that I have not committed, if only by permitting it to flash through my mind. The very possibility of such an impulse of my spirit shows my sinful state. And who can be quite sure that he is beyond the reach of wicked ideas? And where is the guarantee that the moment when a bad thought comes to me will not be transmuted into eternity?

So long as we have life there is the possibility of reformation; but what happens to us after we depart hence, we do not yet know. On the material plane a mass, given a sufficiently powerful thrust, can theoretically, once it has left the sphere of gravity, fly at great speed for ever in infinite cosmic space. Will it not be thus with the soul? Drawn by love for God, having left the body, the soul will go to God; or, contrariwise – having discarded God, she will be 'cast out into outer darkness' [Matt. 8:12], into the never-ending torment which is the opposite of a state of love. Therefore, in so far as we are able to see ourselves, we must throughly confess our sins lest we carry them with us after we die.

Direct resistance to evil or vain thoughts is not always the best way of combating them. It is often wiser to think on the Father's mighty, pre-eternal design for us. To know that even before the foundation of the world we were chosen to be perfect [cf. Matt. 5:48; Eph. 2:10 and 1:4–5] is vital if we are to live as we should. To minimise God's initial idea for us is not just an error but a really black sin. Those who do not see in themselves and, worse, do not see in their brethren any permanent worth become like wild beasts in their mutual relations, and readily take to slaughtering each other. Oh, what a paradoxical mixture is man – on the one hand he inspires delight and wonder; on the other, sad bewilderment at his cruelty and savagery. The soul decides to pray for the world but such prayer never attains its ultimate purpose, since no one and nothing can deprive people of the freedom to yield to evil, to prefer darkness to light.

Prayer offered to God in veritable and proper fashion, 'in spirit and in truth' [John 4:23] is an imperishable, inviolable reality. Psychologically we may forget about it in the bustle of daily life but it is preserved for ever by God Himself [cf. Luke 10:42]. On the day of resurrection and judgment all that we have done of good in the course of our life will stand at our side, to justify us; and, vice versa, all the bad will convict us if we have not repented in due fashion. Ugly deeds and unkind words can be wiped clean by tears of repentance, however odd and logically impossible this may seem. The negative consequences to ourself of our sins are healed; the bad effects of our behaviour towards our neighbours are effaced; fulness of life is reconstructed by divine power – not, though, through the one-sided intervention of God but always in conjunction with repentance and a right disposition, since God performs nothing with man without man's co-operation.

God's participation in our individual life we call Providence. This Providence is not at all like pagan fate. At certain decisive moments we do actually ourselves choose from the various possibilities that are offered. When different paths lie before us, then normally we ought resolutely to move towards the ultimate Good that we are seeking. This choice inevitably implies being ready to accept sacrifice. On such occasions our spiritual freedom is particularly obvious. In most cases, unfortunately, prompted by worldly considerations, people forsake the direction to the Kingdom of Light indicated by God. Thus does man fall into the deceptive round of passions that prevent him from seeing the wished-for dawn. Every choice, however, must involve suffering and self-denial. And when we elect for the will of God, then every sacrifice likens us to Christ: 'Father, if thou be willing, remove this cup from me: nevertheless not *my* will, but *thine*, be done' [Luke 22:42].

Every one of us must *nolens volens* suffer the mystery of death for the sake of becoming more like Christ. After we have crossed that still unknown threshold God our Father will lead us into the realm of eternal *day*. Such is our hope in Christ which must be realised, since all His promises are true and unfailing, as the age-old experience of our Church has shown.

The Gospel ('glad tidings') both begins and ends with a call to repentance. And the teaching of the holy Ascetics and the Fathers of the Church is permeated with the consciousness that every time man prays to God not as a sinner, his prayer fails to reach the Divine Throne, since the Son of God did not come to call to repentance those who think themselves righteous and so stand outside the truth [cf. I John 1:8] but those who acknowledge themselves to be sinners [cf. Matt. 9:13].

'The foul sea that lies between us and our image of paradise, we can cross only in the boat of repentance rowed by the oars of fear. And if the boat of repentance in which we cross the sea of this world to God is not rowed by the oars of fear, then we drown in the foul sea . . . Repentance is the boat, fear is the navigator, and love the divine harbour . . . Into this harbour come all that labour and are burdened with repentance, and when we reach [the harbour of] love, we have reached God' [Isaac of Syria].

41

Repentance lies at the root of our whole ascetic life. Ephraim of Syria left us the prayer to pray – 'Grant me awareness of my own transgressions'. Again and again I repeat that to see one's sin is a spiritual act of extraordinarily great price for all who seek the Face of the Living God. Indeed, this act is the working in us of God Himself, Who is Light.

Over the decades of my ministry as a confessor I have come to the sad conclusion that there are very few people whose hearts have shown them the real nature of sin. Most of us base ourselves on human morals, and if we do adopt higher standards, it is still not enough.

Of the various ways that lead to recognition of our sins the most important is belief in the Divinity of Christ, for which belief the love of the Holy Spirit descends on man. He who has had experience of the sacred fire of Divine love naturally strives to continue in this blessed state. And if he performs any act, or has any impulse, which results in a weakening of the feeling of Divine love, then this very lessening of grace, without words or rational analysis, is enough to indicate his defection from Divine truth. Then he resolutely turns to God in repentant prayer, through which forgiveness comes like a renewal in love. And the greater the grace felt during the hours when the Holy Spirit was with him, the more painful and profound will be his repentance. Such a man lives before God simply, without deliberating with himself, governed by love and fear of God. He could even rise to perfection in holiness, without being aware of it [cf. Luke 17:20].

Another means of recognising sin is to judge oneself against the Divine word. By keeping a mental check on our inner state we see that we are not following the commandments, and therefore offer repentance. If this method is to be successful it is essential to make a fervent study of the Saviour's law, for the commandment of God is 'exceeding broad' [Ps. 119:96] and His 'thoughts are very deep' [Ps. 92:5].

The human conscience and the human mind in their capacity to penetrate into the realm of the Spirit fall far below the commandments that we have been given [cf. I John 3:20]. Fulness of repentance involves both heart and mind which eventually merge into one in an act of genuine eternal life. 'God is love' [I John 4:8] and He knows Himself and us absolutely; and everything in Him is one. So man must attain, first and foremost, the state of Divine love, and then, knowledge of God [cf. I John 4:7–8] and self-knowledge – a penetration into the pre-eternal concept of God for man.

Here is an instance to illustrate my idea: St. Simeon the New Theologian writes concerning himself that over and over again a light appeared to him, and he loved the light and was drawn to it, but for a long time did not know Who this light was. At last, one day when the light appeared, he summoned up the temerity to ask, 'Who art Thou?' And he received the answer, and knew, that what appeared to him as Light was Jesus Christ. After that he not only dwelt in love but also 'knew' this love. The combination of what we experience with what we know brings certainty into our life.

Similar occurrences in the history of other ascetics lie at the root of the Church's teaching on the uncreated nature of the Light that appeared to them.

'And he said unto them, Thus it is written, and thus it behoved Christ to suffer, and to rise from the dead the third day: And that repentance and remission of sins should be preached among all nations' [Luke 24:46–47]. Inexpressibly great is the gift of repentance. It is linked with the ingress of our spirit into the Mysteries of the Unoriginate God, our Father. Only through repentance can we apprehend existentially the revelation of how the pre-eternal Council of the Holy Trinity conceived of man before the creation of the world.

Knowledge of God omnipresent is open to all reasoning creatures everywhere. But schools of theology and theological tomes are far from sufficient for its assimilation. In some inexplicable fashion true knowledge filters into our inmost being when He is with us. The operative in-dwelling of God in us means that we are introduced into the very act of Divine Being.

And this is precisely the way that our spirit is given the lively knowledge of Him 'which shall not be taken away' [cf. Luke 10:42]. The surest means to this good end is prayer of repentance as granted to us through faith in Christ.

Unless we contemplate the primary creative idea of God concerning man – unless we experience the *holiness* of God – regret over the loss caused by our fall will not be strong enough. We may suffer in our given situation; we may partly and at a distance, as it were, feel the Divine Fire, and, in so far as our understanding permits, repent. But quite a different repentance, total now, grips our whole system when the uncreated Light discloses our inner hell and at the same time allows us to sense the holiness of the Living God.

As we shed bitter tears over our sins, in miraculous fashion we become aware of God Himself in us, clasping us close in Fatherly love. No effort on our part can retain this delicate Spirit. It departs and once again we are plunged in the darkness of death. We seek Him but He 'that filleth all in all' [Eph. 1:23] is inaccessibly remote.

When I measure myself against the commandments of Christ – to love God with all one's being and one's neighbour as oneself – I do not possess the means to judge how far distant I am from my purpose. And it seems then that I still have not acquired repentance, though its flame has touched me and made itself known. I remember being impressed by St. Sisoe's plea when the eternal Lord appeared to him as he lay dying, 'Give me time to repent, O Christ'. His brethren standing round his sick-bed asked, 'Have you not repented yet?' And the Saint replied, 'Believe me, brothers, I have not yet begun to repent' – which his brethren interpreted as proof that Sisoe had attained the utmost perfection possible on this earth.

Paradoxical as it may seem, this is just the way in which we sense Divine infinity. Our weary thirst for the Living God torments us past bearing, wrenching our spirit from all created things to transport us into an indescribable pit of spiritual space, where there is nought and no one save the God of love and a vision of His boundlessness. We see no Light, as such, but nor is it dark, since in some strange fashion the abyss is transparent with nothing to hinder the eye from piercing the depths without ever reaching the far brink.

Those who believe utterly in Christ as God our Creator and our Saviour, in their agony of repentance are given the experience both of hell and of resurrection while they are still in the body. Repentance is not just a mental action, like a change in our intellectual approach to everything that happens in the world. This mutation is normally accompanied by a feeling of bitterness over oneself, as one is – the heart is filled with regret at the breach with the Holy God. There is no greater grief than this feeling that I am indeed the most wicked of all men and all things. The whole of our earthly experience is temporal but our relations with God lie outside time. Cast into the expanse of the eternal Spirit through prayer springing from hatred for oneself, we pray without reference to ourselves.

Contemplation of divine realities is possible only if one's spirit is to some extent in harmony with the object of contemplation. How, indeed, could anyone in the clutches of pride expect the *humble* Holy Spirit to dwell in him? Could anyone in a convulsion of hatred or other black passion behold the unimaginable Light of Divinity? Or 'despising even one of these little ones' [cf. Matt. 18:10] preach divine love? So then, it is only when a man consciously abides in the grace of the Holy Spirit that the vision of immortal glory and undying Light is vouchsafed to him.

Every true vision of God is a gift from the High God making us participants in His life, granting us humility and peace, wisdom and knowledge, love and goodness. When the uncreated Light finds a dwelling-place in us life without beginning is imparted to us. By virtue of this, those who are saved become 'without beginning' (not in essence but by grace).

Here on earth the measure of the gift that we have received

is based on the extent of our likeness to Christ in our thinking, our feelings, our supplications. For in us there must be one mind, 'which was also in Christ Jesus' [Phil. 2:5], 'Who in the days of his flesh . . . offered up prayers and supplications with strong crying and tears unto him that was able to save him from death' [Heb. 5:7]. Abiding in Christ's Spirit, we become sons of the Eternal Father and gods while still in this life.

It may not be out of place to emphasise that for the outside observer with no experience of Christian life there is nothing worthy of attention in such a bearer of im-material Light. The believer – often an ascetic in the desert – may be a pitiful creature in appearance, clad like a beggar, defenceless before the prince of this world, but his inmost spirit is that of a truly great man. The kingdom to which he belongs by the gift from on High is not of this world.

At first repentance is all bitter taste but soon we feel the energy of new life producing a marvellous change in our mind. The very movement towards repentance appears like a discovery of the God of love. The inexpressibly splendid image of Primordial Man is revealed to us more and more. Beholding this beauty, we begin to realise how terribly distorted the Creator's primary idea for us has become. The Light proceeding from the Father gives us the 'light of the knowledge of the glory of God in the face of Jesus Christ' [II Cor. 4:6]. He Himself said of this: 'No man can come to me, except the Father . . . draw him' [John 6:44]. The grace of repentance reveals in us the image of the Son of the Father. Oh, how painful the process is! Our heart is pierced as with a white-hot sword. How portray the horror that grips us? And how relate the act of God's recreation in us? The image of the only begotten Son of one substance with the Father, the *Logos*, kindles a strong desire in us to become like Him in all things. And once again we find ourselves in a paradoxical situation: we suffer but in a hitherto-unknown way. This suffering inspires us. It does not destroy. There is uncreated strength in it. We are cast into divine infinity. We are amazed at what is happening to us, surpassed by the majesty of it. We shrink into ourselves, knowing ourselves for what we are, while at the same time God comes forward to embrace us like the father of the prodigal son [cf. Luke 15:20]. Fear and trembling depart from us, giving place to wonder at God. He clothes us in rich garments. He adorns us with great gifts, the noblest of which is all-embracing love. Our initial suffering of repentance is transformed into the joy and sweetness of love which now takes a new form – compassion for every creature deprived of divine Light.

There is rapture, too, in that we begin to perceive God's will for us. We see ourselves drawn into the creative process of God Himself. We have collaborated with Him in our own restoration from our fallen and distorted state. And lo, He accepts us as co-workers with Him in His 'field'. Such are the consequences of our rebirth in the Spirit through repentance.

The Lord 'in the days of his flesh . . . offered up prayers and supplications with strong crying and tears unto him that was able to save him from death, and was heard in that he feared; Though he were a Son, yet learned he obedience by the things which he suffered; And being made perfect, he became the author of eternal salvation unto all them that obey him . . . Of whom we have many things to say' of the deep places of Christian life, 'and hard to be uttered' [cf. Heb. 5:7–11] to people lacking the necessary experience of this wondrous sphere.

'Unto all them that obey him' Christ constituted Himself the one path and does not refuse to make them like Him in prayer. What can I, the least of all men, say? In the course of my long life I have 'offered up prayers and supplications with strong crying and tears'. It was despair over myself, when measured against Christ's commandments, that led to such prayer. Sometimes the bitter self-hatred that cast me into an indescribable abyss would recede, giving place to light and love. I would think that my love was becoming 'sure and stedfast' – it seemed to me that I was on the threshold of that 'which entereth into that within the veil' [cf. Heb. 6:19] and would never want to return to the earth I had left. The Lord, however, did not vouchsafe to take me.

Many a time have I thought of how God called Moses out of the burning bush and sent him to Egypt, where for forty years he languished, struggling the whole while with the shabby passions of those it was his business to save – who themselves were not seeking salvation. Of course, I do not compare myself with the Prophets, or the Apostles or Fathers – it is just that here and there I seize on an analogy without which it would be impossible to find one's bearings. God in His measureless humility did not reject me but gave me to contemplate His Uncreated Light. Christ became my life. I worshipped Him and could imagine no parallel to Him. He is for me the one true Lord and God. I live in almost constant dread of forfeiting His mercy because of my perpetual stumbling. I may argue with Him, make innumerable attempts to avoid His cross, but still I embrace Christ's cross and somehow or other bear my own cross as ordained for me [cf. Matt. 16:24].

And now I bless my God Who has granted me regeneration in fervent repentance.

4

Spiritual Mourning

Here at the very outset I find myself in difficulty. How am I going to discuss tears with my contemporaries, who think it disgraceful to weep about anything at all? Of course, it *is* shameful to cry over transitory matters, like one's career or property, privileges or social position, health, and the like. But the weeping that we are to consider now applies to our relations with the Eternal God. This sort of weeping belongs on another plane of being. It is our response to contact with the Divine Spirit. The Holy Spirit came. One's heart surged with imperishable love, the mind was struck with a new vision, the spirit transported into the sphere of uncreated Being. The fire of Gethsemane prayer – of compassion for the whole suffering creature world – touched our fragile self and we surrendered to the power of Love. Thus did the Apostles and Fathers weep when they received the heavenly blessing. This fire is sent on the earth of our hearts by Christ Himself [cf. Luke 12:49].

Only on rare occasions does the holy power of this Love that proceeds from the Father flow into us to such an extent – it would be too much for our nature in its present state. Our regeneration usually begins with a manifestation of uncreated Light, which opens our eyes to the mystery of our separation from God, and the heart knows no other way save tears to express its sorrowful love before God.

It is naïve to think that one can follow Christ without shedding tears. Take a dry nut, put it under pressure and you will see the oil oozing out. Something similar happens with our heart when the invisible fire of the Divine word scorches it all round. In its brutish egoism and, worse, pride, our heart has turned to stone. But there truly is a Fire [Luke 12:49] able to melt the hardest metal or stone.

Whoever in the course of his life has never really felt the approach within himself of this Fire will not understand what I am talking about. The first Gospel word – 'Repent: for the kingdom of heaven is at hand' [Matt. 4:17] bids us make a radical change in our whole life, a change that can only be realised by the fusion of our ardent desire with the action of the heavenly Fire to soften the heart, which, once softened, is reforged by the blows of a powerful hammer.

Spiritual weeping is totally different from ordinary weeping. It is part and parcel of continuous mindfulness of God, in grievous sorrow at being separated from Him. Violent emotional crying exhausts the body, extinguishing its vitality, whereas spiritual weeping cleanses one from malignant passions and so quickens one's whole being, purging the mind of salacious images. Spiritual courage fills the soul, bringing release from anxiety and fear. The more deeply this penitent weeping takes hold of us, the more radically are we liberated from a whole series of seemingly natural needs, as well as from such destructive passions as pride and anger. The joy of liberation, hitherto unknown, drops anchor within us.

Only the man who has never felt the murderous power of sin within him could hold that the transfiguration of our nature as ordered in the Gospel is possible without tears. Stemming initially from bitter repentance, weeping develops into tears of rapture over Divine love. And this is a sign that our prayer is heard and through its action we are led into new imperishable life.

Spiritual weeping is a phenomenon of a heavenly order. Try as I may, I cannot recall ever crying as an adult, although my life-span has coincided with all the terrible events of our century. Many a time have I found myself not only in difficult situations but in mortal danger. But when Light was manifest to me and I saw the depths of my fall, weeping which I could not stop took hold of me – weeping that despair made insuperable. At first I wept for myself, appalled at my degradation.

Later on I wept over people unaware of God – I was flooded with compassion for them in their disastrous ignorance. And on Mt. Athos, especially in the desert during the Second World War, I would weep bitter tears for the world at large.

For a long while I was haunted by the thought, 'It is a fearful thing to fall into the hands of the living God' [Heb. 10:31]. It is dreadful to be bereft of God. Without the God of love nothing makes sense – the soul sees herself hurled into the darkness of death [cf. I Cor. 13:1–3]. The horror of this pitch darkness lies in the fact that it is not only outside me but inherent in me. But when the uncreated Light releases me from my inner hell, then all passion departs and I realise that the Almighty Lord can make even me like Him – a lord free from any extraneous power, invulnerable to any and every evil.

The changes in my inner state altered the character of my weeping. Sometimes both heart and mind would know a marvellous peace, and tears became 'sweet' because of love. But when the Spirit of the Lord retreated, and the breath of immortal life died away, a kind of distress – alarm, even – invaded my heart. Prayer would become a wearisome despair and for hours I would lie face to the ground. Worn out, I would cross to my hard couch. The tears would continue to fall, while weariness silenced the mind.

I would prefer to speak of these happenings quite unassumingly but then my reader might miss the mighty force of such phenomena which undoubtedly exceed the measure of man, for they are a gift from on High.

'God is a Spirit: and they that worship him must worship him in spirit and in truth' [John 4:24]. Christ's words, 'in spirit and in truth', admit of dual interpretation – 'the Spirit of truth, which proceedeth from the Father' [cf. John 15:26] and a spirit and truth in the man who confesses his sins [cf. I John 1:8–10]. The Holy Spirit descends upon man, who, as the image of God, by the action of the Divine Truth himself becomes true.

Our existential union with the God of Love presupposes the harmonious confluence of two wills – God's and man's. Such union takes place in a state of love. God, the Personal Spirit, and man *qua persona* are joined in one in the eternal Act of Divine Life. Thus do we come to know God.

Acquiring this Love is the ultimate purpose of Christian asceticism. Its achievement demands long and arduous travail. But by a gift from on High one can experience a Divine visitation in great strength at times when the soul, in a burst of repentance for her sins, becomes receptive to the coming of God. However, these preliminary visitations do not mean that once and for all we have achieved the state of salvation. They are still only 'the unrighteous mammon' which may be taken away for unfaithfulness. It is impossible to preserve this grace, to continue faithful in all things that it has taught us, without years of profound weeping [cf. Luke 16:9–12]. Whoever thinks otherwise would not find himself in agreement with the Fathers. We must strive to continue in the tradition of holiness that we have inherited from them.

The way of the Lord is this: He manifests Himself to man, and man apprehends His love in the uncreated Light, in timeless mode. I keep harping on the word 'love' but ontologically it contains wisdom not of this world and grandeur infinite in its boundless humility, all-conquering beauty and deep peace. When this love touches man God thereby makes him a participant in His Being, and this there are no earthly words to describe. We are possessed by one single longing – to acquire this Divine Love in such fashion that it becomes our nature, for ever inalienable.

When God sees that nothing in all the world can separate us from His love [cf. Rom. 8:35–39] there follows a period of trial, arduous indeed but without which we should remain ignorant of the depths of the created and uncreated forms of being. This is a cruel ordeal – an invisible sword cuts us off from the beloved God, from His never-setting Light. We are stricken on all levels. We simply cannot understand why it is that what seemed in prayer – prayer akin to the Gethsemane prayer – a definitive conjunction of love has given place to the hell of abandonment by God. The answer is to be found in the twelfth chapter of the Epistle to the Hebrews, particularly verses 26 to 29. But firstly and lastly we have the 'example' [John 13:15] of Christ Himself – on Golgotha, nailed to the cross, He cried out to the Father, 'Why hast thou forsaken me?', followed immediately by 'It is finished: and he bowed his head, and gave up the ghost' [Matt. 27:46; John 19:30].

And so the mystery of Divine Love is revealed to us – utter self-emptying precedes the fulness of perfection.

Love, the flame of which Christ cast into the soul of man, possesses an amazing attribute. It will lead him into depths and heights inaccessible to anyone else. It will enable him to master suffering of all kinds, even death itself. Time and again it will hurl him into indescribable infinity, where he will be 'alone', yearning to behold again the Light of the beloved God.

Such is the process for cleansing our nature infected by the poison of Lucifer. The way of Christ leads from a relative, constantly vacillating type of existence to an absolute, unshakeable Kingdom. It is natural that man's spirit should be restless when cut off from the perfect love of the Father – the result of the Fall. The image of God – man – seeks holy, immutable, absolute Good. And who can describe love for Him? Where find words powerful enough to express even a shadow of the grief felt by the soul separated from God?

Nothing but sacred love can cause the tears to flow from the Christian's heart. The Scriptures write that Jesus 'having loved his own which were in the world, he *loved them unto the end*' [John 13:1]. And only this 'unto the end' can account for His sweat that fell like 'great drops of blood' as He prayed in the garden of Gethsemane. Where there is no love there are no tears, even when ascetic striving goes to extremes like exhaustive meditation, prolonged fasting, rigorous living conditions faraway from the rest of the world – of all of which both Western Christianity and the non-Christian East provide many instances.

When the spirit of humility takes command of us the tears flow from the depths of our heart. Christ referred to this weeping when He said, 'Blessed are they that mourn: for they shall be comforted' [Matt. 5:4]. Comforted how? By the comfort that proceeds from the Holy Spirit, Whom Christ called the *Comforter* – comfort which is neither psychological nor physiological but *ontological*, having to do with Divine eternity.

Perhaps now we may briefly turn aside from general theological and ascetic arguments to look in more detail at the centuries-old experience of the Christian ascetics. Spiritual weeping varies in character, depending on the state in which the ascetic finds himself. There are the sweet tears which come with closeness to the God of Love embracing the whole man; but more often the weeping is a mixture of joy and sadness. To begin with, repentance brings bitter tears prompted either by the realisation of how enslaved we are to sinful passions, or because our feeling of grace is less acute, or there is the sore affliction of being deserted by God. It is possible to weep out of compassion for all humanity, for all creatures, even. Each of these forms of spiritual weeping cleanses one from all that pollutes in daily life and renews one's longing for the Divine World. Tears of love for God attach one's whole self to the Beloved Master. Mind, soul, and body, too, all flow together into a powerful current towards the uncreated Light. Such weeping shatters the tight coils of earthly existence and carries the spirit into heavenly spheres, liberated from the compulsions of sinful passions. It brings the experience of freedom from passion, of the hallowing of our whole formation.

The absence of weeping, according to the teaching of the Fathers, signifies that our prayer has not yet attained the first rung on the ladder ascending up to God. However, after the physical tears have drained away a different form of prayer may be accorded to us – wordless prayer, like a quiet feeling of the grace of the Holy Spirit within us, when the peace 'which passeth all understanding' [cf. Phil. 4:7] fills the heart. After bringing the utmost sacrifice of love to God, man is generally taken over by a delicate state of contemplation.

54

Spiritual weeping is an abundance of life springing vigorously from potent love, whereas ordinary weeping prostrates mortal man. Providence has installed me in a country whose people are trained from childhood not to cry; where tears are despised as unworthy of a civilized being. It is impossible not to respect such a culture but we must not forget that it is meant for those whose feet are firmly rooted in the earth's crust. The ascetic Fathers did not weep because they were deprived of temporal goods but they do insist on the necessity for spiritual weeping without which man's stony heart is incapable of love as taught by the Gospel. The mind of the Christian who weeps is totally directed towards the sphere of Divine eternity. The commandments of Christ refer exclusively to this. A whole multitude of circumstances unacceptable to those living the banal life of this world are disregarded by him who weeps according to God's commandment. Poverty holds no terrors for him, he will not be dismayed by insults or slights from the sons of this generation, nor by blows of any sort, because not only his mind but his feet, too, are lifted high above ground. He feels compassion for people, sorrows over them before God, but he does not share their interests, inspired as he is by his striving after immutable Truth.

Genuinely spiritual weeping derives from the Holy Spirit. With it the uncreated Light descends on us. The heart and then the mind find the strength to embrace in themselves the whole universe, to love all creation. Spiritual weeping is not aimless, having no object. It is directed to God and, abiding in God, man in tearful prayer for all humanity feels pity for the whole world. The Fathers counsel us to take care of this gift by keeping the commandments, lest we grieve the Holy Spirit through any sort of sin, but it cannot be cultivated because it does not belong to our created nature – it is grace, and the grace of God is not in our control.

There are times when out of love we weep profusely. But when we feel deserted by God tears dry up until only a single drop remains in the eye, like a trickle of warm blood oozing from a wounded heart. If you have not experienced the action of Fire from on High [cf. Luke 12:49], you will not understand this.

Again, I venture to remind my reader that ascetics stand with fear before the Divine judgment. It is not a transitory affair but a matter of eternity either in the Light of the countenance of the All-High or in 'outer darkness' [cf. Matt. 25:30]. Therefore ascetic strivers remain indifferent to their earthly circumstances. Their mind is in God and when this 'comfort wherewith we are comforted of God' [cf. II Cor. 1:4] comes from the Father of lights, he who weeps easily forgives all wrongs done to him, because his spirit is lifted from earth to heaven, and in the Holy Spirit he can love even his enemies.

'Therefore also now, saith the Lord, turn ye even to me with all your heart, and with fasting, and with weeping, and with mourning' [Joel 2:12]. The Lord Himself 'in the days of his flesh . . . offered up prayers and supplications with strong crying and tears unto him that was able to save him from death, and was heard in that he feared' [Heb. 5:7]. And precisely this path – 'strong crying and tears' – confronts every one of us who aspires to Divine eternity.

5

Wavering in Quest of the Unwavering

Christ is Living Truth. '*I am . . . the truth, and the life*' [John 14:6]: life without beginning, life totally unrestricted, unconditioned, co-eternal with the Father, inseparable from the Father, indissoluble. His Love and His Light touched me in the dawn of my life. But even this gift of grace did not preserve me from sliding into the dark abyss of the non-existent. As soon as I became adult I committed a great sin – on a mad impulse of ignorant pride I abandoned Him in favour of another, imaginary Supra-personal Absolute. Repressing the good habit of praying to the God of my childhood, I spent hours of meditation aspiring to absolute being. I stripped myself, so it seemed to me, of all that was relative, of all amalgams visible or invisible, physical or mental. Stubbornly I went into the darkness of ignorance, in order, by divesting myself of everything that was transitory, to arrive at What or Who transcended the boundaries of all that is inconstant. There were times when I experienced a certain peace and solace. In a more forceful impulse towards the unnameable, all-transcending Being-Nonbeing I saw my mind as light. I did not pursue anything on this earth except the Eternal, and at the same time in my painting sought to express the beauty proper to almost every manifestation of nature. It might be supposed that that period of my life was full of inspiration but I recall it far from pleasurably, now that I see how at the time I was indulging in a peculiar easing of the mind that was really suicide in the metaphysical sense.

I could never have got out of this erroneous situation of my own strength but the Lord had pity and caught up with me, perhaps at the last moment. He performed a miracle of mercy and came into my heart, which for a long while I had tried to disregard. I do not know how to relate in due sequence the spiritual events of those days. Suddenly, as it were, it became obvious to me that my artificial absorption in the abstract mental sphere would not afford me authentic knowledge of the First Principle of all principles. My austere 'putting away' of all that was relative had not brought real union with the One I sought. My mystical experiences had been of a negative character. It was not pure being that lay before me but death, complete and final.

The commandment to 'love God with all thy strength; and thy neighbour as thyself' [cf. Luke 10:27] in an unexpected fashion occurred to my mind in its evangelical context: existential fusion with God is effected through love. Thus what had formerly deflected me from the Gospel – when 'love' had appeared to be pitiable psychism that strange day as I walked along a Moscow street – now pierced my heart and mind like the light of true knowledge: existential union proceeds from the act of love. The Gospel conception of love goes incomparably farther than our psychical or sensual comprehension. The God of my childhood returned to me in the light of understanding.

Christian life is the conjunction of two wills: the Divine, eternally one, and the human, which vacillates. God reveals Himself to man in myriad different ways. He does not compel man. If we accept His approach to us with love He will often visit the soul with His meekness and humility. It can happen, as the history of the Christian faith testifies, that He may manifest Himself to man in great Light. The soul, having beheld Christ in the Light of His love, is drawn to Him. She cannot, she would not wish to resist this impulse. But He is Fire consuming us. Every proximity to Him involves painful stress. It is natural for us in our fallen state to recoil from pain, and we falter in our determination to follow after Him. But to remain outside His Light is likewise abhorrent. And so my spirit was faced with the choice between wrongly abasing myself and getting lost in the life of the world around, thus condemning myself to corruption, or accepting Christ's dread summons. When I chose the latter course I was reborn into life in the Living God.

The Lord knows with what fear and dread many of the pages of this my confession are written. Now at the end of my life I have decided to testify that the words of Psalm 34 have proved true for me on more than one occasion – 'This poor man cried, and the Lord heard him . . . O fear the Lord . . . for there is no want to them that fear him'. It is not at all a happy thing to see oneself as a 'poor man', to realise one's blindness. It is painful in the extreme to hear myself condemned to death for being what I am. Yet in the eyes of my Saviour I am blessed because of this very recognition that I am poor in spirit [cf. Matt. 5:3]. This spiritual insight is connected with the 'kingdom of heaven' revealed to us. I must see Christ 'as He is' in order to confront myself with Him and thus perceive my 'deformity'. I cannot know myself unless I have His Holy Image before me. My disgust with myself was, and still remains, very positive. But my aversion begat prayer of singular desperation which plunged me into an ocean of tears. I could not imagine any possible cure for myself – there was no way of transforming my ugliness into the likeness of His beauty.

And this frantic prayer, which shook me to the core, roused the compassion of the All-high God, and His Light began to shine in the darkness of my being. In profound silence it was given me to contemplate His clemency, His wisdom, His holiness.

Through the hell of my hopelessness came heavenly deliverance. New powers opened in me, a different eye, a different ear. I became aware of indescribable splendour. However, all this did not yet 'belong' to me – it was not yet mine. I was not through with wavering. I drifted away from the celestial radiance. I returned to my benighted state. And yet without any shadow of doubt I knew that the Holy Kingdom of Christ was the eternal reality, to be obtained after prolonged prayer.

'The kingdom of heaven suffereth violence, and the violent take it by force' [Matt. 11:12].

We must praise and glorify God when the possibility of perdition, not only temporal but eternal, is revealed to us on the one hand, and, on the other, the inscrutable Light of Divinity. The Scriptures speak of 'everlasting punishment' [Matt. 25:46]. But what does this mean? We do not yet actually know all the various forms of suffering that may come upon us after our departure from this world. But the same Gospel declares that 'the children of the kingdom shall be cast out into outer darkness: there shall be weeping and gnashing of teeth' [cf. Matt. 8:12]. For myself I imagine 'everlasting punishment' to mean that we shall appear unworthy to enter into the Holy Kingdom of Divine Love, the one place natural to our being.

'Repent: for the kingdom of heaven is at hand' is how Christ Jesus began His preaching [Matt. 4:17]. Repentance begets the strength of life in us – renews the dignity that man lost when Adam fell. Tearful repentance restores our capacity, which sin had destroyed, to receive the uncreated Light proceeding from God – from the Holy Trinity. But what did my personal experience show me? It proved to me that long years of weeping over my corpse-like state had not stablished my life in God: sin in one form or another still triumphed. Every sliding into sin saddens the soul. Moreover, we – I mean I – am very often unsure how right I am in my actions, or how far I am from a truly holy life. This is especially so when I find myself in conflict with people. We are haunted by the consciousness of our insufficiency and plead to the Lord, 'Forgive me, Thine unprofitable servant' [cf. Luke 17:10]. Of course, as a monk I am trained to condemn myself for everything – to 'keep my mind in hell'. But this demands much endurance. And only thus can we abate the see-sawing so wearying to heart and mind. Perfect steadfastness is the conclusive gift for eternity of God our Saviour.

There is no one who could embrace in one eternal act heaven

60

and earth and the nether regions save the Only-begotten Son, co-eternal with the Father. If we follow Him, determined to abide in the spirit of His teaching, there will be moments when we, too, will be irradiated by Light and in prayer embrace the earth, the nether regions, even heaven, and meet Eternity. 'Jesus Christ the same yesterday, and to day, and for ever' [Heb. 13:8].

Having delighted in the longed-for Light of Heaven, we then find ourselves in a dreadful predicament: the Holy Spirit leaves our house empty, abandoning us. It had seemed that we had attained the God we sought, that we contemplated the Mysteries concealed since before time in the womb of Divinity . . . and now suddenly we are like naked beggars again. Blessed are we when from the depths of ignorance and death we are transported into wondrous Light; but when we fall from the Light into our former darkness our pain is more acute than ever. It takes not a little while before we begin to understand the ways of our God. In His infinite love for us He hungers to communicate His all-embracing Plenitude but it is not for us to imagine acquiring this Plenitude in the confines of this earth. Here we are always as it were torn: drawn with all our strength to Eternity but convinced of our present body's incapacity to assume and steadfastly bear the fulness. At some point the Light shows infinity to our spirit but then inevitably recedes. True, somewhere in the depths of our hypostatic being this Light, which appeared in a flash but is eternal by nature, lingers, seen 'through a glass, darkly' [I Cor. 13:12]. The Lord rose from the dead and His risen body acquired the attributes of the spirit. This means that so long as we are invested with a body not transfigured by resurrection we cannot avoid painful faltering in our following after Christ.

It would be more normal for a man of my age to be preparing for death rather than writing a book. Besides, who am I to be recounting what happened in my life in the sphere of the spirit? I never had any such idea in the past. Indeed, I was never disposed to reveal my inner life – I considered its course to be the result of my fall, which later showed itself to me in its infernal nature. Many might have seen the inner conflicts that beset me as symptoms of incipient madness but somehow I knew intuitively that my case lay outside the competence of the dreary science of psychiatry. To appeal to professional doctors would have been a truly unforgivable profanation.

On the whole my days have passed without much outside contact. Because of this, I do not quickly arrive at conclusions. Now, however, I am not afraid of being seriously mistaken, supposing as I do that in our time millions of people of the most widely varying temperament and nationality live in a tragic merry-go-round of contradictions to one extent or another similar to mine. To become acquainted with a concrete case like mine may for some of them even prove helpful.

The spiritual life of every Christian has a specific rhythm or progression peculiar to him alone. But at the root of all there is the one Spirit [cf. I Cor. 12:4–11] and, consequently, the same ultimate purpose as contained in the commandments of Christ, summed up in the bidding, 'Be ye therefore perfect, even as your Father which is in heaven is perfect' [Matt. 5:48]. Hence the experience of one may coincide with that of many of the same faith engaged in the ascetic struggle at different times and in different circumstances, not only interior but external also. The same commandment of perfection is given for all eras, to all people. The commandments of the Absolute transcend all that is conditional or relative.

This spiritual life of the Christian is of an exclusively dynamic nature. Never static, its manifestations are innumerable. On the one hand this demonstrates its amplitude. On the other, it is an indication of the perfection we have not yet achieved: in the life of the very Divinity of the Holy Trinity the dynamic and the static merge into a unity that passes our understanding. And this unity contains the real stability as promised to all who genuinely repent.

The world is fast approaching the moment when 'we shall

all be changed . . . in the twinkling of an eye'; when 'the heavens being on fire shall be dissolved, and the elements shall melt with fervent heat'; when 'things that are shaken . . . are removed that those things which cannot be shaken may remain' [cf. I Cor. 15:51–2; II Pet. 3:12; Hebrews 12:26–28; Rev. 21:1]. To man will it be given to dwell in Divine fastness. And this is verily *eternal rest*.

6

The Bliss of Knowing the Way

In the early days of my life on Mt. Athos I remember asking one of the hermits to talk to me about prayer. Discerning in my request a wish to hear about prayer at its most sublime, he replied, 'Let us discuss what we are capable of. To talk of what is beyond us would be idle chatter'. I felt ashamed but still ventured to say, 'I really do want to know about more perfect prayer – prayer that surpasses me. Not because I am pretentious. No. But because it seems to me vital to glimpse a guiding star to check whether I am on the right path. In ancient times mariners took their bearings by an incredibly remote star. In the same way I should like to have a true criterion, however out of reach, so that I shall not be content with the little I have so far discovered'. The holy man agreed that this was not only permissable but right and proper.

As a young man I was constantly tormented by an urgent need to understand why I had been born into this world. Where are we all going? What could we attain to? Where is our 'end'? To be ignorant of all this is an unbearable nightmare, a perpetual torture. The object of my quest was a noble one. But at the very thought of the sheer unattainability of the One Whom I sought, I would lose all inspiration, and despair would envelop my soul. Better that I had never been born. Outwardly calm, inwardly I twisted and turned. I did not avoid alien (non-Christian) paths. But everywhere lay darkness. Eventually, regenerated, I met with Christ, Who had said, 'Be of good cheer; I have overcome the world' [John 16:33]. Likewise, 'The kingdom of heaven suffereth violence, and the violent take it

64

by force' [Matt. 11:12]. And He filled my heart with inspiration which has never since deserted me. Though not over-intimidated by difficulties, I realised the foolishness of daring to follow after Him. To overcome the world? To make Christ's victory my victory, which is what each of us is called to? If He said of Himself that He was 'the way', then it cannot be ruled out that at some time or other we shall be forced to engage in single combat against the entire universe. Was He not forsaken by all, even by the Father [cf. Matt. 27:46]?

The uniqueness of Christ's teaching was soon revealed to me. On the one hand, I am painfully conscious of my nothingness. On the other, I aspire to eternal God. Prayer to Him keeps the spirit steadfast before the Face of the Absolute – not my old abstract philosophical conception but a Living and Personal Absolute. Christ is revealed as having descended into hell and then risen into heaven, sitting on the 'right hand of the Father', containing in Himself all the fulness of Being. And He is our way.

'O Israel, happy are we: for things that are pleasing to God are made known unto us. Be of good cheer, my people' [Apocrypha: Baruch 4:4–5]. And we Christians are endowed by God vastly more than were all the prophets and righteous men before Jesus' coming on earth. When we realise this, we lift our voices and exclaim aloud: 'Blessed are we, the new Israel, hallowed Christians, for the Lord Himself hath desired so to be united with us that He and we are become ONE' [cf. John 17:21–23].

The Very Lord bore witness to this: 'Blessed are your eyes, for they see: and your ears, for they hear. For verily I say unto you, That many prophets and righteous men have desired to see those things which ye see, and have not seen them; and to hear those things which ye hear, and have not heard them.' [Matt. 13:16–17]. St. Peter wrote that to the prophets 'it was revealed, that not unto themselves, but unto us they did minister the things, which are now reported unto you by them that have preached the gospel unto you with the Holy Ghost sent down from heaven; which things the angels desire to look into' [I Pet. 1:12]. And St. Paul asserts that knowledge of the mystery of Christ 'which in other ages was not made known unto the sons of men . . . is now revealed unto his holy apostles and prophets by the Spirit'; that to him had been given grace to proclaim to the people 'the unsearchable riches of Christ; And to make all men see what is the fellowship of the mystery, which from the beginning of the world hath been hid in God' [Eph. 3:5; 8–9]. Like St. Peter he stresses the profundity of the mystery – even to the 'principalities and powers in heavenly places the manifold wisdom of God must be made known by the church according to the eternal purpose which the Father purposed in Christ Jesus our Lord: In whom we have boldness and access with confidence by the faith of him' [cf. Eph. 3:10–12].

It is natural for us to be drawn to the Supreme Good but our progression must begin with a descent into the abyss of hell. St. Paul, having repented of his past, says of Christ: 'Now that he ascended, what is it but that he also descended first into the lower parts of the earth? He that descended is the same also that ascended up far above all heavens, that he might *fill all things*' [Eph. 4:9–10]. And this is precisely our route after the Fall.

We are conscious of descending into hell since from the moment the image of pre-eternal man is shown to us we are more sharply aware of the depths of our benighted state. Our whole self is stricken with grief. The timeless anguish of the spirit surpasses any and every pain of the body. With all our might we pray for help from on High. Slaves of passion, cut off from God, out of the depths we cry, 'Come and heal me from the death which holds me fast . . . Come and drive out the evil in me . . . Come and do Thy will in me, for I am powerless to perform any good deed. I am captive in darkness hateful to me'.

Pride is both wickedness and darkness. Pride lies at the root of every sin. The Lord began His mission on earth with a call to repentance. The Greek word for repentance, *metánoia*, betokens a radical change in our attitude to the whole of life – a transition from our previous philosophy to a converse icono-graphic perspective – through humility ascent to the All-high, since through pride we fell into the darkness of hell. Thus does our repentance begin, which has no end on earth – the end is perfect likeness to the Christ-God ascended to the Father. Our divinization lies in perfect God-like humility.

When God draws us to Him, prayer of sorrowful repentance becomes all-devouring. Mind and heart are consumed with longing for the Holy of holies, for the Lord. And suddenly there is a miracle – something unthought-of, unheard-of, that has never happened before even in the heart [cf. I Cor. 2:9]: a ray of the uncreated Sun penetrates the blackness of the abyss wherein I lie. Is it possible to speak of the Light of this Sun? It comforts the grieving soul in His own peculiar manner. It brings peace to the agitated heart. It illumines the mind with a new vision. The soul that was dying is filled with imperishable life.

Our spirit yearns after the Father's love. Our psychosomatic formation enters into this prayer but can only go so far. When the heart is consumed with thirst for God, prayer purifies us from all that is extraneous and concentrates our longing for the Lord Whom we seek. When this happens we may lose all awareness of our body and the material world around us. I cannot say how this occurs but I do know that it has not been given to every man to cross this threshold. Many, having reached the border, take fright and draw back. Others, engrossed in their prayer, do not notice anything, and in a way which they remain ignorant of are caught up into another sphere of being, and forget the earth. The Divine hand performs this with such caution that man does not detect the moment itself, just as one does not catch the moment of falling asleep. It is only after his return to his normal awareness of the world that he realises that his spirit had departed from its usual state and been united with God. After such an event all the things of the earth are seen as transient and brittle. The soul recognises that the point of her existence is to be with God, in Him, in His eternity.

I once read a newspaper account of an engineer testing the jet engine of a 'plane who carelessly stepped into the air stream, which caught and lifted him high off the ground. Seeing what had happened, his assistant quickly switched off the engine. The mechanic fell to the ground, dead. Something similar happens to the man of prayer: after being caught up into another sphere he returns to earth 'dead' to fleshly interests and worldly gains. He will not seek any career. He will not be too upset if he is rejected, nor will he be elated by praise. He forgets the past, does not cling to the present or worry about his earthly future. A new life full of Light has opened before him and in him. The infantile distractions that occupy the vast majority of people cease to interest him. And if we judge the quality of life, not by the quantity of pleasurable, psycho-physical sensations, but by the extent of our awareness of cosmic realities and, most important of all, of the First and Last Truth, we shall understand what is hidden behind the words of Christ, 'My peace I give unto you' – said to the Apostles only a few hours before His death upon the cross. The essence of Christ's peace is perfect knowledge of the Father. So it is with us – if we know the Eternal Truth lying at the root of all being, then all our anxieties affect merely the periphery of our existence, while within us reigns the Light of life 'coming down from the Father of lights' [cf. James 1:17]. No temporary ease can afford us genuine peace if we continue in ignorance of the Principle of all principles.

Not many souls have the courage to step off the path trodden by the vast majority in this fallen world, to live according to Christ's commandments. Unquestioning belief in the Divinity of Jesus naturally generates spiritual courage. In their eagerness to follow the Lord some believers have suddenly found themselves on the edge of an abyss, too late to draw back. However, we have all got to cross the abyss in order to attain to Divine eternity. But what is it exactly that I have in mind? I am thinking of the deep pit of ignorance, the hopeless anguish of those condemned to death, the power over us of the blackness of this world [cf. I Tim. 1:13; Gen. 2:17; Luke 22:53]. To get across this black pit we need the energy of blessed despair. The action of grace in us takes the form of determination. The Light is seen in the distance. Drawn to it with unsuspected strength, we decide to hurl ourselves into the unknown, having called upon the sacred Name of Jesus Christ, God our Saviour. And what happens? Instead of having our head smashed against the rocks hidden in the darkness, an invisible hand appears, to carry us gently across the gulf. Without this friendly hand of the Living God not one of us could hold out against the storms and vicissitudes that beset the soul at such times. Formed of the dust of the ground, we make up a tiny fraction of the massive body of mankind from which it is not at all easy to escape, especially in our day when practically the whole universe is under the control of officialdom in general. One cannot appeal to the princes of this world for help: a small good turn from them and we risk losing our liberty [cf. John 14:30]. Our best 'gamble' is a childlike trust in God's providence in the pursuit of a life where first place is given to Christ.

'Ye have heard that it was said by them of old time, Thou shalt not kill . . . But I say unto you, That whosoever is angry with his brother without a cause shall be in danger of judgment . . . Ye have heard that it was said by them of old time, Thou shalt not commit adultery [Deut. 5:18]: But I say unto you, That whosoever looketh on a woman to lust after her hath committed adultery with her already in his heart . . . But I say unto you, Swear not at all . . . But I say unto you, That ye resist not evil . . . Ye have heard that it hath been said, Thou shalt love thy neighbour, and hate thine enemy. But I say unto you, Love your enemies, bless them that curse you, do good to them that hate you, and pray for them which despitefully use you, and persecute you. Whosoever . . . shall break one of these least commandments, and shall teach men so, he shall be called the least in the kingdom of heaven . . . *For I say unto you*, That except your righteousness exceed the righteousness of the scribes and Pharisees, ye shall *in no case* enter into the kingdom of heaven' [cf. Matt. ch. 5].

I went in dread of breaking the Lord's commandments and so perishing. At that painful but blessed time, to live according to the Gospel commandments for me meant walking a tight-rope stretched between two precipices. After a short while this changed into a vision of the arms of Christ on the cross stretched out to draw into a whole a world split by enmity between its peoples. It was all so far beyond me that I felt 'crucified' by Christ's teaching. In despair I prayed, and then I saw the body of the Lord hanging like a marvellous bridge between heaven and earth. The way for the Christian is crucifixion. 'If any man will come after me, let him deny himself, and take up his cross daily, and follow me' [Luke 9:23]. For the soul this means both the subtle joy of 'knowing the way' and considerable dismay at the immensity of the task.

Words cannot describe the terrible privilege of walking the mysterious tight-rope. By the same token those who have departed into the next world do not try to appear to us who are still in the flesh, to tell of the majesty awaiting us in the new sphere.

Uniting in Himself both God and man, the Lord calls us to follow after Him. On this exalted path our spirit, having over-come the passions that drag us down, contemplates the hitherto unknown, unimaginable realities of the Divine sphere of Being. Just as a heavy body projected beyond the gravity of the earth finds itself subject to 'celestial mechanics' and moves with a speed impossible on earth, so our spirit enters into the infinity of 'mental' space pierced by Light bearing witness to the unorig-inate Truth and our immortality.

The touch of Divine love on the heart signals the first step on the shore of the heavenly side of the abyss, and new birth from on High into eternity. This love is apprehended as Truth, as Light, as the Kingdom. All thought of death, of enemies, of what pertains to this earth disappears from our consciousness, and, thus liberated, the spirit lives another form of being.

On return to her customary condition the soul feels sad at her loss: she would have preferred not to come back, though the sensation of Divine love is not quite gone.

Christ gave us everything. He revealed to us the glorious mystery of the *Holy Trinity*. He 'shewed us the Father' [cf. John 14:8–9]. Through Him we receive and experience knowledge of the Holy Spirit, and can infallibly determine when it is He, the Third Person proceeding from the Father, Who is acting in us, and not some other spirit which might seem sovereign to the inexperienced. Through Christ and in Him we have a momentously positive expression of man answering to his primordial image and likeness to God. Now there is no longer in us anything or anyone else that could be the foundation of our being, either here on earth or in eternity. And Christ's words, 'All that ever came before me are thieves and robbers' [John 10:8] ring true for us in the clear understanding that has been given to us. But we must interpret them in the same perspective as that other proposition, 'A man's foes shall be they of his own household' [Matt. 10:36]. 'They of our household' love us, and we love them; but we must not listen when they would prevent us from surrendering to God. In so far as they would dissuade us from the one true way, they become our 'foes'. They are 'thieves and robbers'.

By living according to the Gospel commandments we gradually – though painfully – find solutions to many of the age-old problems that confront mankind. Marvel not – it really is so. In Him lies salvation for every separate individual. In Him lies salvation for those who are united in His Name, and so for whole peoples, for the whole world [cf. John 4:42; Matt. 12:21]. There is not, and cannot be, any situation wherein He is power-less to save. In saying this, I do not mean that He will without fail heal this or that malady, deliver us from some disaster or other, physical, moral or material, or from our oppressors or anything else generally considered harmful or destructive – although all that lies in His hands, too. Genuine salvation means in all circumstances standing firm in His love, as He Himself kept His Father's commandments, and abode in His love [cf. John 15:10]. We all know what trials the Lord went through, especially in the last days of His sojourn with us. And yet, immediately before His death, He says to His disciples, 'These things have I spoken unto you, that my *joy* might remain in you, and that your joy might be full' [John 15:11]. And, later, 'Verily I say unto thee, To day shalt thou be with me in paradise' [Luke 23:43].

All love is subject to testing, and true friendship shows up in adversity. When love is stronger than death, it is perfect love. After such 'trying out', which none of us can avoid, love through death on the earthly plane conquers death in eternity and makes man an inheritor of a 'kingdom which cannot be moved' [Heb. 12:28].

To start with, the Christian's ascetic struggle is concentrated within himself; but ultimately it becomes prayer for the whole world, for all Adam. Love's first step is towards God; the second, towards his neighbour. Just as the Incarnate Son's love for God the Father was 'unto the end', so His love for man is also 'unto the end' [cf. John 15:10–15; 13:1]. And this precisely is the love commanded of us.

In their essence Christ's commandments are the Self-revelation of God. Though expressed in seemingly relative terms, whoever would rightly obey them finds himself on the frontier between the relative and the absolute, the finite and the infinite, the determined and the arbitrary. The keeping of these unconstrained prescripts far exceeds our human strength. It is imperative that He Himself, the Almighty Who manifested Himself to us, by His effective abiding within us should lead us into His own sphere of unconditional and absolutely unconditioned

72

Being: 'I am the vine, ye are the branches: He that abideth in me, and I in him, the same bringeth forth much fruit: for without me ye can do nothing' [John 15:5].

Thus speaks the One Omnipotent Sovereign of all creation [cf. Matt. 28:18].

The Divine source of the Gospel injunctions also reveals that those who keep them, irrespective of their cultural level, apprehend the Eternal in their heart: 'I thank thee, O Father, Lord of heaven and earth, that thou hast . . . revealed [these things] unto babes' [Luke 10:21]. To the Apostles – 'babes' in so far as human learning is concerned – Christ gave genuine knowledge of Eternal Truth [cf. John 17:3].

He who knows the Father, Which is in heaven, already has eternal life in him: 'Rejoice, because your names are written in heaven' [Luke 10:20].

To live as a Christian is impossible: all one can do is 'die daily' [I Cor. 15:31] in Christ, like St. Paul. This daily dying, however, is neither easy nor simple – it is the 'strait gate', the 'narrow way, which leadeth unto life, and few there be that find it' [cf. Matt. 7:13–14].

The glad tidings of Christ far transcend anything that the earth knows. How heal the terrible sickness with which the serpent infected man at the dawn of his appearance on earth [cf. Gen. 3:1–6]? How can people be made to see that the utterly uncommon man, the Gospel Jesus Christ, is truly God without beginning, the Creator of all that is, revealed to Moses with the name I AM? Can anyone 'of sound mind' so lose his mind as to acknowledge as God a man who died on the cross, hanging between two thieves? What can I say? Those who are positively unable to believe in the Divinity of Christ will find no other way of attaining their own divinization. Children are capable of believing, as are the pure in heart, or those who for all their recognition of their fallen state, their nothingness, intuitively feel their kinship with God. He who believes in Christ believes in his own divinization. Belief or disbelief depends on an elev-

73

ated or depreciated conception of man. For the believer Christ's death on the cross – how and why He was crucified – is the strongest evidence in His favour. Look how St. Paul, who had persecuted Him, saw it: 'Christ sent me . . . to preach the gospel: not with, wisdom of words, lest the *cross* of Christ should be made of none effect. For the preaching of the cross is to them that perish foolishness; but unto . . . the saved it is the power of God. For it is written, I will destroy the wisdom of the wise, and will bring to nothing the understanding of the prudent . . . Hath not God made foolish the wisdom of this world? For after that in the wisdom of God' (manifest in the creation) 'the world by wisdom knew not God, it pleased God by the foolishness of preaching to save them that believe. For the Jews require a sign, and the Greeks seek after wisdom: But we preach Christ crucified, unto the Jews a stumblingblock, and unto the Greeks foolishness; But unto them which are called . . . Christ the power of God, and the wisdom of God. Because the foolishness of God is wiser than men; and the weakness of God is stronger than men . . . Howbeit we speak wisdom among them that are perfect: yet not the wisdom of this world . . . But we speak the wisdom of God in a mystery, even the hidden wisdom, which God ordained *before the world unto our glory;* Which none of the princes of this world knew . . . But God hath revealed them unto us by his Spirit . . . Now we have received . . . the spirit which is of God; that we might know the things that are freely given to us of God' [I Cor. 1:17–25; 2:6–12].

We are faint-hearted but Christ bids us 'Be of good cheer; I have overcome the world' [John 16:33]. If He overcame the 'world' (in Greek, *kósmos*), it means that even as man He became supra-cosmic, transcending this world. And everyone who believes in Him, who conquers in the ascetic feat of repentance the 'law of sin which is in [our] members' [Rom. 7:23] also becomes supra-cosmic like Christ.

'Father, the words which thou gavest me . . . and the glory, which thou hast given me, I have given them. Father, I will that they also, whom thou hast given me, be with me where I am; that they may behold my glory which I had with thee *before the world was*' [John 17:8, 24, 5].

In order to contemplate this glory it is essential oneself to be in this glory. In order to understand, even if only partly, 'Who this is?' [cf. Matt. 21:10] we must become like Him by abiding in the spirit of His commandments. The man who has not followed Him with absolute faith, who has not come to love Him with his whole heart and mind, and so has not observed His word, must not presume to judge Him or pronounce concerning Him [cf. I Cor. 2:14]. He should keep an honest silence since he is unfit to judge of the Son of God and Word of the Father. Just as in the realm of science or the arts one must not be too remote from the artist or the scientist if one is to appreciate his genius, so is it in the realm of the Spirit. But the man who has based his life on the rock of His teaching [cf. Matt. 7:24–29] will gradually come to understand 'Who this is'.

Christ said, '*No man* knoweth the Son, but the Father; neither knoweth *any man* the Father, save the Son, and he to whomsoever the Son will reveal him' [Matt. 11:27]. We may conclude, then, that souls do exist to whom the Son reveals knowledge of the Father. '*No man* can come to me, except the Father which hath sent me draw him.' The Father, therefore, does draw one. '*No man* cometh unto the Father, but by me' [John 6:44; 14:6]. So one 'comes' to the Father through Christ.

Man is indeed a great mystery. Created from nothing, he is lifted up to the fulness of uncreated Being. God so loved man that He gives Himself without measure, without limit. Just as God transcends the whole of cosmic reality, so man, divinized through the coming into him of the Holy Spirit, is more precious than all the galaxies. This is the way the Christian feels – otherwise, he could not 'walk worthy of the vocation wherewith [he] is called' [Eph. 4:1].

Is not such temerity a sign of excessive pride? Certainly not, if we follow Christ's example, 'For I have given you an

example, that ye should do as I have done to you' [John 13:15]
– if we tread in the steps of the Apostles and Fathers. 'Be ye
followers of me, even as I also am of Christ', said St. Paul [I
Cor. 11:1].

The sixteenth chapter of St. Matthew's Gospel sets out this
teaching in full:

'Jesus asked his disciples, saying, Whom do men say that I
the Son of man am? And they said, Some say that thou art John
the Baptist: some, Elias; and others, Jeremias, or one of the
prophets. He saith unto them, But whom say ye that I am?
And Simon Peter answered and said, *Thou art the Christ, the
Son of the living God.* And Jesus answered and said unto him,
Blessed art thou, Simon Bar-jona: for flesh and blood hath not
revealed it unto thee, but my Father which is in heaven. And
I say also unto thee, That thou art Peter, and upon this rock I
will build my church; and the gates of hell shall not prevail
against it. And I will give unto thee the keys of the kingdom
of heaven: and whatsoever thou shalt bind on earth shall be
bound in heaven: and whatsoever thou shalt loose on earth shall
be loosed in heaven. Then charged he his disciples that they
should tell no man that he was *Jesus the Christ.* From that time
forth began Jesus to shew unto his disciples, how that he *must*
go unto Jerusalem, and *suffer many things* of the elders and chief
priests and scribes, and be killed, and be raised again the third
day. Then Peter' (ignorant as yet of the mysteries of the ways
of our salvation) 'began to rebuke him, saying, Be it far from
thee, Lord: this shall not be unto thee. But he turned, and said
unto Peter, Get thee behind me, Satan: thou art an offence
unto me: for thou savourest not the things that be of God, but
those that be of men. Then said Jesus unto his disciples, If any
man will come after me, let him deny himself, and take up his
cross, and follow me. For whosoever will save his life shall lose
it: and whosoever will lose his life for my sake shall find it. For
what is a man profited, if he shall gain the whole world, and
lose his own soul? or what shall a man give in exchange for his
soul? For the Son of man shall come in the glory of his Father
with his angels; and then he shall reward every man according

to his works. Verily I say unto you, There be some standing here, which shall not taste of death, till they see the Son of man coming in his kingdom' [Matt. 16:13–28].

This extract from the Gospel provides us with the radical, vital features of the 'strait gate and narrow way, which leadeth unto life'. When many of the people started to honour Christ as a great prophet, and the Apostles accepted Him as 'the Son of the living God', He began to 'shew unto his disciples' His imminent sufferings and death. Countering Peter's natural human reaction with a decisive 'Get thee behind me,' He went on to expound the necessity, for all who would follow Him, of taking up the cross, even going so far as to declare that whoever would save his soul for eternity in the Kingdom must 'lose his life' in this world. The importance of the soul is such that if the price of gaining the whole world impairs her on the Divine plane, all the treasures of the earth will not make up for the spiritual damage incurred. He builds His Church, against which the gates of hell shall not prevail, on the confession of His Divinity. If we detract from the fulness of His Divinity, then neither the Church nor anything else can overcome the world or the abyss of hell. And He goes on to speak of His eternal glory and power, which will be revealed to some standing there at the time – a dictum fulfilled on Mount Tabor, where Christ prayed, 'and spake of his decease which he should accomplish at Jerusalem' [Luke 9:31]; where the uncreated Light of the Holy Spirit shone on the Apostles and they saw Moses and Elias as servants of the Lord, and heard the searchless voice of the Father testifying to Christ's eternal Sonship.

Almost concurrently – descent into hell and infinite glory! *And this is the way for Christians:* they condemn themselves to torment and, in return, receive the gift of the Father's mercy, which there are no words to describe. Such is the *abundance* of life brought to us by Christ [cf. John 10:10]. Christ-life embraces both hell and the Kingdom. It incorporates in itself extremes of suffering with the heights of bliss. It makes the little man great, universal, god-like in all things . . . Unhappily, 'few there be that find it' [Matt. 7:14].

The Father's gifts are more than we can bear. When immeasurable strength descends on mortal man it may happen that Lucifer, who fell in the paroxysm of his pride, will approach. How can we avoid this fall? Here, too, we have Christ's example to teach us, when He was tempted in the desert. We remember His words again: 'And thou, Capernaum, which art exalted unto heaven, shalt be brought down to hell' [Matt. 11:23].

In order to depict our Christian path more clearly, let us adopt the method of the Fathers and make an analogy. When we look at an ancient tree reaching high up to the clouds, we know that its roots, deep in the ground, must be correspondingly powerful. If the roots did not stretch down into the dark depths of the earth, as deep, perhaps, as the tree is high; if the mass and strength of the roots did not parallel the size and weight of the visible part of the tree, they could not nourish the tree or keep it upright – the lightest breeze would blow it down. So it is in man's spiritual life. If we recognise the greatness of our calling in Christ – that we have been chosen before the foundation of the world [cf. Eph. 1:4] by the eternal Divine Providence to receive the adoption of sons [Gal. 4:5] – we shall be, not puffed up but genuinely humble. A downward movement, into the blackness of hell, is indispensable for all of us if we are to continue steadfast in the Christian spirit. So we must be ever conscious of our primeval nothingness, continually condemning ourselves harshly in all things. And the more man abases himself in self-condemnation, the higher will God exalt him. 'I tell you . . . every one that exalteth himself shall be abased; and he that humbleth himself shall be exalted' [Luke 18:14].

Vast numbers of people with no experience of the beneficial action of prayer do not know that a world of indescribable magnitude is disclosed to the spirit of man through prayer. Prayer unfolds both the dark depths of hell and the luminous heavenly spheres. Without faith in the resurrection almost all suffering is unmeaning, pointless. It may subdue the obstinate soul but does not cure her of the pride hidden in her depths. Suffering may enrich one's experience but in the absence of prayer it does not rid the soul of passion. Suffering gradually destroys the body, the heart and the mind, without perfecting them in the knowledge of God. But when the Light of Supreme Being approaches the soul, all is changed: earthly passions die away and the spirit rises to contemplation of the Eternal. The man endowed with this blessing regards worldly status, whether social, material or even cultural, as a sort of temporary 'extra', and does not worry about a career. And if he persists in his humble opinion of himself, the more knowledge will he be given of the mysteries of the world to come.

Uniting himself through prayer with Christ, man within himself, in his heart and mind, is made aware that in eternity the whole content of God-man will be given to him imprescriptibly. Because of this, every good deed on the part of anyone whomsoever gladdens him here and now with the joy of salvation for all [cf. Luke 15:31–32]. A brother's renown will be his renown. He will delight in seeing others glorified by Divine Light; and the more radiant they are, the lovelier the vision. In the Kingdom to come of the saints there is a wealth of love, of which God grants us a foretaste here on earth. Divine love embraces hell, too. *And we know now that our descent into hell in the course of this life is the true road to perfection.*

There are two stages to victory over hell. The first is the mastery of the blackness within us ourselves; the second, compassionate love, natural to Divinity, for all creation. Yea, this love through the Holy Spirit is conveyed to all who are saved. Eternity knows no duration of time but contains in itself the full compass of the centuries. Eternity without space includes in itself all the expanses of the created world.

Though our earthly experience is incomplete – we know 'in

part' – it is nevertheless reliable. St. Paul tells us, 'Charity never faileth: but whether there be prophecies, they shall fail; whether there be tongues, they shall cease; whether there be knowledge, it shall vanish away . . . But when that which is perfect is come, then that which is in part shall be done away . . . For now we see through a glass, darkly; but then face to face: now I know in part; but then shall I know even as also I am known' (by God). 'And now abideth faith,' – the beginning of love – 'hope,' – the ripening of love – 'charity,' – the perfection of love. 'But the greatest of these is charity' [cf. I Cor. 13:8–13].

Knowing the way keeps us alive even in hell but it does not make our suffering imaginary: we are benighted by the passions, like all the heirs of fallen Adam; but we are not devoured by the flames of hell – we 'despair not'. We must not be over-daunted by this plunge into darkness, since without it, after the Fall, fulness of knowledge is unattainable.

However successful a man may be in his chosen field of science, he must never lose sight of the 'fundamentals' – of the root-propositions of his subject. Similarly, while in this body we cling firmly to the method taught us by our Fathers, and the action in us of the Divine Spirit. The law of sin is still active in us, and with anger and detestation towards ourselves we condemn ourselves to hell-fire, since there is no other fire that could extinguish the working of the passions in us. And what happens? When sorrowful prayer consumes the heart, and endurance fails, suddenly there is a cool breath of heavenly comfort. When awareness of our perishability plunges our spirit into hopelessness, suddenly new strength descends on us from on High and clothes the soul in incorruption [cf. I Cor. 15:54]. When thick darkness fills us with dread, in some inexplicable manner the wondrous Light turns night into bright day, lifts us on high and leads us like sons into the Father's house.

How explain such apparent contradictions? Why does our angry self-condemnation justify us before God? May it not be that in this recognition of the mighty power of sin that imprisons us there is existentially-genuine truth? And this our repentance, reaching back to the source of the world's tragedy [cf. Gen. ch. 3], opens a place within us for the coming of the Holy Spirit, the Spirit of truth, which leads us, restored, into the light of the Kingdom.

How wondrous are the Divine ways! Man himself cannot uncover them but the Spirit, proceeding from God, by His appearance illumines for us this ineffable approach to eternal salvation.

'But when the Comforter is come, whom I will send unto you from the Father, even the Spirit of truth, which proceedeth from the Father, he shall testify of me . . . he will guide you into all truth' [John 15:26; 16:13].

Impossible not to sing hymns of praise unto God when we emerge from the flames of repentance that, unremarked, transport us to a new mode of being, having consumed all that was perishable in us, that weighed us down like a heavy burden. Who can describe what it is like to be caught in this fire? To whom, and how, can one propose this experience? To wish each and every man that he may rise into Divine Being is natural; but who will endure the torments of hell without falling into utter despair? When I look at myself, condemned to live in this appalling century, I am inclined to think that for many of my contemporaries there may be no other solution.

I have made bold to speak more than once of my own experience: that prayer of total repentance before our Creator meets with every trial possible for beings created 'in the image of God'. The image of man and his likeness to the Lord state clearly that each of us may become a 'lord' only by overcoming the world – not, of course, through our own strength but by faith in Christ [cf. I John 5:4–5; John 16:33]. In the Book of Job [Septuagint version 1:7] we read: 'And the Lord said to the devil, Whence art thou come? And the devil answered the Lord, and said, I am come from compassing the earth, and walking up and down in the world'. There is nowhere on earth, nor in the whole universe, where it is possible to avoid encounter with the devil. And if the devil controls not only our world but all the rest of creation, as 'prince of this world', wherever we happen to be 'geographically' and spiritually, he will come and put us to the test. Discussing this, Blessed St. Silouan said, 'Mind wrestles with mind . . . our mind with the mind of the enemy'. Even to Christ in the wilderness the devil came to tempt Him [cf. Matt. 4:1–11; Luke 4:1–14]. But before His prayer in Gethsemane the Lord said to His disciples: 'The prince of this world cometh, and hath nothing in me' [John 14:30]. What exactly is my point? This – that at every stage of our ascent to God the enemy will pursue and tempt us. And when we ail in every part of our being, when we give ourselves over to proud thoughts, he endeavours to turn us away from God.

During the actual period of trial the soul cannot accept it as a manifestation of Divine mercy; as a sign of God's *trust* in her; as God's wish to communicate to man holiness and plenitude-of-being in Himself. The soul knows only one thing: God has abandoned her after having manifested His Light to her, and thereby has immeasurably increased her sufferings. And when, weak and exhausted, she does not find God inclining His mercy toward her, *thoughts and feelings come about which it is better to keep silent.*

'We wrestle . . . against principalities, against powers, against the rulers of the darkness of this world, against spiritual wickedness in high places' [Eph. 6:12]. This spirit of 'wickedness in high places' rushes to attack the contrite heart and mind now stayed on God. Brazenly it invades us, creating the impression that the thoughts and feelings brought by the enemy are our own. Indeed, after the Fall there is something in us that does respond to demoniacal suggestions. This engenders such a surge of repentance that our spirit departs from the actual world into mental infinity, there to stand naked and alone before God, in silence discerning the character of our degradation and of Divine eternity.

82

Paul, who had persecuted the Church and slain believers, had much to repent of. I presume, not irresponsibly, that his conversion or rapture happened in a surge of desperate repentance. He himself writes about it: 'I know a man in Christ . . . (whether in the body, I cannot tell; or whether out of the body, I cannot tell: God knoweth;) such an one [was] caught up to the third heaven . . . into paradise, and heard *unspeakable* words, which it is not lawful for a man to utter' [II Cor. 12:2, 4]. And to the Romans he wrote, 'Who shall separate us from the love of Christ? shall tribulation, or distress, or persecution, or famine, or nakedness, or peril, or sword? As it is written, For thy sake we are killed all the day long; we are accounted as sheep for the slaughter. Nay, in all these things we are more than conquerors through him that loved us. For I am persuaded, that neither death, nor life, nor angels, nor principalities, nor powers, nor things present, nor things to come, Nor height, nor depth, nor any other creature, shall be able to separate us from the love of God, which is in Christ Jesus our Lord' [Rom. 8:35–39].

It is not difficult to conceive that Paul went through the fiery trials that he describes. In my book about Saint Silouan I explored the words of the great Apostle in the light of contemporary ascetic experience. I wrote:

'His reason would pluck the ascetic striver away from Divine love: he cannot contain or accept the law of Christ's Spirit which is foolishness to the natural man [cf. I Cor. 2:14]. In times of abandonment such protests can acquire extraordinary strength.

'The ascetic striver may be distracted from love of God by desire for life, or fear of death; by the attractions of worldly pleasures, by illness or hunger, persecution or other suffering; by the eminence and light of other revelations, the profundity and majesty of other conceptions; by the grandeur of various other possessions, or the breadth of other possibilities; by the vision of angels and similar heavenly beings; or because of the violence of the powers of evil.

'It can be stated on firm grounds that the Christian on his

83

progress towards Divine eternity will meet with a whole series of trials and temptations. All the paths will be familiar to the Christian but his ways are hidden from the outsider' [cf. I Cor. 2:15–16].

I know that I am nothing worth. But still I do not think my pain, my suffering unworthy of attention. And the Lord Who bade us 'Take heed that ye despise not one of these little ones' [Matt. 18:10] did not disdain my appeal 'and heard [me] and saved [me] out of all [my] troubles' [Ps. 34:6]. I was unrestrained in my frantic prayers, audacious even, but He responded softly, gently, without putting my ignorance to shame. Praying, I looked for an answer and at the same time did not dare to rely on one. Beyond all my expectations – He came. The manner of His coming was particularly unexpected. The enemies retired. The Lord conquered both them and me. Strange – for the first time I knew the unspeakable joy of being vanquished.

God is searchlessly great. We hear and read of His greatness but it is quite another matter to live it, this greatness. No one and nothing can in any way diminish His eternal Sovereignty but He, even God, made Himself lowly to a degree that we cannot understand: in our frail flesh He attained absoluteness. Now I know from my own experience: He hungers for our perfection. In sanctioning our grievous struggle against the enemy and against our own selves in our fallen state, He would have us victorious. If we do not abandon Him in the worst moments of our humiliation by the enemy, He will most certainly come to us. He is the conqueror, not we. But He will attribute the victory to us, because it is we who have suffered.

Nature never repeats herself exactly. Still less is man, a reasonable being, standardised. All the sons of men have a heart 'fashioned' by God 'alike' [cf. Ps. 33:15]. It is the heart given to the person-hypostasis, and as such – unique. At the last trump every man will receive a new *name* for ever, known only to God and to him that receiveth it [cf. Rev. 2:17]. Thus, although the life of all who are saved will be *one* like the One Kingdom of the Holy Trinity [cf. John 17:11, 21–22], the personal principle in each of us will never be transferable to anyone else.

If the testimony in the book of The Revelation is true, the proposition is understandable that there is and can be no single system, programme or sequence of growth applicable to all of us. But this does not mean that we have no common foundation. So we observe a phenomenon that almost invariably repeats itself in the course of our spiritual life – not in detail but in principle – to wit: When he turns to God man receives grace which accompanies and enlightens him, instructing him in many of the mysteries of life in God. Then, *inevitably*, grace departs, at any rate in its 'tangible' strength, and God will wait for a response to the gift that He has poured out. This testing of our faithfulness has a dual purpose – firstly, and imperatively, to allow us to manifest our freedom and our reasoning power and to educate and, if possible, perfect the gift of freedom for self-determination in the eternal sphere. And secondly, to give our Heavenly Father the occasion to commit to us *all* that He has [cf. Luke 15:31] for our eternal use, since every gift from on High is assimilated by us inescapably through suffering. When we have demonstrated our steadfastness God comes again and makes His abode for ever in the man who has proved himself *able* to contain the fire of the Father's love [cf. John 14:23; Luke 16:10–12].

So then, though there is no general prescription for life in God, there are certain basic conditions which we must keep in mind if we would make our way intelligently and not be victims to ignorance of the road to salvation.

'O God our Saviour, hide not from me the mysteries of the ways of Thy salvation.'

For the Christian, as we see him, the only way to the Father is through the Son. 'All things that the Father hath are mine'

[John 16:15]. In the eternal birth of the Son the Father poured into Him the plenitude of His Being. Accordingly, the Son is in all things equal to the Father. He is the consummate fulness of the revelation of the Father. He is the life of the Father, His strength, power, might, kingdom, wisdom, omniscience, creativity, love . . . 'He that hath seen the Son hath seen the Father' [John 14:9]. 'He that hateth the Son hateth the Father also' [cf. John 15:23]. 'He that believeth on the Son hath everlasting life: and he that believeth not the Son shall not see life; but the wrath of God abideth on him' [John 3:36].

Through the Holy Spirit, 'Which proceedeth from the Father' and reposes in the Son, we know the Son in His Divinity and in the nature of man that He assumed. It is in the Holy Spirit that we live the Father.

Every word spoken by Christ is truth beyond human judgment. Everywhere we are shown that the Son, the Word of the Father, is unique, unparalleled. And He Himself emphasises this, categorically: 'All that ever came before me are thieves and robbers' [John 10:8]. And concerning those who had appeared and were to appear after the coming of Christ, He warned, 'Take heed that no man deceive you. For many shall come in my name, saying, I am Christ*; and shall deceive many . . . Then if any man shall say unto you, Lo, here is Christ, or there; *believe it not*. For there shall arise false Christs, and false prophets, and shall shew great signs and wonders; insomuch that, if it were possible, they shall deceive the very elect. Behold, I have told you *before*. Wherefore if they shall say unto you, Behold he is in the desert; go not forth: behold, he is in the secret chambers; *believe it not*. For as the lightning cometh out of the east, and shineth even unto the west; so shall also the coming of the Son of man be' [Matt. 24:4–5; 23–27]. There can be no doubting that the Lord stands aloof from *all* other so-called 'teachers of mankind': 'One is your Master, even Christ; and all ye are brethren' [Matt. 23:8].

* *Christ* – Greek word, corresponding to the English, 'The Anointed'; in Hebrew, 'The Messiah'.

History tells of many an attempt in the past to relegate Christ to the ranks of other teachers, prophets and founders of religions. This happens even more so in our day and we must expect the same in the future. They all have the one thing in common – refusal to accept the Divinity of Christ; that is, to recognise His absolute authority (as did the First Ecumenical Council in A.D.325).

The unoriginate Light is communicated to us through the incarnation of the Word of the Father. When this 'great mystery of godliness' [I Tim. 3:16] is rejected one should not expect to receive knowledge of Truth. In Christianity we have the maximum concreteness together with the ultimate inscrutability of God. We eat the Body of the incarnate God and drink His Blood. Our bodies become 'members of His Body' [cf. Eph. 5:30]. In the communion of His Word our human mind merges with the eternal Mind of God [cf. I John 1:1–2]. Nevertheless, 'no man hath seen God at any time' [I John 4:12]. 'The King of kings, and Lord of lords . . . dwelleth in the light which no man can approach unto; whom no man hath seen, nor can see' [I Tim. 6:15–16].

God, Who in His essence is far beyond all understanding, all naming, all portraying, the Church of Christ knows in her age-old experience. And our Fathers, through the ultimate experience possible to man, became partakers of this knowledge, which they bequeathed to us as a precious, imprescriptible inheritance. Our humble God does not despise our nothingness and did not refuse us the blessedness of knowing Him, in so far as is possible for mortal man [cf. Matt. 11:27].

Our way to knowledge of God lies not through books but through faith in Christ's word. This faith brings our mind down into the heart, consumed by the flame of love for Christ. We descend into the bottomless ocean which is the heart of man. We know the arduousness of this immersion, the weight of suffering that it entails. There in the depths the Divine arms embrace us tenderly and lift us to heaven. (*A propos*, ascent even to heaven is possible if we have the energy of the pain of love.)

I frequently speak of 'pain' and am often worried that not everyone will rightly understand this ascetic term. The pain I write of is the *leitmotiv* of my life in God. I cannot ignore it. It is not at all like physical or mental pain, although it often includes these inferior forms. It is the pain of the love of God which detaches the one who is praying from this world to transport him into another. The fiercer the spiritual pain, the more vigorous the attraction to God. The more dynamic our plunge into the depths of the shoreless ocean of suffering, the surer our spirit's ascent into heaven. When the spirit is introduced into the radiant sphere of the heavens pain is transformed into the equally unbearable joy of love victorious. Again, in essence we have the same thing: extreme suffering coupled with utmost joy. This is exactly what happens to the man who repents: the Holy Spirit transports him to unforeseen frontiers, where he experiences a foretaste of divine universality. Consider Christ – how He lived on earth after the fall of Adam. In Him Divine power was combined with the weakness of the flesh. Something similar happens with us: 'I can do all things through Christ which strengtheneth me' [Phil. 4:13]. What the Lord is by His essential Divinity, men have through grace. And he who is like unto Christ in his earthly manifestations is naturally like unto Him on the Divine plane, too.

Spiritual suffering is a reality which cannot be measured and is invisible to the majority. Divine love begets in us a whole gamut of different torments for the spirit, which can be discussed only on supernatural, metaphysical lines. Outwardly, those so afflicted may live in circumstances no worse than other people's but their soul finds no satisfaction in wealth, luxury, privilege, power or even fame in this world. The soul pulling away from her normal confines and stretching up to the eternal God suffers. Having felt the breath of the Holy Spirit, she sorrows more acutely.

The first thing the Lord said when He emerged from His forty days and forty nights in the wilderness was, 'Repent: for

88

the kingdom of heaven is at hand' [Matt. 4:17]. He Himself is this Kingdom. And lo, we – people – see Him: He stood before us, so close that we could not only see but feel Him with our hands [cf. I John 1:1]. And when the 'tangible' form of the pre-eternal God in the greatness of His love wounds our soul, we can never forget the miracle. 'The kingdom of heaven is like unto treasure in a field; the which when a man hath found, he hideth, and for joy thereof goeth and selleth all that he hath, and buyeth that field. Again, the kingdom of heaven is like unto a merchant man, seeking goodly pearls: Who, when he had found one pearl of great price, went and sold all that he had, and bought it' [Matt. 13:44–46]. In these parables the Lord is speaking of what I have in mind at this moment. Having seen in spirit the beauty of God, man abandons all that he has on this earth in order to acquire the 'treasure', the 'pearl'.

When the Holy Spirit manifests, in uncreated Light, the Divine reality, the soul needs courage to credit the vision given her, which far surpasses anything that happens in everyday life. He who has had this experience recognises the Virgin Mary's hesitation at the Archangel Gabriel's message. Only after she realised the suffering entailed in her service to the world could she respond, 'Behold the handmaid of the Lord; be it unto me according to thy word. And the angel departed from her. And Mary arose in those days, and went into the hill country with haste, into a city of Juda; And entered into the house of Zach-arias, and saluted Elisabeth. And it came to pass, that, when Elisabeth heard the salutation of Mary, the babe leaped in her womb; and Elisabeth was filled with the Holy Ghost: And she spake out with a loud voice, and said, Blessed art thou among women, and blessed is the fruit of thy womb. And whence is this to me, that the mother of my Lord should come to me? . . . Blessed is she that believed: for there shall be a performance of those things which were told her from the Lord'. Having received this confirmation of the veracity of the revelation given her, Mary said: 'My soul doth magnify the Lord, And my spirit hath rejoiced in God my Saviour' [Luke 1:38–47]. 'And when they saw him, they' (the disciples) 'worshipped him: but some doubted' [Matt. 28:17], since what had happened was too much for man to take in. [cf. also Luke 2:35; Matt. 20:22; Acts 9:15–16].

The uncreated Light to begin with shows us the state we are in, which is appalling; and we descend in our consciousness into the abyss of our hell and see ourselves in our degradation, as we are. But when the Light comes after another fashion, now, in glory, the humbled soul wants God to take her in His hands and give her strength to bear the ineffable gift.

Sin begins with delectation and ends in tragic downfall. Deliverance from the power of sin over us starts with painful repentance but the end is – *joyous victory*. More than once have I heard people say, 'I am ready to accept religion if it will bring me happiness'. But they expect happiness from the very outset of their believing, which is not always possible. Yet the same people will put up with all sorts of difficulties to make a base for themselves for their striving after their daily bread, or for some advantage or other. Artists who would perfect themselves in their chosen field have to struggle even harder. Poets, painters, writers and musicians often willingly throughout their lives undergo every sort of deprivation for the sake of their art. So will the man who has been singled out for contact with the heavenly fire be even more prepared to endure all things.

Let us consider Christ's teaching: 'Blessed are the poor in spirit: for their's is the kingdom of heaven.' Are they blessed now, or only in the kingdom to come? 'Blessed are they that mourn: for they shall be comforted.' When? 'Blessed are they which do hunger and thirst after righteousness . . . Blessed are the merciful . . . the pure in heart . . . the peacemakers . . . Blessed are they which are persecuted for righteousness' sake . . . Blessed are ye, when men shall revile you . . . and say all manner of evil against you falsely, for my sake. Rejoice, and be exceeding glad: for great is your reward in heaven' [Matt. 5:3–12]. Is it possible to make all this come true without a tremendous battle against one's passions – without bitter weeping, much sorrow, searing distress? Of course not. But however strange it may seem, the luminous rays from the heavenly kingdom begin to reach us the moment we start to believe in Christ-God. 'Verily I say unto you, *There is no man* that hath left house, or parents, or brethren, or wife, or children, for the kingdom of God's sake, Who shall not receive manifold more *in this present time*, and in the world to come life everlasting' [Luke 18:29–30; cf. Mark 10:30].

Everything that the Lord speaks of is acquired by much suffering on the part of the soul seeking God, drawn to Him by the power of love. This love directs man's spirit to God with such force that many of his old reflexes and reactions cease to affect him. Man's spirit stands as mind (*nous*) before the First *Nous*, divested of all that is visible, that is transient. Ascetics term this state '*pure prayer*'. In pure prayer man is outside all earthly categories: he is not old, not young; 'neither Jew nor Greek, neither bond nor free'; neither rich nor poor, learned nor ignorant. And 'neither male nor female'. He is 'a new creature' in Jesus Christ [cf. II Cor. 5:17; Gal. 6:15; 3:26–28].

When his repentance reaches the utmost limits the Christian begins to wrestle against 'the prince of this world' [John 12:31; 14:30]. The enemy's mind is of cosmic dimensions. An invisible struggle goes on between us. It may be asserted without contradiction that the Christian who throughly repents will encounter all the content of the spiritual world. It must be thus because repentance approximates man to the likeness of Christ as *Lord* of all. In order that fulness of likeness to God in His seigniory be imparted to him, man is tested at every level. He will be confronted with manifold visions, including, possibly, non-Christian mystical experiences. But he meets with all of them in an, as it were, inverse perspective: what adherents of other disciplines seek and strain after – what they accept as truth – the Christian sees as a falling away from true life. The Divine Light that has appeared to him shows him the bottomless pit of hell; but in such a way that he discerns the *phantoms* of truth that attract the inexperienced ascetic. 'Take heed that no man deceive you' [Matt. 24:4]. On alien paths the states of the Christian spirit are unknown – especially so is the love proceeding from on High to envelop all creation in suffering.

Love for God may stab at us like a sword-thrust in the heart. But – still another 'but' – the pain dissolves into inexpressibly sweet and verily all-embracing love. It is clear then that both pain *per se* and joy without pain would be fatal for our psychosomatic organism.

In my final analysis, after long years of penitent prayer, I am convinced that it would be an irreparable mistake to confuse the pain of the love of Christ, that I have described, with manifestations of a pathological kind. The sufferings of one who repents are neither a nervous disorder nor the consequence of unsatisfied desires of the flesh; neither the result of psychological conflict or loss of mental control. There is nothing at all pathological about them. Absolutely not. By their nature these sufferings belong to another plane of being. In certain initial periods they affect the entire man – that is, both his soul and his body – so that the *whole* entity suffers. But spiritual travail in connection with God quickens and does not destroy. By this means man is victorious over the consequences of the Fall and is delivered from the 'law of sin which is in his members' [cf. Rom. 7:23].

The way to rebirth, to a return to our primordial state, is not easy. But there is no justifying any shirking of the ascetic effort required. Let me take as an illustration our epoch with its revolutionary movements. The experience of the last half century or more has proved convincingly to the whole world how difficult and painful it is to change from one inequitable social order formed in the dreadful circumstances of the Fall of humanity to another, likewise distanced from Divine Truth but seemingly less harsh. In this fearful struggle millions of people will accept any risk, including death itself. And everyone 'understands' them. May we not take this as a parallel to justify the 'risk' run by the Christian ascetic? Yes, indeed, it is not a simple or easy matter to transform our life from corruption to incorruption, from the temporal to the immortal.

We must choose one of two paths: either, in our pursuit of psycho-physical delights and comfort, shun God and so die spiritually; or, in our striving for a supra-natural form of being, let ourselves die to this world. In this 'dying' lies our cross, our crucifixion. Many perish in their efforts to attain their ideal, though it be only a question of temporary triumph. But the Christian, in the freedom found in God for his immortal spirit, is ready to suffer in order to realise the supreme truth. In this lies the virtue of the Christian, the like of which is not met with in the natural world.

'And there was war in heaven: Michael and his angels fought against the dragon; and the dragon fought and his angels, And prevailed not; neither was their place found any more in heaven. And the great dragon was cast out, that old serpent, called the Devil, and Satan, which deceiveth the whole world . . . And I heard a loud voice saying in heaven, Now is come salvation, and strength, and the kingdom of our God, and the power of his Christ . . . They overcame him by the blood of the Lamb, and by the word of their testimony; *and they loved not their lives unto the death.* Therefore rejoice, ye heavens, and ye that dwell in them . . . ' [Rev. 12:7–12].

To love God to the point of hatred for oneself is perfect love. 'Greater love hath no man than this, that a man lay down his life for his friends' [John 15:13]. This is love 'unto the end' [John 13:1]. He who approaches this noble threshold has found the door into the 'kingdom which cannot be moved' [Heb. 12:28].

If we would obtain this kingdom we must remember that every spirit created in the Divine image will have to cross the threshold of suffering – voluntary suffering for the sake of holy love. Without this testing of our freedom we cannot realise ourselves as truly free persons. On the other hand, in order to abide for ever with God and in God we must learn the love natural to Him. Christ, the incarnate Logos of the Father, revealed this mystery to us. Without His example no one would ever have known this sacrament. 'To cross the threshold' means to be born again, radically – to become a 'new creature'. It means to receive the gift of divine eternity. Godlike life will come to be our inalienable possession. Uncreated grace is so joined to our created nature that the *two* become one. And this is *divinization*.

The bliss of knowing the way includes all that we have been discussing. The Christian who keeps these things in mind will endure 'the fiery trial' [cf. I Pet. 4:12], maybe even joyously, like the holy martyrs. Not to be aware of this is dangerous, since the soul may waver in her love toward God, in her trust in Him, at such moments of temptation, and refuse to follow Christ to Golgotha.

To summarize this truly noble doctrine of the Spirit: We must overcome all earthly suffering by immersing ourselves in even more profound suffering. 'Keep thy mind in hell.' We must condemn ourselves to hell as unworthy of God but we must 'despair not'.

This ascetic effort will lead to victory over the world [cf. John 16:33]. It will bring us to the 'kingdom which cannot be moved' [Heb. 12:28].

Is there a limit to this noble science on earth? We have the answer in Christ Who 'conquered death by death'.

Blessed be the Name of the Lord from this day forth and for ever more.

7

Summation of the Life of our Spirit

Authentically Christian life means living 'in spirit and in truth'
[John 4:23] and so is practicable anywhere, at any time, in any
historical epoch. Christ's divine commandments are absolute in
character. There are no circumstances in all the world – nor
could there ever be any – which might make it quite impossible
to observe these commandments. As Divine Spirit and Truth,
Christian life, of course, in its eternal essence transcends all
mundane forms. But since in this world man is *tabula rasa*, called
upon to 'grow, wax strong in spirit, be filled with wisdom' [cf.
Luke 2:40], so the necessity arises for *cadres* of some sort, of
disciplines to coordinate life in common and educate far from
perfect human beings. Our Fathers, the Apostles – and, indeed,
Christ Himself – who trained us to venerate the true God, knew
very well, on the one hand, that the life of the Divine Spirit
surpasses all worldly institutions, and, on the other, that this
very Spirit creates a habitation for Himself possessing within
the confines of the earth certain contours which express the
Spirit and are the vessel for the preserving of His gifts. This
wondrous dwelling-place of the Holy Spirit is the Church,
which down the centuries – all so turbulent – has borne the
precious treasure of Divinely-revealed Truth. Let us leave aside
those who, lacking in wisdom, become immoderate adherents
of outward 'forms', and, consequently, are diverted from the
spiritual quintessence contained in them. 'The Lord is . . .
Spirit: and where the Spirit of the Lord is, there is liberty. But
we all beholding . . . the glory of the Lord, are changed into
the same image from glory to glory' [cf. 2 Cor. 3:6, 17–18].
The Church is appointed to lead her children into the sphere of

Divine Being. She is the spiritual centre of our world, the focus of the whole history of mankind, from the creation of the first to the last man to be born of a woman. The Church is the bond of Christ's love by virtue of her indissoluble unity with Him. Those who have matured in her bosom through long ascetic struggle to keep the Gospel commandments and find the liberty of sons of God are no longer bound by any geographical situation or local tradition. Established conventions neither hamper nor harm them. There is the example of Christ Himself Who observed the commandment of the Father without contravening the 'grievous burdens' [cf. Luke 11:46] of the law of Moses.

Time and again have I interrupted my task, dissatisfied with what I had written. I tried to find the reason for my lack of success and now perhaps I begin to understand. I had set myself an impossible task – to put into a book all that I had gone through during the decades of my 'hell of repentance'. Obviously, I am no writer. When I looked back on those events in my spiritual life that clung most in my memory, I was not seldom brought up short by the nature of my experience. I think this must be not only my own case but that of all other ascetics and writers in the long and not so long ago past. Each recurrence over a sometimes protracted period of what was essentially the same phenomenon almost every time followed a different ritual, or varied in composition and detail. Fresh elements would appear in my state, previous ones would no longer be there. Diversities would arise impossible to write about in a book, which *ipso facto* requires methodical organisation of all the material. Looking through my first drafts for a more extensive treatise, time after time I noticed that a single page would be a coagulum of divers themes. Some of them could have fitted equally well into various other chapters such as *On Repentance, Concerning Prayer, Contemplation, Light, Persona, et al.* If I had written down each idea on a separate sheet of paper I could almost have manipulated them like a pack of cards, shuffling them into different combinations – one and the same thought could apply to a dozen closely-related problems. Do not think that I exaggerate. The life of the spirit is like living water – sometimes just a small brook, at others a broad river or confluence of rivers. Or it can be a vast sea. Now there is the music of a stream bubbling over stones; now the continually vibrating but steady flow of a mighty river. There is the swirl of waters where two mountain torrents converge in a rush. Or the smooth surface of water reflecting the sun and blue sky. Now storms rage over vast stretches of deep sea, to be followed by a majestic calm in the silence of a moonlit night. And through it all the water remains the same.

In contact with God man's spirit can always apprehend new outpourings of another being, another cognition. He reaches frontiers of time, moves into other dimensions, with the help of the Divine Spirit embraces the terrestrial world, cosmic being, the ages of ages; touches on the unoriginate in his prayerful upsurge to the Unoriginate.

I do not know of an experience that might serve as a sum total of all others, especially where initial and intermediate states are in question. Even if for a moment or two our spirit approaches perfection of vision in Light, the perfection is still only relative and in our earthly career does not continue fixed. In short, the extraordinary opulence of bestowments from on High cannot be depicted chronologically, in due sequence, and I abandon the attempt.

St. Silouan's method is to place us before the general principle and then leave us to work out and diagnose our own case. To give a few examples: 'One should eat only so much as allows prayer and the feeling of the Divine presence to continue uninterrupted after taking food'; 'Better defer each and any undertaking on which the soul is not prepared to solicit God's blessing – abandon any project which cannot be prefaced by untroubled prayer'; 'If prayer is interrupted by some alien thought, then that prayer is not "pure" '; 'Where hostility – rancour – persists in the heart, our salvation is not assured'; 'If we do not love our enemies, we are still in the embrace of death and have not come to know God as He ought to be known'. And so on.

I have decided to continue with my writing and make fewer demands on myself, propounding my fifty and more years of experience of fragmentary manifestations relative to the basic tenets of our faith as I see them: the God of Love is Trinity consubstantial and undivided; Absolute Being is Personal, and our relations with the Personal God are likewise first and foremost personal; sin is always an offence against, or digression from, the Father's love; only repentance can restore the purity and unfading immutability of our union of love with God; apart from Christ and without the Light of the Holy Spirit no one can ever arrive at a comprehensive vision of sin; the way to the Father of all that exists – is Christ, and our adoption of sons is only and solely through Him and in Him, as the only-begotten Son, co-eternal with the Father and the Spirit. Weeping with our whole being is the normal state where there is true repentance. The more shattering our fear of being eternally cut off from God, the more we are appalled by our ugliness – the more total the striving of our spirit in prayer.

The magnitude of the task ahead must in no way deter us from carrying it out. If we believe that Christ, the Creator of our nature, is absolutely aware of our ultimate potentiality, we shall be inspired to ascetic struggle. According to revelation we are chosen in Christ 'before the foundation of the world'. The Apostles and Fathers recognised this, so why should we falter before such a marvellous calling, compared with which all other concepts and aims pale? Furthermore – aside from this notion everything collapses and life becomes foolish vanity. Christ revealed Himself to us as man, the implementation of holy eternity in the bosom of the Father. We cannot refuse to follow after Him [cf. John 16:22, 33]. Of course, we are no sturdier than the Apostles, who 'were afraid' as they 'followed the Lord going up to Jerusalem' where He would be judged and condemned to a shameful death [cf. Mark 10:32–33]. And we know that we are at war. But our one and only war, which we elected for, is the sacred battle with the common enemy of all people, of all mankind – against death [cf. I Cor. 15:16]. In effect man has no other enemy. Our fight is for resurrection – our own and each of our fellow-men's. The Lord 'sent us forth as sheep in the midst of wolves' [cf. Matt. 10:16].

Of the spiritual states of the Christian and, more especially perhaps, of the monk, the lowest is 'outer darkness' [Matt. 8:12] and the loftiest – 'the kingdom of God come with power' [Mark 9:1]. Complacent narrow-mindedness prevents an enormous number of people from accepting real Christianity, and even alienates them. But it is still possible in our time, too, to find ascetics striving for sanctity whose experience approaches the universal. They have suffered the agony of mental see-sawing; tortures of conscience because of their depravity and iniquity before God; soul-destroying uncertainty and dolorous combat with the passions. They have known the torments of hell, the blackness of despair, the fetters of death-dealing despondency, the anguish that defies description and the distress of being forsaken by God. The ascetic who has sought and found true repentance will similarly be familiar with numerous categories of spiritual joy and peace, of inspired faith and healing hope. The fire of Divine love touches the heart and mind of him who prays and with it a vision of the unfading Light of the 'city to come' [cf. Heb. 13:14]. Refined by fasting and prayer, the heart through grace becomes clairvoyant when the depths of fellow souls are revealed to it. Attention is not stayed on other aspects of intuition. Generally, to begin with, comes the grace of 'mindfulness of death'. This is an especial state when eternity knocks at the heart living in the darkness of sin. Here the Divine Spirit, still unrecognised, still unknown and concealing itself, imparts to the spirit a vision, difficult to explain, of the outside world – the world, the whole of cosmic being, stamped from the very outset with the seal of corruption, where all is meaningless, engulfed in the shadow of death. The Gospel word becomes intelligible to the experienced

Christian. What used to seem contradictory is now revealed as Divine universality, as sacred Mystery, secret since the foundation of the world. The contrast between this new understanding and our preceding blindness is too vast to be explained in our words. The spirit arrives at two frontiers – of *hell* and the *Kingdom* – between which the whole spiritual life of the reasoning individual oscillates.

When his spirit is contracted within, either from sheer exhaustion or because of the heavenly glory that has come to him, the Christian's prayer is like lightning cutting from end to end through the universe in a single flash. Freed from the power of all that is ephemeral, the spirit is transported to the immutable world. Deathly suffering meets with unendurable bliss.

Man cannot for long tolerate such extremes, which are accorded to only a few, and only *once*. But the experience for a tiny instant reveals such spheres of Being, which people generally never even suspect. Their hearts are closed to the holy Life of God.

The first step to success in the struggle against sin is to distance oneself from places or people and circumstances connected with our fall. To retire from the world, retreat into the desert, is a positive stage in this respect, since there, in the desert, many sins – violence, deception, calumny, covetousness, debauchery, intemperance, *et cetera* – are not feasible. Of course, this is far from enough. The attentive Christian feels the very presence in himself of passions as yet not overcome because the thought of them may still intrude, as servitude to iniquity and death. Moreover, there are many sins, such as pride, vanity, rancour and the like, which may destroy us, whether we implement them or not. Combating them can be a grievous business even in the absolute solitude of the desert. The secret of victory lies in humility likening us to the humble Lord.

God is holy and those who have found salvation in Him are hallowed. Christian holiness means being free from the 'law of sin' [cf. Rom. 8:2]. The state of being free from the passions is distinguished by the constant presence within a man of the grace of the Holy Spirit, Which bears witness that we 'have passed from death unto life' [I John 3:14] incorruptible. Love is the indication of the Divine Spirit's action in us, for 'God is love; and he that dwelleth in love dwelleth in God, and God in him' [I John 4:16]. This love is by its origin immortal. It cannot be diminished by suffering, compassion is proper to it. Setting man outside death, this love is *naturally* all compassionate pity even for enemies. It has no 'fear of them which kill the body' [cf. Matt. 10:28] but sorrows for them because they are without the Light of true life. This is the understanding that our holy Fathers teach us, and we accept and live it as true.

Born into this world, we are bound to it by the strong bonds of kinship. We love the world. Within its bounds we fashion our eternity. But we suffer in it – it cramps the love commanded of us. We cannot fail to love it but this does not mean walking its fallen ways. We cannot help loving the world but when our attraction to it triumphs over our love for God, we must find the strength in ourselves to act like Abraham – 'take the fire in our hand, and a knife', and offer in sacrifice all that we hold dear for the sake of the victory of Divine love in us [cf. Gen. 22:6].

The Creator's blessing rests on this world wherever He is gratefully accepted. But even the blessed side of the world cannot be our ultimate goal. We languish here with a holy grief, drawn by the summons of the celestial Father. We are aware that the part of ourselves that would hasten to Him, itself becomes celestial. We know that God has summoned us to collaborate with Him in the Act of creation by Him of immortal gods. We ourselves are created beings but the Lord Jesus by His appearance on earth, His teaching, His example, creates us like unto Himself. The coming in to us of the Holy Spirit perfects in us the likeness of the only-begotten Son. Thus do we, too, become sons of the Highest [cf. Luke 1:35]. And everything that Christ says of Himself in His incarnation can apply to us, also. 'The Son can do nothing of himself, but what he seeth the Father do: for what things soever he doeth, these also doeth the Son likewise. For the Father loveth the Son, and sheweth him all things that himself doeth' [John 5:19–20].

Man is twofold – on this earth, he at the same time transcends the natural world. In the lower forms of his material existence he is a 'thing' of this world, and as such – determined. As hypostasis, image of the Hypostatic God, he is beyond definition. Hence our dual perception of ourselves – we are nonentities, created from nothing, and yet we are of great consequence in the grace of salvation. Dependence cohabits with freedom in us, decay with immortality, servitude with lordship. In their fall men fell victim to the fatal aberration of 'highly esteeming that which is abomination in the sight of God' [cf. Luke 16:15]. They shun and despise that 'which is in the sight of God of great price' [cf. I Pet. 3:4; Luke 1:52].

To be a Christian requires a fortitude that outdoes all other kinds of courage. 'The man Christ Jesus' overcame the world and He invites us to share in His eternal victory [cf. I Tim. 2:5; John 16:33]. After His ascension as Man He sat 'on the right hand of God' [Mark 16:19]. We need the immense strength of the faith of the disciples, or the simplicity of a child, to accept this vocation without hesitating. 'To him that overcometh will I grant to sit with me in my throne, even as I also overcame, and am set down with my Father on his throne. He that hath ear, let him hear . . .' [Rev. 3:21–22]. 'For whatsoever is born of God overcometh the world: and this is the victory that overcometh the world, even our *faith*' [I John 5:4].

Whoever tries to follow Christ 'whithersoever he goeth' [Rev. 14:4] will inevitably be rent again and again – at every rise from a lesser to a wider cognition, from a small measure of love to a greater. Our heart cannot contain His omnipotence. Our mind cannot grasp His infinitude. 'My thoughts are not

your thoughts, neither are your ways my ways, saith the Lord'
[Isa. 55:8].

How often are we brought up short, incapable of understanding His will, His first and last thought for us. We do not
easily abandon 'our ways' and with enormous difficulty search
out 'His ways'. The instant it seems to us that *now* I begin to
see . . . He demonstrates how immeasurably distant He is. My
soul is strained to the limits of her strength, my spirit fails. I
am appalled at the endless profundities of the knowledge of
God that stretch before me. I look for sustenance in the Divine
word, and what do I come on? 'Yet once more I shake not the
earth only, but also heaven'. Why? 'For the removing of those
things that are shaken, as of things that are made, that those
things which cannot be shaken may remain' [Heb. 12:26–27].

O LORD, I am weak. Thou knowest this.
In fear I seek the way to Thee. Despise me not.
Forsake me not in my fall.
Draw near even unto me, who am of no account, yet I
        thirst after Thee.
Take up Thine abode in me and do Thou Thyself
perform in me all that Thou hast commanded of us.
Make me Thine for ever and ever, in love unshakeable.

Divine life is unimaginable for us, which is why we generally
speak of *Divine Mysteries*. This, however, does not mean that
the Lord deliberately conceals from us certain aspects of His
eternal Being. Of course not. As creatures created from
'nothing', and therefore only 'potentials', we are faced with the
familiar process of maturing and becoming established in Truth,
through gradual cognition of the Mysteries. This is the way of
it: every gift of the Creator is pure gift, for we had nothing
before coming into this world, and, indeed, our very existence
we received from His hands. But assimilation of the talents, the
gifts, entails painful effort of our whole being. Only when it is
so can God attribute the attainment to us, putting into our full

possession for all eternity the life that proceeds from Him. His life becomes our life.

The Unoriginate Absolute – God – revealed Himself to us as Personal Being. And we are created as potential *personae*. Cognition of God by us, created *personae*, is a twofold act – of Giver and receiver. This cognition is always personal, never objective. We, who are in the Divine image, bear within ourselves an insuperable urge to find the meaning of the Self-existent Divine Being that is revealed to us.

With the creation of man the Lord acts no longer by Himself but always in concordance with His creature. The process of our perfecting requires two wills – the Creator's and that of the created; two *personae*, God and man. Cognition of the living God comes in the act of our uniting with Him in His very Being. Such an act of union emanates from mutual love that opens up the whole fulness of our heart, of our entire being. But if we only give God a part of our life, we must not expect Him, the Unoriginate, to manifest Himself to us in all His Plenitude, and imprescriptibly, moreover, for all eternity. The Lord is inscrutably munificent but He takes into account the measure of our surrender to Him. In other words, He gives Himself to us to the degree that we are *ready* of our free will to accept Him.

God so fuses with man that man lives Him as his own life, and not in the least as an 'object' of cognition. The scientific, objectifying approach can in no way be applied to Him. In the union between God and us both He and we invariably remain *personae* conscious of being linked by love. He says of Himself, 'I live'; He names Himself, 'I AM', and imparts to us exactly this life, so that we, too, may say feelingly of ourselves, 'I am'. He is Self-existent but we have our being from Him. In so far as we are in Him, so are we beyond death – that is, eternal.

His Name is – '*Alpha and Omega, the beginning and the ending*' [Rev. 1:8]; '*the first and the last*'[vv. 11, 17]. He is the initial principle both of Himself and of all that exists. Until He touches us with His finger; until His energy of eternal life traverses our heart, our mind and even our body, we are lost in conjectures about Him. As creatures – we cannot comprehend the possibility of Existence in general. We register the fact but can go no further. He revealed Himself first to Moses on Sinai with the Name 'I AM', but incomparably more potently through His appearance in this world, in our flesh. And He gave us the blessing of knowing him as PERSONA, and of seeing ourselves lifted to this form of being through faith in Him, through meeting with Him in truly existential union, through the coming of the Holy Spirit into our hearts.

One of the most important events of my life was my encounter, by God's good providence for me, with St. Silouan. It was given to this humble man, from on High, to pray for the whole world as for himself. Predominantly, however, he sorrowed for those who had already passed over. His soul was riveted on the vision of hell beyond the bounds of this earth. He contemplated this hell by virtue of his experience of the reality of the spiritual state of the human spirit. He did not let time or space condition his prayer, for his spirit looked always on eternity. Personally, I was possessed by the vision of hell here, in history. Life in the desert, far from releasing me from this torment, increased my suffering over the events of our age, most of all the Second World War. The desert gave me freedom to devote myself to prayer for mankind, especially during the night. I was somehow obsessed by all the suffering in the world. My experience of the First World War and the ensuing Revolution in Russia contributed to this. I had lived for years in the stifling atmosphere of the fratricidal hatred – at first of conflict between nations and then of civil war. Since that time I would rather hear of maybe thousands of victims of earthquakes, floods, epidemics and so on – catastrophes which normally inspire widespread compassion, whereas wars drag practically everyone into moral participation in the slaughter. There is no worse sin than war. In those years I lived the

Liturgy, pondering on Christ's night in Gethsemane and the fearful day of Golgotha. I knew despair – I understood the enormity of the First Fall of man. I cannot think how I survived.

'When Jesus . . . had received the vinegar, he said, *It is finished:* and he bowed his head, and gave up the ghost' [John 19:30]. What was Christ aware of when He said, *It is finished*? No one has the power wholly to uncover the eternity wherein our Lord dwelt. But it would not be mistaken to suppose that His global vision included not only extreme Self-emptying to the extent of descent into hell but the spectacle of His victory over death. He beheld the multitude of them whom He had saved in the Light of the Father's Kingdom. What the creative mind of God had designed for man 'before the foundation of the world' is now possible and accomplished. The 'work' which the Father had given to Christ to do – He has finished [cf. John 17:4].

We are fearful, we are appalled, when we see the dreadful extent of the suffering that lies before us. But the peculiarity of the Christian way lies precisely in the fact that descent into the domain of torment may parallel the human spirit's ascent into the sphere of uncreated Light. When we are seized by what seems to us unbearable anguish, suddenly the possibility of really measureless abundance of life opens out before us. Then it is that we begin to cognize Christ more deeply, both as Man and as God. And our spirit rejoices, marvelling at the miracle that God has performed with us. Just as the Gethsemane prayer continues eternal in its operative puissance; just as Christ's death at Golgotha has for all time seared the body of the created world; just as the Lord's deeds and words can never be effaced from the history of man – so will our labours to follow after Christ stay engraved in us for eternity, but transfigured by the power of Divine Love.

To the faithful believer states of being are accorded that liken him to the Incarnate God – we do not speak of complete identity but we do not deny an analogy. (It would be folly to claim identicalness; profanity and ingratitude to reject similitude.) And if it were never given to anyone to live in prayer be it only a faint likeness to the spiritual states of the God-man, how could people ever manage to recognise God in Him? 'This is life eternal, that they might know thee the only true God, and Jesus Christ, whom thou hast sent' [John 17:3]. The whole point of our arduous striving is to know the one true God. Our spirit is focussed, not on ephemeral phenomena but on eternal Being. Our mind aspires to Him, Who IS, the foundation of all that exists, the First and the Last. And how could we ascribe such attributes to the *historical* Christ if following His commandments did not bring the fruits of which the Fathers from generation to generation speak with such reverence and rapture; if He were as hidebound as we are? But . . . 'the Son of God· . . . hath given us an understanding, that we may know him that is true and may be in his Son Jesus Christ . . .' [cf. I John 5:20]. And St. Paul says that in us must be 'this mind which was also in Christ Jesus' [Phil. 2:5]. And again, Paul 'bows his knees unto the Father of our Lord Jesus Christ . . . That he would grant us to be strengthened with might by His Spirit in the inner man; That Christ may dwell in our hearts; that we . . . may be able to comprehend with all saints what is the breadth, and length, and depth, and height; And to know the love of Christ, which passeth knowledge, that we might be filled with *all the fulness of God*' [cf. Eph. 3:14–19].

So then, if at the beginning of Christianity the Spirit put these words into the mouth and heart of St. Paul, the same Spirit right up to this day never ceases to move the hearts of the faithful to like prayer for the whole world, that every man may know through and through that the Lord calls each and all of us 'into his marvellous light' [I Pet. 2:9].

Our mind does not take in what the salvation of the world signifies; or 'what the rising from the dead should mean' [cf. Mark 9:10]. But in prayer even we are given an inkling of the mystery of the next world. We believe that the moment will come, to be called 'the fulness of times' [Eph. 1:10], as the completion of all that the Creator conceived for us. Eternity knows no duration, although it embraces the whole expanse of time and space. One can only call it an eternal instant, imposs-ible to determine or assess, either in time, space or logic. In this ineffable moment even we, by the gift of the Holy Spirit, in a single brief, deathless act of our whole being will embrace everything that ever was, and God will be all in all [cf. I Cor. 15:28].

Reasonable man has to become perfect after the image of the Triune Divinity. This is the meaning, the purpose and the task of Christ's Church. 'That they all may be one; as thou, Father, art in me, and I in thee, that they also may be one in us . . .' [John 17:21]. It is clear that every member of the Church must come to fulness of likeness to Christ, even to identity. Other-wise, there will be no unity of the Church in the image of the oneness of the Holy Trinity.

8

Concerning Spiritual Liberty

'Stand fast therefore in the liberty wherewith Christ hath made us free, and be not entangled again with the yoke of bondage' [Gal. 5:1].

The start of our life in the body, 'formed . . . of the dust of the ground' [Gen. 2:7] provides us with experience of being dependent on the forces of nature, with which necessity and determinism are connected. It is only through Christ that we can know the kingdom of the liberty of the Divine Spirit [cf. II Cor. 3:17] and then also of the human spirit [cf. John 8:31–32]. The human spirit, as the image of the Spirit of the Lord, created by God in some searchless way, is engendered, as it were, in the material of our body but by its essence stands above cosmic matter. Meeting with Christ causes it to grow in its hypostatic cognition to such maturity that it ceases to be dependent on the physical laws of the earth and begins effectively to breathe the breath of Divine eternity.

The freedom of the man who believes in the Divinity of Jesus Christ, and who dwells in the sphere of His word, belongs to a plane of other dimensions. It is a freedom in no way determined from without. Such a man, approaching 'unto the measure of the stature of the fulness of Christ' [Eph. 4:13], although he is a creature created by God, the Creator treats not as His 'energy' but as a definite *fact* even for Himself. God will never force anything from him, not even love for Him as His Father. He reveals Himself as He is, leaving man free to react as he chooses. So the Church avoids even Divine – that is, Origenist – determinism, whereby God of His goodness will, without infringing the principle of freedom, find a way for all men and all things to be saved.

This liberty, experience of which is given to the Christian, belongs to the personal principle in man. The *two* – *persona* and liberty – are indissolubly related: where there is no liberty, there is no *persona;* and vice versa – without *persona* there is no liberty. This kind of eternal being uniquely concerns the *persona*, in no way the individual [cf. I Cor. 15:47–50].

We are created by God 'in His image' for life 'after His likeness' – that is, for our ultimate divinization, for the communication to us of Divine Life in all its plenitude. Relations between God and man are based on the principles of freedom: our final self-determination with reference to God depends on our own discretion. When in our liberty we opt for sin, we then sever the ties of love, and withdraw from Him. The possibility of negative self-determination in connection with our Heavenly Father constitutes the tragic aspect of liberty. But this fateful free will of ours is nevertheless an essential condition for the created *persona* in his progress towards the assumption of Divine Life.

Yes, we are free. But not to the absolute degree in which God Himself is free: He determines His own Being in all things. We, however, created from 'nothing', in ourselves have no life. We cannot produce any other sort of being which we might wish for in our wisdom or our folly. Before us is the *fact* of the Primal Self-existence of God besides Whom nothing self-existent can be. We are faced with the choice between 'the adoption of sons' [Gal. 4:5] by our God and Father, or withdrawing from Him 'into outer darkness' [cf. Matt. 22:13]. *There is no middle way.*

The Christian is called upon to have the temerity to believe that we can become possessed of Divine Being. It does not belong to us, since we are creatures. We have not the power to originate this being: it can only be given to us as the pure gift of the Father's love.

What am I talking of at this point? I am trying to find a kind of parallel in our everyday life that might explain what happens when the Lord comes to dwell in us. Man is born a blind, helpless infant. His weapon in his struggle for existence are tears by which he expresses his discomfort, his hurt, whatever the reason for it. His parents – his mother especially, out of love for the child of her womb, hurries to his help. At the start of his life the infant clings to his mother. Gradually he learns to distinguish objects, pronounce words, begin to understand certain things, grow stronger and able to stand, walk and run. Finally he reaches maturity – physical, moral, intellectual. He can become a parent himself. He enters on an independent life. Everything experienced in infancy disappears from his memory: he knows who his father and mother were but no longer feels dependent on them: he lives as if he had issued from no one. He is free in his activities and decisions. He senses himself as a complete individual entity. In short, 'I exist'. How this has come about, I do not know, but the fact is utterly convincing for me myself . . . Only my reason knows that the life that my parents had was given to me, became mine, flowed in my veins.

So it is with us in relation to God: 'For as the Father hath life in himself; so hath he given to the Son to have life in himself' [John 5:26]. 'As the living Father hath sent me, and *I live by the Father:* so he that eateth me, even he *shall live by me*' [John 6:57–58]. 'Because I live, *ye shall live* also' [John 14:19]. When this immemorial life is communicated to us existentially, we feel it like our own life. We know from previous experience that this life is given to us by God. It is not ours by its nature; but given as their imprescriptible property to those who are saved. It does indeed become *our life*. One can speak of it in the words of St. Paul: 'And yet not I live, but Christ liveth in me' [cf. Gal. 2:20]. Again, I repeat – I know that it is He Who lives in me, but His life has become the kernel, the intrinsic kernel, of my whole being, so that I can speak of it as *my* life: the Lord lives, and I, too, live.

'He that hath my commandments, and keepeth them, he it is that loveth me: and he that loveth me shall be loved of my Father, and I will love him, and will manifest myself to him . . . and we will come unto him, and make our abode with him' [John 14:21,23]. 'Make their abode', of course, not temporarily but for eternity.

Our entry into possession of this immortal life is conditional upon the keeping of the Lord's commandments.

'If ye continue in my word, then are ye my disciples indeed; And ye shall know the truth, and the truth shall make you free' [John 8:31–32].

The likeness of our nature to God generates a thirst in us to know the Truth, to aspire to Divine perfection. This perfection is not in us ourselves but in the Father, the Source of all that exists. Following Him in all things is not in the least like being subjected to the dictates of some alien power. It is our love attracting us to Him. We continually pine for His perfection. And Christ did give us the commandment, 'Be ye therefore perfect, even as your Father which is in heaven is perfect' [Matt. 5:48].

The sacred will of the Father, eternally existing in Him, is not foreign to us, who are His 'image'. It is kindred to our spirit, even though it surpasses our created nature. The superiority of the Father explains the necessity for our struggle to assimilate it; and we freely accept this ascetic striving, at one and the same time both agonizing and inspiring. Through prayer strength from on High comes to us. The Holy Spirit, not our struggle, achieves in us what we seek and aspire to. We grieve painfully because we do not contain His fulness in ourselves. And we ache, and suffer, but are blissful, too, in our suffering; and we revere Him and bow down before Him in our love. In its purest form our prayer is nothing other than our spirit's rapture before Him.

'Lord, teach us to pray . . . He said unto them, When ye

pray, say, Our Father' [Luke 11:1–2]. 'After this manner therefore pray ye' [Matt. 6:9–13]:

'Our Father which art in heaven, Hallowed be thy name'. Thou didst give my spirit to scent the fragrance of Thy holiness, and now my soul thirsts to be holy in Thee.

'Thy kingdom come': I pray Thee, let me, who am poor and destitute, be filled with thy royal life, and may it be my life, for ever and ever.

'Thy will be done in earth, as it is in heaven' – in the earth of my created being . . . let even me, a mortal, be included in the mighty stream of this Light as it is in Thee Thyself from the beginning.

'Give us this day our daily bread', and before all and after all 'the true bread . . . which cometh down from heaven, and giveth life unto the world' [John 6:32–33].

'And forgive us our trespasses, as we forgive them that trespass against us' . . . I beseech Thee, send down on me, held fast in the bondage of corruption, the grace of the Holy Spirit to give me strength to forgive all things to all men, that nothing remain in me to hinder me from receiving Thy forgiveness for my manifold sins.

'And lead us not into temptation' . . . O Thou, to Whom all hearts are open, Who knowest my vileness, my disposition to sin, I pray Thee, send Thine angel with his sword drawn in his hand to stand in the way of my fall [cf. Numbers 22:22 *et seq.*].

'But deliver us from evil'. O Holy Father, Almighty and good, deliver me from the power of our enemy and Thine adversary. To battle alone against him is beyond my strength.

To begin with, we pray for ourselves. But when the Holy Spirit increases our understanding and broadens our knowledge, our prayer takes on cosmic dimensions, and in invoking our Father by the word 'our' we think of all mankind and implore grace for all men as earnestly as for ourselves.

'Hallowed be thy name' amongst all peoples. 'Thy kingdom come' into the souls of all men, that the Light of the life that proceeds from Thee may become the life of our whole world.

'Thy will be done' – the one holy will that unites all in Thy love, on the earth wherein we live, as it reigns among the saints in heaven. 'Deliver us from evil' – from the evil 'murderer' [cf. John 8:44] who sows seed of enmity and death everywhere [cf. Matt. 13:27–28].

According to Christian understanding evil, like good, is present only where there is personal form of being. Without this kind of life there is no evil but only determined natural processes.

In connection with the problem of evil in general and particularly in the human world, the question arises of God's participation in the historical destinies of peoples. Vast numbers of men reject belief in God because it seems to them that, if God existed, there could be no place for such savage evil everywhere, so much undeserved suffering, such chaos and absurdity. They forget, or simply do not know, that the Creator cherishes our freedom as the basic principle in the creation of god-like beings. If God were to interfere every time men felt drawn to evil it would be tantamount to depriving them of the possibility of self-determination and the end result would be to reduce everything to cosmic impersonal laws.

God, of course, saves both individual sufferers and whole peoples if they will set their feet on His paths and call upon Him for help.

Not everyone holds the same conception of the meaning of the word *salvation*. For Christians waging unrelenting battle against sin salvation signifies that God Himself gives Himself to man in the immensity of His eternity. Their whole lives may be marked by adversity but inwardly they stand before the Invisible [cf. II Tim. 4:7; Phil. 1:29; Acts 9:16; I Cor. 15:30; II Cor. 6:4]. Any attempt to describe the state of such a Christian would be useless: he surrenders to the will of God, and in this self-abnegation resembles Christ [Luke 22:42]. In its essence this act is a free manifestation of kenotic love, making man like God: ' . . . the hour is come; behold, the Son of man is betrayed into the hands of sinners' [Mark 14:41]. There is no greater love than this: we give ourselves into the sacred care of our Creator, and thereby enter into the fulness of Divine life.

Prayer is more important than any other activity, whether social or political, in the field of science or the arts. He who knows this by experience finds it easy to sacrifice material well-being for the sake of leisure to converse with God. It is a great privilege to be able to concentrate one's mind on the permanent, the intransitory – on the things that are superior to, and reach higher than, all the most outstanding achievements of science, philosophy or social service. At first the struggle for spiritual freedom may seem inordinately hard and risky; but all diffi-culties are overcome when prayer takes entire possession of the soul.

Prayer of profound repentance may lead to a state in which we receive the experience of freedom in the Spirit of Truth: 'and the truth shall make you free' [John 8:32]. Unfortunately, this holy freedom is unknown to the majority of people. The first symptom of liberation is an unwillingness to dominate. The next rung of the ladder is to unshackle oneself from the authority of others – not because one scorns powers ordained by God, or the temporal rulers of the life of the community, but because fear of the Lord precludes trespassing against the commandment to love one's neighbour.

God without beginning revealed Himself to us in His inef-fable humility. He, the Creator of all that exists, does not rule over us. True, no one has power over Him either. Man is the image of this humble and free God. It would be normal for us to strive to become like Him in His form of Being: to avoid commanding others, and ourselves to 'stand fast in the liberty wherewith Christ hath made us free' [cf. Gal. 5:1].
When God's light enters the soul in prayer it brings release from slavery to the passions and leads up into the luminous sphere of god-like freedom, which is all love and excludes any

tendency to play the tyrant – which is the opposite of love. Where freedom and love are absent, nothing has any meaning. Even gifts like the gift of prophecy, the understanding of all mysteries and the strength to perform miracles lose their value in the absence of love [cf. I Cor. 13:1–3].

Great and marvellous is the world of spiritual liberty. Outside it, salvation, as the divinization of man, is impossible. It is essential that man should freely determine himself for eternity. Every creature strives to 'be delivered from the bondage of corruption into the glorious liberty of the children of God' [cf. Rom. 8:21–23].

Nowadays all over the world fighting goes on for freedom and independence but it is hard to find anyone to whom the mystery of the godlike freedom of children of the Heavenly Father has been revealed. Words fail to describe the virtue of this state – it can only be known by the gift from on High. Once again I cannot help recalling the Apostle Paul, who undoubtedly knew this divinely-royal liberty: 'The earnest expectation of the creature waiteth for the manifestation of the sons of God. For the creature was made subject to vanity, not willingly . . .' [Rom. 8:19–20].

'Stand fast therefore in the liberty wherewith Christ hath made us free, and be not entangled again with the yoke of bondage' [Gal. 5:1]. It is easy to understand that the craving to dominate soon leads to loss of one's own independence, accompanied – and this is fearful – by retreat from the God of love, and dispossession of the grace of the Holy Spirit. The despot prepares his own downfall into the void of non-existence. Likeness to the Lord of lords precludes the subjection of others, in which there is no eternal or even temporal life. Domination is generally achieved by force and slaughter. Those who have not shown mercy will be judged at the Last Judgment on the principle, 'With what judgment ye judge, ye shall be judged' [Matt. 7:2]. And again, 'He shall have judgment without mercy, that hath shewed no mercy' [James 2:13].

'Where the Spirit of the Lord is, there is liberty' [II Cor. 3:17]. Liberty in its absolute form is peculiar only to God. But to man is given the blessing to know it partly in prayer conjoined with life according to the commandments. Prayer – a priceless gift from Heaven – requires 'leisure'. For the sake of an encounter with the Living Christ it is not too difficult to give up the pleasures that delight man, and prefer converse with Him to all else. This priceless privilege – I make bold to say, blessedness – was given to me most of all in the desert. The ascetic conception of the desert has nothing to do with geography: it is a form of life which means living remote from other people, where no one sees or hears you, or has power over you, and you do not rule over anyone else. This freedom is imperative if one's spirit – indeed, one's whole being – is to be absorbed in the Divine sphere. Then divine *apatheia* – more precious than aught that the earth has to offer – may be communicated to us. There will be no more thought of dominating one's brother; no seeking after honour or renown, still less material riches. I do not understand why in the desert I was granted the blessing of 'the glorious liberty of the children of God' [Rom. 8:21]. I cannot say that I absorbed this gift to its highest degree – when man verily outruns the power over him of sin and death. But at times I did approach this state which made me see that complete liberation comes when death is vanquished. He who is not afraid of death is on the way to freedom. In bondage man is held back if he is attached above all to earthly things. 'Behold I and the children which God hath given me. Forasmuch then as the children are partakers of flesh and blood, he also himself likewise took part of the same; that through death he might destroy him that had the power of death, that is, the devil; And deliver them who *through fear of death were all their lifetime subject to bondage*' [Heb. 2:13–15].

I only partially experienced the rapture of spiritual liberty, losing it when I was ordained priest and confessor. Love not infrequently subjugates me to those whom the Lord has entrusted to me. Still, somewhere in the depths of my soul there lingers a trace of what I knew in the past. The experience began in France – in a very vague form – when I felt an urgent need to withdraw from the world. I thanked God's providence for me that I was free to take the step, since there was no one in the whole wide universe whose life depended on me. In my thirst for God I could afford any risk. Nothing held me back. I could face all and every difficulty. This was my soul's initial experience of imperial freedom. Christ in the freedom of His love surrendered Himself to death, thereby opening to us the road to consummate knowledge, to Divine immortality.

9

Inspiration

Although conscious of my extreme unworthiness – or perhaps precisely because of the anguish it caused me – for years on end I prayed that the Lord would grant me the inspiration to follow Him 'whithersoever he goeth' [cf. Rev. 14:4]; be it into the wilderness to test the fidelity of my love for the Father [cf. Luke 4:1 *et seq.*]; or the torture of preaching the Kingdom of the Father's love; whether to Mount Tabor where three of the chosen disciples heard the Father's voice, saying, 'This is my beloved Son' [Matt. 17:5]; but first of all and most of all to Gethsemane and then Golgotha. Inspiration meant for me the presence of the power of the Holy Spirit within us [cf. John 4:13–15; 7:37–39]. This kind of inspiration belongs to a different plane of being from that which the artist or philosopher knows, though his, too, can be seen as a gift from God. But it does not bring union with God Himself, or even intellectual knowledge of Him.

Truly holy inspiration, proceeding from the Father on High, does not impose itself. It must be obtained, like every other gift from God, by an urgent effort of prayer [cf. Luke 11:9–11]. This does not signify that God gives some sort of 'reward' for effort made but that what one has acquired through cognizant suffering becomes an inalienable possession for eternity. It is imperative for every one of us to be totally reborn by the action of grace; that the ability to apprehend divinization be restored in us. But all this is possible in no other way than by our return to Him – a return involving much torment. God does indeed give His life in the fullest sense into our personal keeping. His eternal glory is committed to those whom He has redeemed –

and not as something improper to our nature, an alien presence [cf. Luke 16:11–12]. No. True divinization communicates the unoriginate life of God Himself, effectively and for ever. In other words, God's Life is 'hypostasised' by man just as God, having become incarnate, assumed into His Hypostasis the form of our being that He Himself had created. In the age to come God's union with men will be complete in all the content of His Being, except, of course, identity of Essence. This last cannot be conveyed to mankind and will forever remain inconceivable for all created beings – angels and humans.

The Kingdom of the Father is the ontological union of all who are saved and, as such, 'cannot be shaken' by anyone or anything [cf. Heb. 12:27–28]. Inspiration from on High depends to a considerable extent on us, on whether we open our heart so that the Lord – the Holy Spirit Who 'stands at the door and knocks' – does not have to enter forcibly. If anyone hears His voice and opens the door, He will come to him, and will sup with him, and he with God [cf. Rev. 3:20]. The Lord preserves the freedom of those created 'in His image'. And we have to know what is acceptable to Him. Hence the need for each and all of us to ban deeds and impulses which may grieve the Spirit of God. Honest abiding in the sphere of Christ's commandments heals our sinful mortality, and all life becomes penetrated by the Uncreated Light of Divine Eternity.

When the soul existentially comes in contact with this Eternity base passions fall away and we turn aside from fratricidal struggle over worldly advantages – the peace of Christ descends on us and we receive the strength to 'love our enemies'. 'My peace I give unto you' [John 14:27]. Christ's peace is the most precious of all riches, of all the delights and joys on earth. It constitutes sure knowledge of the Living God – of our Father. It is enough for us to have something to eat, a roof over our heads, raiment to protect us from cold and embarrassment [cf. I Tim. 6:8], provided our spirit be free to devote itself to contemplation of Divine Being as revealed to us by Christ. Longing after the celestial world, fond striving for it, is our delight and fills even sickly old age with the splendid hope of the Father's merciful embrace [cf. Luke 15:20].

10

Emptiness: God has Withdrawn

I.

'Blessed are the poor in spirit: for their's is the kingdom of heaven' [Matt. 5:3]. 'Blessed' because when we recognise our poverty of spirit strength comes from on High to lift us to God. Without this recognition there is no impulse to reach up to heaven. Self-satisfaction is the symptom of either spiritual paralysis or decline. Constant judging of ourselves against the Divine commandments intensifies our awareness of being distanced from God and deepens our understanding that pride is the root of all evil. Pride is hostile to God. Pride runs counter to Divine Love. Through pride mankind became captive to corruption. If we would be born again in God, in pristine spiritual beauty, we must be guided by the Gospel teaching. Only strong faith that Christ is Almighty God will help us cling to the firm rock of His commandments. Now starts the grievous struggle against all that we brought upon ourselves in our fall. Faith that Christ is the only true Saviour of man will not allow us to defect when the unforeseen and unimagined process begins of delivering ourselves from the cult of sin. The Apostles imparted to us what they heard and learned from the Lord Himself [cf. Matt. 28:19–20]. The Fathers of the Church with their unparalleled asceticism kept all that was commanded of God and handed down to us their priceless experience and knowledge. Thanks to them, to the Apostles and Fathers, we know the *mystery* of the ways of salvation. These invisible paths are suspended across an abyss. No other power, no other wisdom – only unshakeable belief in Christ-God can save us from being storm-tossed and hurled into the black depths. 'And this is the victory that overcometh the world, even our *faith*' [I John 5:4].

Let me make a clumsy attempt to describe this mystery. The commandments place us face to Face with Absolute Being. All our efforts to observe these commandments inevitably fail. We discover our utter incapacity. We see such artfulness of mind and spirit in ourselves, such horrors in our heart, that we feel destroyed. Dread of falling away from God, in Whom we believe, is immense. We are in anguish over ourselves. Everything that we set store by in the past, we cast away, and find ourselves stripped of earthly ties, of our learning, even of our will. We become poor and 'empty'. And the worst ordeal of all is that, despite our utmost straining to be faithful to God, there are periods when we feel forsaken by Him. Our spiritual poverty, together with the pain of God's absence, plunges us into despair. It seems as if some terrible curse hangs over us. We suffer, maybe, on every level of our being – spirit, mind, heart, body. Now we understand the tragedy behind the Bible account of the Fall of man, and belief in Christ's love impels us to the fullest possible repentance. The more profound our repentance, the more clearly do we see into our own previously hidden depths. Realising the desperate state that we are in, we begin to detest ourselves as we are.

This form of self-emptying, or humility, is not achieved by human effort. It is the gift of God our Saviour – the grace of repentance for the remission of sins [cf. Luke 24:47]. We do not understand His action within us. We are reduced to nought. We are troubled. He is not with us. He, our one desire, our only love, is hid from us.

In this manner are we cleansed from the 'curse' of our inheritance [cf. Gen. 3:14–19]. New, uncreated energy begins to penetrate us; we make our communion with Divine Being. God's Light comes to embrace us. The Spirit of Truth proceeding from the Father and reposing in the Son descends into our heart as *Comforter*. 'Blessed are they that mourn: for they shall be comforted' [Matt. 5:4].

When we return to 'nothing' we become material which our God can create from. He Himself, none other, revealed this sacrament to us. Having abandoned ourselves into His sacred hands, experiencing Him at work on us, we see how immeasurably it all transcends us – 'Eye hath not seen, nor ear heard, neither have entered into the heart of man, the things which God hath prepared for them that love him' [I Cor. 2:9]. And there is no end to our wonderment before Him. Oh, how He knows man! Only the One Who created us could have such knowledge of the possibilities of our nature. (I am trying to find words to express the mystery that people have mislaid. I pray God to inspire me. I beg my reader to forget about me, who am of no account, and only concentrate on the essence of our theme. I did not invent this teaching but by God's providence I learned through His chosen one.)

'If any man come to me, and hate not . . . his own life' (soul) 'he cannot be my disciple' [Luke 14:26]. The birth within us of this holy 'hate' indicates our approach to contemplation of the great mystery. He to whom this dread blessing is given begins to 'know the only true God, and Jesus Christ' sent by Him [cf. John 17:3], and takes his first step towards the immovable Kingdom. (The twelfth chapter of the Epistle to the Hebrews offers a splendid description of the way to salvation.)

'What hast thou that thou didst not receive? Now if thou didst receive it, why dost thou glory, as if thou hadst not received it?' [I Cor. 4:7]. The Lord, Who in my early years let me behold His Light with a child's simplicity, allowed me to fall as Adam fell. But He did not altogether abandon me: He made me understand the 'far country' whither I had gone away from Him [cf. Luke 15:13–24]. At the same time, in my floods of tears, He poured down on me the grace of contrition. Initially I was completely ignorant of the teaching of the holy Ascetics. What was happening to me was utterly beyond my comprehension and I sobbed with remorse, knowing that I was unworthy of forgiveness. I ached with yearning for the Father. So much so that, when the flame that consumed me was translated into Light, I was unable to take account of this gift and went on condemning myself to 'outer darkness'. Shame devoured me: I had abandoned Him because He was no use to me – I had gone beyond Him in my understanding of First Being. I prayed, lying prostrate, not daring to look up to Him. I loathed myself.

Man in isolation, as a separate individual, cannot follow after Christ – the panorama spread before him is too grandiose. If he is sound in mind he will not trust himself but seek out reliable witnesses, lest he 'should run . . . in vain' [cf. Gal. 2:2]. The witnesses, of course, must be chosen from past followers of Christ and contemporaries of the same faith. Would I check with Buddhists or Mohammedans whether I understood the Lord's commandments correctly? So I started to study the New Testament chiefly, consulting ministers of the Church, professors of theology. I read the Apostolic Fathers and the great Ascetics, not neglecting the works of recent authors. At the time the latter were not of much direct help. Acquaintance with the writings of the Ascetics, however, did answer my need. In them I found not only inspired guidance along my chosen path but likewise many wondrous explanations of inner spiritual happenings already familiar to me. On the one hand, I was confirmed in my knowledge of the spiritual world; on the other, I was plunged into a complex struggle with my self-conceit. Finding a parallel with my own experience, I would feel a rush of satisfaction which would wrap round my heart like slime. I would then lose the vision of heavenly Light, perhaps for a long time, and suffer deep sadness. My case would appear hopeless: I could not be self-sufficient but when I began to understand what was sent down to me by the Right Hand of God, my 'left hand' ruined everything [cf. Matt. 6:3]. 'O wretched man that I am! who shall deliver me from . . . this death?' [cf. Rom. 7:24]. Time and again I would pray, drowning in tears of repentance, and then somewhere close by, in the air still, a vain thought would come and I would rise to my feet bereft – tears gone, soul desolate, body vigorous, spiritual life no more. After many such disasters the slightest sign of the enemy's approach would fill me with dread and I would redouble my cries of repentance – 'O Lord, the murderers are come, save me'. Then it was that I understood why the Fathers disliked praise: if praised, even the most perfect of them did not escape damage to their love of God.

'Blessed are the poor in spirit: for their's is the kingdom of heaven' [Matt. 5:3]. These words of Christ's lie at the root of Christian asceticism, leading to salvation understood as *divinization*.

I beseech Thee, O Word that wast in the beginning with God and the Spirit: Instruct me now that I may somewhat describe the precious mysteries Thou dost teach us by Thy withdrawal from us. Thou only art our Teacher and Master*. Thou art Light; Thou art wisdom. Thou only art the way to the Father.

Placed squarely before the inexpressible majesty of Divine love made manifest to us by the incarnation of the Logos of the Father, in our anxiety to follow in His steps we must first go through the bitter experience of ever more clearly seeing ourselves 'of no reputation' [cf. Phil. 2:7]. It is a grievous and at the same time wonderful process, the deep-laid meaning of which, however, becomes clear only at the end of the road.

In Christ we meet with Absolute Being. Only through His strength can we overcome all that is incapable of assuming eternity, that is contrary to His love. It is hard for us at every step to have to admit our unstrength. Our minds are too limited to understand His sacred commands. But sooner or later our dolorous striving after Him will begin to echo with the inspiring appeal of the Eternal Divinity. Not blissfully yet, but we have

* cf. Matt. 23: 8, 10.

come to love Him in His splendour, and this love is stronger than death. Painful as it may be to keep His commandments, we cannot relinquish the goal before us – to become for all eternity the habitation of His Light. And so, pain in our every fibre, we plunge into a sea of tears of whole-hearted repentance, aware that there is no other way to rid ourselves of the ugly passion of pride inherited at the Fall. In this state of repentance we become open to the action within us of the Holy Spirit – powerful action giving us a foretaste of eternal union with God.

The transition from the corruption inherited from Adam to the realm of Christ's undeclining Light is a more important event than all other earthly realities. When we begin to hate ourselves [cf. Luke 14:26] it is a sign of approach to this great mystery. It is said: Nothing that defileth shall enter into the Kingdom of the Lamb of God [cf. Rev. 21:27]. We put ourselves sternly on trial and without mercy condemn ourselves to hell as being unworthy of God. Only in this way can we repress our disposition to be indulgent towards our weaknesses and easily forgive our transgressions, especially if they occur in thought only. Our gamble is a tremendous one – our whole being lies at stake. The prize is immortality in eternal Light. 'The kingdom of heaven suffereth violence, and the violent take it by force' [Matt. 11:12].

Christ's teaching cometh down from the 'Father of lights' [Jas. 1:17]. Inherent in it is divine perfection. It belongs to another plane of being. No mortal man can accord his life with the Gospel in all its strength. However much we strain, the commandment in its perfection remains out of reach. At some moment or other it may be given to us to approach this Fire [cf. Luke 12:49] but we cannot stay in it for long. Concerning the experience of dispassion [Gr. *apatheia*] it must also be remarked that it may be given to the ascetic but it is not a permanent state and may fluctuate, depending on environment and the type of his ministry to his fellows. There is no absolute perfection on this earth, and it is dangerous to be satisfied with what we have attained.

Unbelievers have no idea of what it means to be bereft of God. Only those who have already experienced God's goodness and try their utmost to abide in and with Him know this grief. The more a man has tasted of the joy of unity with God, the more profoundly he suffers on being parted from Him. The supreme example of this – which we learn of from the Gospels – is the Lord Himself. After His prayer in the garden of Gethsemane, where 'his sweat was as it were great drops of blood falling down to the ground' [Luke 22:44]; after He had given His all to the Father, hanging on the cross, He 'cried with a loud voice, saying . . . My God, my God, why hast thou forsaken me? . . . and when He had cried again with a loud voice, yielded up the ghost' [Matt. 27:46, 50]. Such complete 'self-emptying' on the part of 'the man Christ Jesus' [I Tim. 2:5] is transfigured into equally perfect divinization of our nature which He assumed in the act of incarnation. And to Him, as Man, was given 'a name which is above every name that is named, not only in this world, but also in that which is to come' [cf. Phil. 2:9; Eph. 1:21].

The Christian must somehow approximate to this state before he can assimilate the measure of salvation that corresponds to the depth of his self-emptying. This is the mode of Divine love: in eternity it comprises constant, maximum tension of being, together with complete forgetting of self. It is humble – humble towards all who come ('him that cometh to me I will in no wise cast out' [John 6:37]). In the Kingdom of God the Father no one selfishly concentrates on himself. 'Charity . . . seeketh not her own' [I Cor. 13:5] but is entirely concerned with others, embracing the whole world – the Divine and the created – in humility. Thus all that is forms the content of this love. In the splendour of love lie incalculable riches, inexpressible blessedness.

Conceit and self-absorption, on the contrary, mean destitution and hell. Haughty concentration on self translates into hate for God.

Only after long practice at self-emptying does Divine love come. The revelation is given in brief moments of visitation from on High, to be followed inevitably by days – years – of being forsaken by God. The soul deserted by God is seized with dread. We may not know why this has happened. We are faced with danger – the love, which appeared to us in Light, departs, hiding itself like the setting sun. Dark night approaches. In this fashion we learn to follow Christ descending into hell – follow Him 'whithersoever he goeth' [Rev. 14:4].

No one genuinely seeking salvation can escape the experience of being bereft of God. At some moments this feeling of having been abandoned becomes so acute that even a fleeting instant of it seems timeless. The ascetic does not suffer such extreme states very often but a moderate testing of our faith can occur over long years in the second stage of a Christian's spiritual life – that is, when he providentially sustains a lessening, and even the departure, of the grace he first knew. The purpose behind this withdrawal of grace is to give him the opportunity to manifest his freedom and fidelity to God.

But how avoid despair if not a single prayer reaches the ear of the All-Highest? However confirmed one may be by a living communion with the One True God in previous years, to be abandoned by Him, Whom we have come to love, makes our spirit wonder painfully – what did happen to me 'then'? Can God – the God Whom I knew – really so withdraw that no lamentation of a wounded soul touches Him? . . . Thoughts like these confuse and agitate the mind. And yet it may be long before the answer comes.

When my actual experience made me see that Christ's commandments are, by their very essence, the projection of Divine life on our plane, I understood the meaning of His words 'Without me ye can do nothing' [John 15:5]. In difficult times when, despite all my efforts, I failed to co-ordinate my life with the Gospel teaching, I would pray thus:

'Come, O Lord, and perform Thy will in me.
Thy commandments find no place in my cramped heart,
and my poor mind cannot discern their content.
For if Thou wilt not come and abide in me, I perish.
I know that Thou dost not coerce but I pray Thee,
in power enter into my house and give me new life.
Transform my benighted pride into Thy humble love.
By Thy Light transfigure my all-perverted nature,
that not a single sinful passion possess me
to prevent the coming of Thy Father and Thee,*
to make of me an holy abode for the life
which Thou Thyself hast vouchsafed me to behold.
Yea, O Lord, I beseech Thee, perform in me
this token of Thy goodness . . .'

Often I would spend long hours in such prayer.

Later on, the faithful soul will see his torments as a sign of
his election by the Good Father. Without such testing no man
could penetrate the depths of God's initial design for us, or the
measure of the love of which Christ spoke. Being forsaken by
God indicates that all our efforts hitherto are far from adequate
for salvation – blessed eternity is not yet ours. Bitter dissatisfaction with – revulsion from – oneself is the first sign that we
are approaching the fulness of love commanded of us by God
– surmounting the terrible obstacle of self-centredness. In prayer
born of hatred for self, new being, not of this world, unfolds
within us and we contemplate Divine majesty.

Christian perfection is super-human, divine. The Lord made
this manifest by His incarnation. No one has departed hence in
like measure with Him [cf. Phil. 3:12]. A certain degree,
however, has been granted to a few [cf. Matt. 7:14] and their
teachings and example inspire us to the rare feat of Christ-like
humility. This heavenly fire, present in the life and sacraments
of the Church, preserves through the centuries faith in the

* cf. John 14:21–23

Gospel, which is 'not after man and not of man . . . but by the revelation of Jesus Christ' [cf. Gal. 1:11–12].

Many will be saved, will rejoice in the ocean of Christ's love, but only a few such receive, though not without fear, the flame while still in the flesh. I remember Blessed St. Silouan in his gentle patience with me once saying that our earthly being cannot sustain the fulness of grace, and so the manifestation of God in His eternal glory is possible for only the briefest moment; and this only if body and psyche be fortified by the grace of the Holy Spirit. It is easier to carry burning coal in one's bare hands for a hundred yards, say, than to hold on to this grace and stay alive.

The bearers of such knowledge make their mark on the whole mass of the faithful. Thanks to them, a living tradition of the spirit of life continues through the centuries.

Only those living an inner life like His earthly life 'know' Christ. In the words of the Apostle, we must have the same mind as was in Christ Jesus, Who, 'being in the form of God made himself of no reputation, and took upon him the form of a servant, and humbled himself, and became obedient unto death, even the death of the cross' [cf. Phil. 2:5–8]. He is the 'corner-stone' rejected by the rulers of this world but which in reality lies at the root of all that is. When the Fire which He sent down on earth touches his heart – and only then – man finds the strength to follow Him to Gethsemane and Golgotha. Follow in spirit, of course, in profound suffering of his whole being. This kind of knowledge of the Lord, Who 'came down from heaven' to the world, and then into hell, includes a partial experience of resurrection.

The Christian travels this inexplicable path into endless distances stretching before him. At one and the same time he beholds the dark depths of the pit and the Light of the Kingdom. This Kingdom is present everywhere but entrance into it depends wholly on God, for it is not something that exists 'objectively' but is He Himself, Who has the power to take us to Himself or – which is the same thing – come to abide in us with an eternal abiding. Then we are in Him, and He is in us; and His Life becomes our imprescriptible life.

II.

The abandonment by God that St. Silouan was given to experience before the Lord appeared to him is, in spiritual fact, the Saint's own *kenosis*. In this abandonment by God which he expressed in the words, '*God cannot be moved by entreaty*', we see the Divine Providence that allowed Silouan to plunge into black despair – to be reduced to nought by God's withdrawal from him. But it was this very descent into hell that prepared his soul to meet with Christ, Who appeared to him with great force. The Light of Divinity illumined him and the grace of the Holy Spirit flooded his whole being. Despair and emptiness were transformed into 'Christ-like humility which is indescribable'. Let us look how Silouan writes of what happened.

'The Lord taught me to keep my mind in hell, and not despair, and thus my soul is humbled. But this is not yet true – that is, Divine – humility, which is *indescribable* . . .

'Christ-like humility dwells in the *little ones*. They rejoice that they are *of no account*. The Lord gave me to understand this.

'I write of these things because *my soul knows the Lord*. The Lord manifests Himself through the Holy Spirit only to the humble.

'Humility is the light in which we can behold the Light Which is God.

'He who has learned to know God through the Holy Spirit has learned humility of Him (Christ-God) and become like unto his Teacher, Christ, the Son of God' [cf. Matt. 11:29].

No mortal man can attain the fulness of Christ in this world. Christ is an astounding miracle: God all-powerful 'makes himself of no reputation' through the incarnation with all its attendant sufferings, even to death on the cross and descent into hell. The miracle is that 'being found in fashion as a man' [Phil. 2:8] He displayed the perfection of Divine Self-emptying love:

'*It is finished*' [John 19:30; 17:4]. No one can compare with Him but there must be some, if only a few, who are similar, and '*know God by the Holy Spirit*'.

'I Paul, the prisoner of Jesus Christ for you . . . Ye have heard of the dispensation of the grace of God which is given me . . . How that by revelation he made known unto me the mystery . . . Whereby, when ye read, ye may understand my knowledge in the mystery of Christ . . . Whereof I was made a minister, according to the gift of the grace of God given unto me by the effectual working of his power. Unto me, who am *less* than the least of all saints, is this grace given . . .' [cf. Eph. 3:1–8].

'Pray always with all prayer and supplication . . . for all saints; And for me, that utterance may be given unto me, that I may open my mouth boldly, to make known the mystery of the gospel' [cf. Eph. 6:18–19].

St. Paul begged the Ephesians to pray for him, that utterance might be given to him, that he might open his mouth boldly, to make known the 'mystery of the gospel'. How much more do I need the prayers of each and all that I may truly present one of the most important aspects of Christian life. In my case it is not a question of some exceptional revelation, though it is a very important one as my experience as a confessor has proved to me, by reminding me that people in the mass have forgotten the ways to salvation. And so, I earnestly beg of you, pray for me.

Great was the spiritual genius of Blessed St. Silouan to whose feet the Divine Providence led me. He spoke and wrote of his experience in words that were simple, yet intelligible only to those who lived in the same atmosphere as he did. I have had the opportunity in my life of discussions with some outstanding representatives of academic theology. It was obvious that even those who were familiar with the works of the holy Ascetics of ancient Egypt and Palestine possessed no personal experience of the things concerning which the Fathers testified. This is why I have decided to try and show the grandeur of the world in which St. Silouan's spirit dwelt; to indicate something of the reality concealed behind his 'simple' words – such as, for instance, 'I began to do as the Lord had taught me; and my mind was purified and the Spirit bore witness to my soul of salvation'. What exactly do a 'pure mind' and the 'witness of the Spirit' mean?

The fact that by his, St. Silouan's prayers I, too, was placed in the same spiritual perspective allows me to venture on this task. To be sure, I did not receive in full measure the blessing that the Lord poured out on him; but nevertheless it was given to me, the least of men, to live approximately the same experience. Because at certain times in my life I have known something of the spiritual climate in which St. Silouan lived, I presume now to discuss this vastly important matter – though it will involve broaching profound dogmatic problems.

'*God cannot be moved by entreaty*,' thought the Saint. He had fallen into despair: it seemed to him that God had rejected him finally, that there was no longer any salvation for him. He saw *eternal perdition* for his soul. 'This spirit of despair is so oppressive and wearisome that even to think back on it is terrifying. The soul has not the strength to endure it for long . . . I went into the church . . . and looking at the ikon of the Saviour said, O Lord Jesus Christ, have mercy upon me, a sinner. At these words I saw, in place of the ikon, the *Living* Lord, and the grace of the Holy Spirit filled my soul and my whole body. And thus through the Holy Spirit I knew that Jesus Christ is God. And I yearned to suffer for Christ.'

The very *fact* of the *Living* Lord's appearance to Silouan shortly after his time of trial shows that at that moment his state was not far removed from Christ's condition on Golgotha: 'My God, my God, why hast thou forsaken me?' [Matt. 27:46]. We know that to contemplate anything divine one must oneself be in harmony with the object of contemplation.

After His cry Christ yielded His Spirit into the hands of the

Father. And what happened with Silouan? In mortal sadness he goes into the church, and hardly has he uttered the prayer, 'Lord Jesus Christ, have mercy upon me', before he sees Him Living; and his whole being is filled with the fire of the grace of the Holy Spirit, to the limits of his strength. The vision exhausted him, and the Lord vanished. But the Divine Spirit had lifted Silouan to heaven where he heard ineffable words.

Afterwards St. Silouan confirmed that when the Lord Himself appears in great Light the soul cannot fail to recognise in Him her Creator and God: 'My Lord and my God', exclaimed Thomas the Apostle to the risen Christ [John 20:28]. And Saul-Paul on the road to Damascus in the same Light recognised Christ-God. Strange and quite extraordinary is the life of the Christian: desertion by God and the darkness of eternal perdition are interwoven with the appearance of God in Uncreated Light.

The Lord Jesus cried to the Father, 'Why hast thou forsaken me?' We know quite surely that on the Divine plane ontologically this could not happen – that is, that the Father could have withdrawn from His co-eternal Son, of one substance with Himself, in Whom He had poured the plenitude of His eternal Being. How then are we to interpret what exactly did happen with 'the man Christ Jesus' [I Tim. 2:5]? Looking at St. Silouan's experience, like that of all the other pious ascetics down the ages, we see a painful state of feeling bereft of God coinciding with a maximum effort to observe God's commandments [cf. John 5:30; 10:18; 14:31; 15:10; 18:11]. We remark this phenomenon but can give no explanation for it, especially when it is a question of the God-Man Christ. In the main these infrequent instances of providential abandonment by God must be seen as an immeasurably great Divine gift. Otherwise, it is difficult to understand the promised divinization of fallen men.

The event that we are now discussing is a 'Self-emptying' of Divine love. Christ Jesus, 'being in the form of God' – that is, being in His essence God – made Himself of no account, so humbling Himself in the act of obedience to the Father as to renounce His human will altogether and go to death on the cross.

'My soul is exceeding sorrowful, even unto death . . . And he went a little farther, and fell on his face, and prayed, saying, O my Father, if it be possible, let this cup pass from me; nevertheless not as I will, but as thou wilt . . . And his sweat was as it were great drops of blood falling down to the ground' [Luke 22:44] . . . 'He went away again the second time, and prayed, saying, O my Father, if this cup may not pass away from me, except I drink it, thy will be done . . . And he prayed the third time, saying the same words' [Matt. 26:38–44]. And precisely for this 'God also hath highly exalted him, and given him a name which is above every name' [cf. Phil. 2:6–9].

The Christ-Man is exalted: no one can come up to Him in the act of His Self-emptying – to go to an infamous death appointed for evil-doers; to hang stripped naked on the cross in the presence of His Mother, of the women who had attended Him; to be deserted by the disciples; to see the final failure of His preaching . . . But who can reckon all that He suffered inside Himself during those days?

So then this kind of abandonment by God is another pole of Divine love. This love is commanded of us by Christ in such terrible words: 'If any man come to me, and hate not (all that is dear to him), yea, and his own life also, he cannot be my disciple' [cf. Luke 14:26,33].

There can be very few in the whole history of the Church to whom it has been given to live the grace-bearing abandonment by God to such a degree as the servant of the High God, Silouan. When the great Light shone on him in his vision of Christ, the abandonment by God that had felt like a deadly pain was translated into 'Christ-like humility, which is indescribable'; which is the ontological aspect of the eternal love of God the Three-in-One. God, absolute in His incalculable might, in some searchless fashion is also absolute in His Self-emptying humility.

Everyone who ardently loves Jesus Christ, God our Creator and Saviour, without fail experiences two states of being that would seem to be diametrically opposed: descent into hell and ascent into heaven. St. Paul wrote of it like this:

'Unto me, who am less than the least of all saints, is this grace given, that I should preach . . . the unsearchable riches of Christ; And to make all men see what is the fellowship of the mystery, which from the beginning of the world hath been hid in God, who created all things by Jesus Christ: To the intent that now unto the principalities and powers in heavenly places might be known by the church the manifold wisdom of God, According to the eternal purpose which he purposed in Christ Jesus our Lord: In whom we have boldness and access with confidence by the faith of him. Wherefore I desire that ye faint not at my tribulations for you, which is your glory. For this cause I bow my knees unto the Father of our Lord Jesus Christ, Of whom the whole family in heaven and earth is named, That he would grant you, according to the riches of his glory, to be strengthened with might by his Spirit in the inner man; That Christ may dwell in your hearts by faith; that ye, being rooted and grounded in love, May be able to comprehend with all saints what is the breadth, and length, and depth, and height; And to know the love of Christ, which passeth knowledge, that ye might be *filled with all the fulness of God*' [Eph. 3:8–19].

The diapason of Christian life ranges far beyond ordinary human hearing – farther both below and above. Regrettably, very many of us are deaf to the wondrous cadences of the divine hymn coming to us from the ineffable depths of eternal Being. To the man who believes in the Divinity of Christ, and so constructs his life on the rock of His teaching [cf. Matt. 7:24–27], hidden mines of treasure are revealed that are impenetrable for those who have not accepted Christ as Very God, as the all-holy and absolute Authority [cf. Matt. 23:8] – *Authority*, not compulsion but *true eternal fact and perfect love.*

Blessed St. Silouan distinguished two kinds of humility:

ascetic and Divine. When, not long before his death, I asked him, 'Staretz, are you going to die?', he answered, 'I have not yet learned humility'. I have no doubt at all that he was thinking of the Divine humility of Christ, which he could never forget. With this in mind he had written, 'Blessed is the man who remains pure in soul and body: the Lord loves him and gives him the grace of the Holy Spirit; and this grace so commits the soul to love of God that, for delight in the Holy Spirit, she cannot tear herself from God, and aspires insatiably to Him, since there is no end to Divine love. Though I know someone' (he was thinking of himself) 'whom the Merciful Lord visited with His grace, and if the Lord had asked him, "Wouldest thou that I give thee more grace?", his soul, infirm in the body, would have said, "Lord, Thou seest that if there were more, I could not bear it and would die".' To those still in the body, such extreme tension is given but rarely, and then just for a brief instant – enough, however, to unveil eternity where time is not.

I explain poorly. I see that not only the 'humility of Christ', as the perfection of Divine love, is inexpressible but for me many other aspects of this life are equally impossible to put into words. We are bidden to 'be perfect, even as God is perfect' – a perfection we do not attain but the very desire for which makes us sense with our whole being the touch of Absolute Divinity. He draws the soul to Himself, and the soul suffers that she has not the strength to contain this life, and thus, crucified, lives out her time on earth. And she cannot come down from this cross because every time she considers 'coming down' [cf. Matt. 27:40] the flow of real eternity decreases in her.

Christianity, it may be said, is not some philosophical doctrine but actual *life*. Life and love 'to the end' – to hate for oneself. This is the *'great mystery of godliness'* [I Tim. 3:16] 'made known unto us by revelation' [cf. Eph. 3:3] in Christ, set forth in His word, made manifest in the example of Christ that 'our hands have handled' [I John 1:1], and yet remaining impenetrable, inviolable, 'indescribable'.

St. Silouan in many different ways expressed this same idea – that God and all that is of heaven can only be known through the Holy Spirit. And it is by the gift of this Holy Spirit, proceeding from the Father, that we in our Church existentially, by actual experience, know the *Self-emptying* of the Son of the Father in the act of incarnation, in the wilderness, in the prayer in Gethsemane, and on Golgotha. He, the Holy Spirit, shows us the self-emptying that lies before us, too, in our death.

Through faith in our Lord and God Jesus Christ this self-emptying is possible for us to a certain extent, but can we go further? . . . We are taught in the Church to live the birth of the Son in the Holy Trinity as the Self-emptying of the Father giving all of Himself, in the whole plenitude of His eternal Being, to the Son. And so the Son is equal with the Father in absolute fulness of Divine Being. Then we see the reverse movement: the Son in like fulness of Self-emptying love gives Himself to the Father both in His Divinity and His humanity.

Is it permissible to venture beyond one's own experience and in mental contemplation conceive of the participation of the Father and the Holy Spirit in the Son's death on the cross?

The Son, by Whom all things were made [cf. John 1:3] is the Creator of man; He became incarnate; He took into His Divine Hypostasis our 'form of a servant' [cf. Phil. 2:7] and, consequently, the sufferings of mankind after the Fall. In the pre-eternal Council of the Trinity this way of redemption for fallen man was decided on. Is not this the Self-emptying of the Father Who 'so loved the world, that he gave his only begotten Son, that whosoever believeth in him should not perish, but have everlasting life' [John 3:16] in the bosom of the Divinity? And the Holy Spirit, proceeding from the Father, lives the same love as is in the Father. Thus the Father and the Spirit eternally participate in 'the work' [John 17:4] which was given to Jesus to do. The kenotic character of perfect love is discovered to us by God. And now we *know* that there is no other way to fulness of divinization for us. 'It is finished: and he bowed his head, and gave up the ghost' [John 19:30] . . . 'For in that he himself hath suffered being tempted, he is able to succour them that are tempted' [Heb. 2:18]. So we live in the hope that at the hour of our death He will be with us if we were with Him in our ascetic striving.

11

Love – to the Point of Self-hatred

Jesus Christ, God without beginning, gave us commandments capable of opening the mind and heart of man to infinity. At first, however, the believer in the intransient significance of the Gospel word [cf. Matt. 24:35] is introduced into the inner realm of the soul by a constant placing of himself before the judgment-seat of God: 'He that rejecteth me, and receiveth not my words, hath one that judgeth him: the word that I have spoken, the same shall judge him in the last day. For I have not spoken of myself' (as man); 'but the Father which sent me, he gave me a commandment, what I should say . . . And I know that his commandment is life everlasting' [John 12:48-50]. The natural consequence of pious striving to keep the commandments will be a frank recognition of one's own impotence. But the arduous struggle to abide in the spirit of the Lord's prescript will persuade man that in their spiritual essence Christ's testaments are the uncreated Light of Divinity. Not a single action on our part can achieve the perfection demanded by the All-holy God.

The Light of the Gospel teaching that came down from heaven sharpens our inner eye-sight and refines our capacity to imbibe, so that what was formerly beyond our grasp can no longer escape us: every impulse of the heart or mind is swiftly grasped and we see ourselves as we are. The more intense our dread of being unworthy of God, the more 'naked' our inner world becomes, both for ourselves and, of course, before the Face of God: 'Neither is there any creature that is not manifest in his sight: but all things are naked and opened unto the eyes of him with whom we have to do' [Heb. 4:13]. Vigilance of mind and heart leads to a conclusion that many who are inexperienced may find incredible or exaggerated: the Christian discovers present in himself every sort of evil, either explicit or, at least, potential, and sees himself as indeed the most wicked of all men and all things.

Before the Divine Light appears to us we live like the blind. Without this Light we fail to recognise sin. Without it we do not realise the magnitude of the Fall of man. Only the inspiration of the Holy Spirit can enable us to perceive the calamity within ourselves – and then live the great drama of the whole history of the human race. The consequence of the Fall is disease which no earthly doctor can cure. We cannot of our own strength conform our heart and mind [cf. Phil. 2:5] to the spirit of Christ's commandments. On the other hand, the painful experience of our fight against 'the law of sin' [cf. Rom. 7:23-25] acting within us shows us *whence* came the Gospel word [cf. John 7:17].

For all its torment this is a precious period in our life: we are enveloped on all sides by the flame of the passions taking the form of 'fiery trial' [I Pet. 4:12]. But grace comes to our aid, which at first we do not see as Light but feel as a heavenly fire consuming in us the roots of sin.

How many times did my soul hang in terrible fear suspended over the abyss like a small helpless being! Not earthly fear – I did not hanker after any interminable prolongation of this life. My dread sprang from the fact that after God had appeared to my soul I saw the deep sores on the whole body of my life and realised how utterly unfitted I was for the Kingdom. I cannot describe the grief which plunged me into prolonged, profound weeping. But, foolish as I was, I did know that I was in the hands of my Creator – and 'it is a fearful thing to fall into the hands of the living God' [Heb. 10:31]. I twisted and turned, struggling to tear myself from His holy hands [cf. John 10:28]. But all my efforts were in vain because there was nowhere else to go – nothing in the whole wide world attracted me or promised to satisfy my spirit.

The Lord said, 'Be not afraid of them that kill the body, but . . . fear him, which after he hath killed hath power to cast into hell; yea, I say unto you, Fear him' [Luke 12:4-5]. Having committed Himself to death on the cross, the Lord did not indulge in empty, meaningless words. And I had no wish to minimise the categorical emphasis of this pronouncement. The life-giving fear never left me. And what is more, something strange would happen: so soon as the fear abated, I would feel a slackening of the vital strength within me. Prayer grew weak, my mind was distracted, the sense of the divine disappeared in the mist – my spirit began to die. Only much later on did I realise that the Lord was schooling me, and my torment was turned to incalculable good: the dread of eternal damnation and my tears of repentance in some mysterious fashion converted the whole of me into prayer. Freely, with no especial effort, my spirit rose to a state of contemplation of hitherto-unknown realities – of the infinite spaces of being, the sombre regions of hell, but also heaven illumined by the uncreated Light.

Blessed be His Name for ever more.

Do not expect an orderly, properly-constructed account of the life of my soul during the long years of the past. Sometimes I would descend into the depths of hell; at others the Lord would raise me even to the heavens. Or I would be standing on the indefinable boundary whence one contemplates both the ineffable Light of Divinity and the 'outer darkness' that fills the soul with dread – dread of an especial kind, nothing like the fear of physical death. Something qualificatively different. A blissful eternity would open before my spirit though it was still a long way off; and a timeless tenebrity likewise made its presence felt within me. I was torn in two: captive to the tyranny of the passions, I suffered, and thirsting for immutable good, I strained towards God. Prayer of repentance absorbed me utterly. A weightless, invisible force transported me into spiritual space. There, I was alone: the earth vanished; there was no sun, there were no stars; no people, nor any creature; and I was not aware of my body. I did not see light as such, though my eyes penetrated into fathomless depths. In sick despair my soul pined for God. Yes, yes, I am a sinner but I long for God, holy God. I was conscious, not of concrete acts in my past, only of a piercing awareness of having defected from God, Whom I had known in my childhood and early youth. He had turned away from me after I departed from Him in mad search for something supposedly superior – the supra-personal Absolute.

Impossible now to say how long I prayed in those nights in the desert. I remember that when my soul became conscious again of the material world, the spiritual feeling of having been in soundless, indescribable depths remained with me, in me. In that infinity there is no up, or down; no forward, no backward; neither right nor left. Yet there came a moment when it seemed to me that I was beginning to move and it felt like a falling; and a choked cry would burst from my throat, 'Lord, save me . . . Thou alone canst reach me in the bottomless pit . . .'. And He saved me.

But why did it feel as if I were falling? Was it not because my mind could no longer stand in the Eternal? For after that the vision ended.

Conditions in the desert favoured this kind of prayer since I was alone and had only myself to consider. But that does not mean that prayer in its essence depends on external circum-stances – it is a gift from God bound up with another gift, that of repentance [cf. Luke 24:46–47]. I was acquainted with its elements even before settling on Mt. Athos. I knew it there in the monastery, too, but less intensely, less frequently. It takes one out of the framework of time, of earthly categories. In the actual state of prayer, totally unaware of the outside world, one thinks only of God and, alone, stands before Him alone.

In the solitude of my grotto I had the unique privilege of being able to devote myself entirely to this prayer, free of earthly cares. It possessed me for months on end. It would be interrupted in daylight hours by mundane concerns but when the working day came to an end, with the silence of the night in my retreat prayer would embrace me anew, and again I would be oblivious to all else, conscious only of a terrible sense of sin which engendered in me sorrow, shame, abhorrence and even hatred of myself. And once more I would drown in tears of repentance, and my spirit would enter a nameless infinity.

I have always been very slow at interpreting what is happening inside myself. I spent long periods without reasoning. Thoughts would occur to me in discussions with other people but not when I was alone before God. I did not theologise, I did not analyse myself. I did not cling to the states of mind that I experienced, although I dwelt in a formless mental sphere. Could this be labelled insanity? But when the 'madness' left me, only then did I comprehend the irreparable loss to my spiritual being. Through that prayer the meaning had partially been revealed to me of Christ's words, 'If any man come to me, and hate not . . . his own life . . . he cannot be my disciple' [Luke 14:26].

God's mercy toward me was manifest in that He granted me a potent agony of repentance which drove me to insatiable prayer – the sort of prayer where the soul is unremembering, thinks of nothing, but, unbridled, reaches out to God, invisible yet beloved; inapprehensible yet known; inaccessible yet near. I cannot find words to describe the riches that the Lord gave me.

I will try and list briefly the thoughts which occurred to my heart in the grievous hours when I recalled the prayer that I had forfeited. The normal consequence of keeping the Lord's commandments is an extreme reduction of ourself – a self-emptying. Without sincere recognition that we are indeed devils incarnate in our fall, we shall never arrive at fulness of repentance. Through total repentance we break loose from the deadly embrace of selfish individualism and begin to contemplate the divine universality of Christ, Who 'loved us unto the end' [cf. John 13:1]. When we hate ourselves for the evil that lives in us, then it is that the boundless horizons of the love commanded of us are revealed. Apart from Christ we shall never embrace the whole world in the vivifying flame of the grace that cometh down from on High; nor perceive the ontological dimensions of the 'second commandment' – 'Thou shalt love thy neighbour as thyself' [cf. Matt. 22:37–40]. It was given to Blessed St. Silouan to pray for the whole world as for himself. May the Lord grant to each and all to behold the light of such prayer, through which the primordial image of man is restored. Whoever has not come close to this state should hesitate to call himself a Christian, knowing and feeling shame for his unworthiness. 'If any man will come after me, let him deny himself' (meaning all his old notions and concepts) 'and take up his cross, and follow me . . . If any man come to me, and hate not . . . his own life, he cannot be my disciple . . . He is not worthy of me' [cf. Matt. 16:24; 10:37–38; Luke 14:26,33].

It frightens me to wonder where and in what lay my iniquity before God which barred my way to the plenitude that was poured out on St. Silouan. The thought of my past straying is linked with an acute sense of my general unworthiness to stand before *such* a God. And if at certain moments of my life I have approached the borderlines of repentance – when the whole man is sanctified – this was only made possible by St. Silouan's prayers. I have not reached his measure but I do know that what I write about is *true*.

'God is love.' He is 'light, and in him is no darkness at all' [I John 4:8; 1:5]. Christ's love is by its nature life-giving fire sent down from heaven by the coming on earth of the Son of God [cf. Luke 12:49]. This love is the uncreated life of God Himself. Within the confines of our earthly existence it burns away all that is alien to it, and at the same time fills us with the energy of new being, till then inconceivable. It is essential that strength from on high should come to us, to make us worthy of knowing this love existentially. Without such experience no man born of woman can understand the seemingly paradoxical Gospel commandment, 'Love your enemies, bless them that curse you, do good to them that hate you . . .' [Matt. 5:44], but 'hate' your kin and brethren.

In our urge to apprehend Christ's commandments in their global entirety, again and again we return to these two seemingly conflicting injunctions. The inconsistency is eliminated once it is given us to experience both these states. Then the Spirit bears witness in us that death is vanquished, and we anticipate the grace of our promised resurrection [cf. John 6:40].

'Our God is a consuming fire' [Heb. 12:29]. Divine love is the kernel of eternal Being. In it all the other attributes of Divinity – the Wisdom, the Kingdom, the Power, the Light – find their loftiest expression. It contains the beauty of the eternally unshakeable Kingdom. Christ's love is the revelation of the Mystery of the Father's love, too.

Having found a heart ready to accept its flame, Christ's love takes up its abode therein. But this exceptional blessing in our world allows its servant no rest until the work is finished [cf. John 17:4]. It is a fearful thing to preach the prayer generated by this love.

Painful is the way that leads to the acquisition of holy love – which may be why so many renounce Christianity, preferring other roads to the cross of this love. But there is no other truth, just as there is no other God [cf. John 14:6].

'The spirit indeed is willing, but the flesh is weak' [Matt. 26:41]. At selected moments the uncreated Light of Christ's love may touch the earthborn heart. In it is Divine Eternity. It is the sole and ultimate purpose of our striving.

Without the action of Love that proceedeth from the Father neither our mind in its fallen state, nor our heart, can follow Christ to Gethsemane – still less, to Golgotha. The profound weeping of our whole being, because of the presence of this love aflame within us when we pray for the world, can be too much for our powers of endurance. Then our spirit enters into Divine eternity, and prayer is stilled. So painful is the prelude to the blessed going forth of our spirit to God. But afterwards the soul feels sweet repose and the peace 'which passeth all understanding', of which St. Paul wrote [Phil. 4:7].

The return to everyday consciousness, everyday life, is

accompanied by a certain subtle sensation of grief. The soul soon encounters the same situations as before, and again suffers many a wound. In following Christ with its whole strength man's spirit feels this visible world like a narrow prison cell – every good impulse meets with the savage opposition of the dark powers.

'God is love . . . He is a consuming fire.' It is not at all easy to approach this Fire, and far from safe to enlarge on the subject. The soul shrinks with the dread of finding herself unworthy after her departure from this life.

For many years, especially on the Holy Mountain, in the desert as in the monastery, my mind in its reaching up to God separated itself from the past. 'Separated', not through any ascetic effort but because prayer of repentance was all engrossing. But since I was appointed spiritual confessor I have sometimes had to think back on my life. And now, engaged on writing my 'confession' and spiritual biography in one, I note, not ungratefully, how the touch of Divine Fate has left so many indelible marks on the body of my life. The Spirit of the Living God writes 'not in tables of stone, but in fleshy tables of the heart' [cf. II Cor. 3:3]. That which God has written has become the content of my being.

What exactly do I want to say? Here is my theme song: that through repentance granted to me, even to the point of hate for myself, I unexpectedly experienced a wondrous peace, and uncreated Light enveloped me, penetrating within, making me, too, light like itself, giving me to live the Kingdom of the God of Love – the Kingdom of which 'there shall be no end' [Luke 1:33].

I marvelled, and shall never cease marvelling, at the humble condescendence of Almighty God to me, a thing of nought. But He gave us the commandment, 'Take heed that ye despise *not one* of these little ones; for . . . it is not the will of your

Father which is in heaven, that one of these little ones should perish' [cf. Matt. 18:10–14].

We see that He Himself lives in accord with His own commandments. The Gospel precepts contain God's revelation of Himself. The more deeply we enter into their spirit, the more specific will be our vision of God. And when these commandments, by His good providence, come to be the one and only principle of our whole being, both temporal and eternal, *then* we, too, 'shall be like Him; for we shall see him *as he is*' [I John 3:2].

GOD IS LOVE

12

The Uncreated Light

I.

Christian life is founded on the fact of the incarnation of God. In our flesh, created by Him, He made manifest His pre-eternal perfection, thereby enabling us to judge the extent to which we either fail to reach His stature or approach His supreme Being. If we resemble Him in the inner workings of our heart, in the manner of our thinking, in our reactions to all that happens to us on the earthly plane, we shall *ipso facto* become like unto Him in His Divinity, too. The Gospels furnish a clear enough picture of Him, while the Epistles describe the experience of life in Him. His commandments are the uncreated Light in which He particularly reveals Himself to us 'as he is' [I John 3:2]. 'I am the light of the world: he that followeth me shall not walk in darkness, but shall have the light of life' [John 8:12].

The effect upon us of this Light is amazing: we behold and marvel at the searchless miracle of our appearance in this world. The act of the creation of all things is a mystery drawing us to Him. But prior to this enlightening from on High, caught in the darkness of ignorance, lost and bewildered, we struggle, step by painful step, towards our affirmation in being. Why this intricate process – the genesis of our spirit in a body made of the dust of the earth – for the creation from non-being of sons of God? How is it possible to conjoin spirit – the likeness of the Absolute – and the material world? It is not easy for our spirit, by nature immortal, to be held fast in a body subject to disintegration and death. Hence the unremitting conflict between the spirit straining up towards God, anxious to have the body likewise incorruptible and able to follow in the ascent, and the body pulling downwards, to the earth from which it was taken, and communicating its mortality to the spirit.

Unable to understand myself, weary of endless conflict and insoluble contradictions, I tried the experiment of putting myself in the Creator's place, and pondered how I would have ordered the world. Shutting myself up in the dark and quiet, I concentrated my thoughts on the task. Starting from my own experience of being, and keeping in mind the difficulties that constantly beset me, I proceeded from the ephemeral to the ever-widening horizons of cosmic being. And what happened? Instead of rectifying the 'incoherencies' in God's work I soon found myself marvelling at the Mind which had created heaven and earth with such '*know-how*'. And it was disagreeable and at the same time a delight to discover my own impotence. My infantile mind smiled at the Father, in the way a child in the cradle smiles at its mother. My soul overflowed with wonder at the unfathomable *wisdom* of God. Somewhere far away in the vast heavens a faint light shone, inspiring songs of praise and begetting a hunger in me to be associated with the great creative work of the Father. (Sometimes when I was engaged in landscape painting people would come and stand quietly behind me, watching me work. In the same way I wanted to stand close to the Almighty and delight in contemplating His creative inspiration.)

Something similar may happen when death stares one in the face, or threatens to carry off those dear to one. My presumption was naïve but it contained elements of dissatisfaction with God. In the Book of Job I found passages that paralleled my case. 'The Lord answered . . . out of the whirlwind, and said, Who is this that darkeneth counsel by words without knowledge? Gird up now thy loins like a man; for I will demand of thee, and answer thou me. Where wast thou when I laid the foundations of the earth? Who hath laid the measures thereof? . . . Whereupon are the foundations thereof fastened? or who laid the corner stone thereof; When the morning stars sang together, and all the sons of God shouted for joy?' – [in the Septuagint version: 'When the stars were made, all my angels praised me with a loud voice']. 'Hast thou entered into the springs of the sea? or hast thou walked in the search of the depth? Have the gates of death been opened unto thee? . . . Where is the way where light dwelleth? and as for darkness, where is the place thereof? . . . Who hath put wisdom in the inward parts? or who hath given understanding to the heart? . . . Moreover the Lord answered Job, and said, Shall he that contendeth with the Almighty instruct him? he that reproveth God, let him answer it . . . Then Job answered the Lord, and said, I know that thou canst do every thing . . . therefore have I uttered that I understood not; things too wonderful for me, which I knew not . . .' (Heretofore) 'I have heard of thee by the hearing of the ear: but now mine eye seeth thee. Wherefore I abhor myself, and *repent*' (of my foolishness) '*in dust and ashes*' [cf. Job: chapters 38–42].

When we examine ourselves in the light of the Lord's commandments we see that we are utterly corrupt and devoid of any capacity for good. Aghast, we repent before God and implore Him to restore us from the death with which we are stricken. We are ready to break the chain of our self-will and give ourselves over entirely to His holy and perfect will. But oh, how hard this is, especially at the outset! Yet it is the means whereby we may join the stream of His eternity. To trust in God in times of danger concentrates our spirit in Him, and we can feel His immortal breath upon us. This great gift comes through humble but searing repentance. A miracle – the more I 'see' God, the more ardent does my repentance become, since I the more clearly recognise my unworthiness in His sight. And this miracle is repeated, invariable, from age to age. Consider this from the Old Testament: 'I saw also the Lord sitting upon a throne, high and lifted up . . . Above it stood the seraphims . . . And one cried unto another, and said, Holy, holy, holy, is the Lord of hosts: the whole earth is full of his glory . . . Then said I, Woe is me! for I am undone; because I am a man of unclean lips . . . for mine eyes have seen the King, the Lord of hosts. Then flew one of the seraphims unto me, having a live coal in his hand, which he had taken with the tongs from off the altar: And he laid it upon my mouth, and said, Lo, this hath touched thy lips; and thine iniquity is taken away, and thy sin purged' [cf. Isa. 6:1 *et seq.*].

The New Testament gives us the remarkable instance of the Apostle Paul. He recognised his sin only after the Lord had appeared to him in the great Light of His Divinity, on the road to Damascus. (Afterwards he retired to the desert [cf. Gal. 1:17] to repent before Him Whom he had persecuted.) Paul had a terrifying past history. Until his encounter with Christ he could have echoed the prophet Elijah: 'I have been very jealous for the Lord God of hosts' [cf. I Kings 19:10]. And then suddenly what he had up to then thought of as light and Divine truth now appeared to be darkness and 'enmity with God' [cf. Luke 11:35; James 4:4]. And in bitter grief he called himself a sinner worse than any other. 'Christ Jesus came into the world to save sinners; of whom I am *chief*' [I Tim. 1:15]. 'Christ died for our sins . . . was buried . . . and rose again the third day according to the scriptures . . . he was seen of Cephas, then of the twelve: After that, he was seen of above five hundred . . . And last of all he was seen of me also, as of one *born out of due time*. For I am the least of the apostles, that am not meet to be called an apostle, because I persecuted the church of God' [I Cor. 15:3–9]. 'And I thank Christ Jesus our Lord, who hath enabled me, for that he counted me faithful, putting me into the ministry; Who was before a blasphemer, and a persecutor, and injurious: but I *obtained mercy*' [I Tim. 1:12–13]. And Peter after denying Christ 'went out, and *wept bitterly*' [Matt. 26:75].

The inner state of those who have come to know the divine manifestations in strength may seem incomprehensible, even paradoxical, to many. They genuinely consider themselves worthy of hell but the Lord to them continues blessed for all time. The vision of the infinite sanctity of the humble God, on the one hand, and the feeling of the infernal darkness within us, on the other, contracts a man's whole being into an irresistible, *painful* reaching up to God Who is Holy. This is accompanied by self-loathing; and the soul is drowned in tears. The pain is spiritual, metaphysical, unbearable. The longing for forgiveness and reconciliation with God is like a deadly thirst – a condition difficult to explain to those who do not know it. By its very nature spiritual weeping is quite different from ordinary tears over some catastrophe in our finite life [cf. I Cor. 15:42–46; James 3:15; Jude v. 19].

When a man weeps with his whole being from the *pain* caused by the knowledge of his vileness, his torment far exceeds any outside suffering, and he sees himself as the worst of men. The Light of God's Kingdom, whether seen on Mount Tabor, on the road to Damascus or anywhere else, draws one to itself but it appears unattainable, infinitely beyond our merit or, rather, demerit. Prayer in this holy *pain* can sweep man's spirit into another world. Everyday life is forgotten and the body no longer makes itself felt. The desert ascetics termed this the hell of repentance that likens us to Christ descending into His hell of love. However acute the Adamitic torment, however profound the suffering, it is accompanied by the joy of the Divine summons and the light of new life.

Our Fathers of the Church, with the gift of grace repeated from generation to generation down the ages, explicitly declare that there is no other way to the Father of lights. The grace of such repentance is given to the world through the prayer of Gethsemane, the crucifixion on Golgotha and the resurrection of Christ [cf. Luke 24:17].

There is a risk in speaking frankly of such matters with unbelievers who, *ergo*, are unduly ignorant of them. It is typical of St. Paul's 'natural man' to distort. 'For what man knoweth the things of a man, save the spirit of man which is in him? even so the things of God knoweth no man, but the Spirit of God. Now we have received, not the spirit of the world, but the spirit which is of God; that we might know the things that are freely given to us of God. Which things also we speak, not in the words which man's wisdom teacheth, but which the Holy Ghost teacheth; comparing spiritual things with spiritual.

But the natural man receiveth not the things of the Spirit of God: for they are *foolishness* unto him: neither can he know them, because they (must be) spiritually discerned. But he that is spiritual judgeth all things, yet he himself is judged of no man' [I Cor. 2:11–15].

Before proceeding to describe, in so far as I am able, the action of Divine Light, perhaps it may not be inappropriate to begin with a brief description of light phenomena which were given to me to encounter. As a young man I was much preoccupied with the mysteries of Being, and more than once I felt – I saw – my thinking energy like a light. The world of mental contemplation is essentially a radiant one. Indeed, our mind is an image of the Primal Mind, which is Light. The intellect, concentrated on metaphysical problems, can lose all sense of time and material space, travelling, as it were, beyond their boundaries. In just such a situation my mind would seem to be light. This state of being is naturally accessible to man but later it became clear to me that it differs qualitatively from the event of the manifestation of God in uncreated Light.

> Lord, forgive me – I am feared to speak. Heal me, hearten me. Withdraw not from me.

The Apostles on Mount Tabor were found worthy to enter the realm of Light proceeding from the Father, and hear His voice bearing witness to His beloved Son. But this became possible for them only after they had confessed the Divinity of Christ [cf. Matt. 16:13 *et seq.*].

It has been granted to me to contemplate different kinds of light and lights – the light the artist knows when elated by the beauty of the visible world; the light of philosophical contemplation that develops into a mystical experience. Let us even include the 'light' of scientific knowledge which is always and inevitably of very relative value. I have been tempted by manifestations of light from hostile spirits. But in my adult years, when I returned to Christ as perfect God, the unoriginate Light shone on me. This wondrous Light, even in the measure vouchsafed to me from on High, eclipsed all else, just as the rising sun eclipses the brightest star.

Confession of the *Divinity* of Christ Jesus is the *rock* on which the Church is built [cf. Matt. 16:18]. 'Great is the mystery of godliness: God was manifest in the flesh' [I Tim. 3:16]. 'In the beginning was the Word . . . And the Word was made flesh, and dwelt among us . . . full of grace and truth' [John 1:1, 14]. The Son, unoriginate with the Father, became the Son of man. He was born of the Virgin Mary. Her greatness as the Mother of Jesus-God is beyond human measure. It is impossible to isolate her from the Christ-God – and yet at the same time she is *of one substance* with us in all things. The Christmas canticle tells of all creatures bringing the gifts peculiar to their kind, 'but we (men) offer the Mother'. Without this the 'historicity' of the incarnation could be queried, and doubts arise concerning the human nature of Christ (Docetism).

The fact of the incarnation occupies a central place all through the history of mankind, in the whole of the created world. The event upset all human attempts to know the Unoriginate Principle, even when occasionally the effort seemed to be a stroke of genius. Now we are taught to avoid attributing to God the inventions of our brain and sick imagination. All our ideas, all our acknowledgments or rejections in no way modify God in His ageless Being [cf. Isa. 55:8-9].

Where am I with Him? With Him Who revealed Himself to us and said – not like a lunatic but with absolute knowledge – 'I am the truth' [John 14:6]? And the vast majority of His hearers were appalled. He in no way fits into the framework of our natural thinking. His injunctions are quite beyond us. His life is laden with such suffering that the soul is dismayed. And yet He says that there is no other way but to follow Him. So what are we – what am I – to do?

I tried out other ways and ended up convinced that Truth was not to be found in them. I returned to Him, like a prodigal son, though with new understanding of man and being in general. His words now sounded differently in my ears. I believed in Him utterly. And not because He fitted into my pattern of thought; or because His commandments did not seem too difficult to me; or because I felt light-hearted about accepting suffering like Him. No. But even now I am unable to describe the process that took place deep within me. I do not know what to call the power that was guardedly but effectively healing my mind and heart. In the most secret places of my heart something mysterious stirred – mysterious though familiar to me since my early childhood – which developed after its own fashion. Now the progress would be slow and laborious, now a sudden upsurge would sunder me from everything that was not He. It seems to me that this was nothing other than God's revelation of Himself within my spirit [cf. Matt. 11:27].

'No man can come to me, except the Father which hath sent me draw him' [John 6:44]. Does His Father seek out only the great? Or the 'little ones', too, and if so, why should I exclude myself, although I am less than the least? Was it not He Who impregnated me with a minute degree of intuition which nevertheless ran deeper than all my other thoughts and was more trustworthy than all my other knowledge? Be that as it may, when I accepted belief without the faintest shadow of doubt in the Divinity of Christ I was irradiated by Light not of this world. And to a certain extent, like Paul, in His Light I knew Him. At first I believed with a lively faith. Afterwards Light appeared to me. Was it not the same with the Apostles Peter, James and John? When they confessed His Divinity, through Peter as their mouthpiece, He replied, 'Verily I say unto you, There be some standing here, which shall not taste of death, till they see the Son of man coming in his kingdom' [Matt. 16:28] – a prediction shortly to be fulfilled on Mt. Tabor. Paul, likewise, bore Christ in his heart Whom he had persecuted, and therefore the Light of the Godhead appeared to him in strength. And I make bold to say that the vision of uncreated Light is indissolubly bound up with belief in the *Divinity* of Christ – bound up with, though in a curious manner one depends on the other. In *one* Light both Christ and the Holy Spirit appear. This witnesses to the Divinity of Christ, since it is impossible not to recognise God in this Light of which we are speaking. Its action is indescribable. In it lies eternity; in it, the inexpressible goodness of love. In it our spirit contemplates immeasurable horizons and – not all at once but gradually – discovers more and more that is new in this *luminous breakthrough* into Heaven 'where God is' [cf. Exod. 20:21].

'Now are we the sons of God, and it doth not yet appear *what* we shall be; but we know that, when he shall appear, we shall be like him; for we shall see him *as he is*' [I John 3:2]. In actual fact, in His every manifestation to man God remains one and the same; but we do not apprehend Him as we should; we do not include Him in His Absoluteness in the confines of the earth. Yet we 'see' Him, be it only 'through a glass, darkly' [I Cor. 13:12]. And this 'glass' is not always equally 'dark', depending on the extent to which we keep the commandments of Christ, in which God's revelation of Himself is given to us. The Spirit of the Father lives in the commandments. 'The words which *thou gavest* me, I have given unto them; and they have received them, and have known surely that I came out from thee' [cf. John 17:8]. Also, 'If ye continue in my word, then . . . ye shall know the truth, and the truth shall make you free' [John 8:31–32].

Reception of Truth must happen in freedom: no one and nothing can force it on man. Nor can it be forcibly removed. Faith by decree cannot be perfect in its roots, though it may progress to true faith – that is, faith through which Truth comes to dwell in us as something sought after and longed for, and for all eternity.

Truth is Self-Being. It is revealed to us as Personal Absolute – One Being in Three Persons. Union with Him imparts to us, too, the Divine form of Being, immutable for all time. In so far as we continue in it, the Gospel word becomes crystal-clear and is assimilated by us to such an extent that we possess it as we possess our mother tongue. When it becomes our very life-blood, then are we approaching likeness to Christ, Who gave us this treasure [cf. John 17:8]. And as I have often said before, our likeness to the incarnate God is transmitted by analogy from this visible plane into eternity, as our divinization – our eternal dwelling in the sphere of Divine Being.

Conversely, it must be observed in the same connection that when the Gospel word is not translated into action in our lives it not only remains incomprehensible in its eternal essence but becomes an opaque screen between God and us.

We cannot attain to the fulness of the perfection of Christ. Therefore all our conclusions concerning Him fall short. But it is of momentous importance that His hidden world be revealed to us, even if only partially. In the experience of grace given to us in our long ascetic struggle, peering, as it were, through a slit in a fence, we do glimpse the Light of Divinity [cf. I Cor. 2:9–12]. And what can I say? My life is based on the conviction that God, the Creator of the world, my Creator, too, absolute in His primordial Being, came down to us, made known to us the path to His eternal life; disclosed to us the enigma of death – of sin, that is; and made manifest to us the *purport of life*, which is *love*.

The manifestation of Light affords man existential knowledge of God in which heart, mind and body participate. But we cannot contain all its plenitude, which fact stimulates an eager desire to expand our communion with Him and throughly penetrate with our whole selves. There is an alluring strength in this yearning after God which brings joy and at the same time pain. Aware of being still so inexpressibly distanced from the longed-for Father, our spirit grieves, and prayer streams forth in a torrent – prayer of richly-varying experience. Our days and nights are taken up with the vital quest of ways to Him.

In our heart of hearts – subjectively – we cannot for an instant doubt the divine provenance of the holy love that may breathe in us at this time. But, despite the overwhelming uprush of this wondrous love, manifest in Light, it would be not only wrong but dangerous, too, to trust oneself. We know from the Scriptures how the most holy Virgin Mary hurried to the blessed Elisabeth to hear from her whether the revelation was true that she would bear a Son, Who 'should be great, and be called the Son of the Highest . . . and of his kingdom there should be no end' [cf. Luke 1:32–33]. Paul is another instance. He was 'caught up into paradise, and heard unspeakable words, which it is not lawful for a man to utter' [cf. II Cor. 12:4]. 'It pleased God . . . to reveal his Son in me' [Gal. 1:15–16]. Nevertheless, twice he journeyed to Jerusalem to communicate to Peter and others 'which were of reputation' the 'gospel that he preached' and receive confirmation that he was not 'running in vain' [cf. Gal. 2:1–2]. There is no end to similar instances in the history of our Church which insists on the inflexible rule that one must submit to the appraisal of other and far more experienced elders recognised as faithful. And we hold to this tradition.

Our being is stamped through and through as having been formed of nothing – 'of the dust of the ground' [Gen. 2:7] – which effectively prevents us from making any individual judgment concerning the Self-Existence of the Absolute Being. Moreover, we carry in ourselves the consequences of the fall of Adam which finds expression in a tendency to self-divinization. Our freedom for self-determination of course testifies to our absoluteness, and we may easily lose our awareness of having been created, but created 'in the image of the Absolute God', and that our 'absoluteness' is no more than a reflection of the First-Absolute. Aberration on this count may be both intellectual and psychological. We may become victim to our imagination and regress from actual reality, which is not individual but 'collective'. We are called upon to contain in ourselves the whole fulness of being, human and even Divine, but we must recognise that we are still a long way distant. And so it remains imperative for each one of us, whatever prophetic gift we may or may not possess, to make sure that we are included in joint being, after the image of the Triune God, through the witness of other *personae*. We naturally seek such witnesses, who are only to be found in the Church, whose age-old knowledge immeasurably surpasses any individual experience. In the distant past the Apostles were able mentors who bequeathed to us in written form the message that they had received directly from God. After them innumerable Fathers (teachers and ascetics) handed down from generation to generation first and foremost the 'spirit of life itself', which they often confirmed in their writings, too. We believe that every given historical moment in the Church has its living attestors; that until the end of time mankind will never be bereft of genuine *knowledge of God*.

Solely after finding authoritative confirmation can we rely on our individual experience, and then only in due measure. Our spirit must not pause in its *élan* towards God; and at each fresh step it is essential to remember that self-confident isolation of our personality may mean sinning against Truth.

> O heavenly King and Comforter, Spirit of Truth, [John
>   14:16–17]
> Which proceedest from the Father [John 15:26]
> And dost repose in the Son,
> Come and abide in us.
> Guide us into all truth [John 16:13]
> And save our souls, O Thou who art good.

'Howbeit when he, the Spirit of truth, is come, he will guide you into all truth' – so the Lord promised us before going to His death on the cross.

It is torture to realise that one is distanced from God – God mysterious yet beloved. Now when I think back on what did in fact happen with me in those blessed years my mind remarks three tendencies. First, there was my consuming hunger for God which seemed to be the only *natural* thing – the 'one thing needful' [Luke 10:42] in my benighted state. Secondly, I was weak, irresolute in all things . . . so whence the prayer that exceeded my strength? And thirdly, was it not the Lord Himself Who drew me with His? Were not *two* wills conjoined: His and mine, in so far as our Creator and Father performs nought with us without our consent and cooperation?

My anguish of soul continued unceasing, day and night. The torment swelled into the same uninterrupted prayer even in sleep or when other people were about, although then something kept me from giving any outward sign. But as soon as I was back in my room, almost before I could shut the door, the tears would overwhelm me. There were moments when the pain of being separated from God cast me to the floor, and in the silence of the night I would weep for hours over my dreadful loss. The whole of me – mind, heart, even my body – contracted into a single tight knot. And when the weeping exceeded a certain limit, the earth – the whole visible world – disappeared from my consciousness and I was alone before God. The intangible Light, proceeding from the Unoriginate let me see myself, not as I appeared outwardly, not in my everyday circumstances, but in some strange fashion which I cannot describe, standing before my Creator, naked to the bone. And there was nothing in me hid from His eyes.

If the ascetic struggle be interpreted as the determined surmounting of our evil inclinations, then the life that is truly blessed with grace knows *no* struggle. The advent within a man of divine strength means that everything he does becomes a positive act, free of all inner contradictions. Both mind and heart, inspired by the love of Christ, are immune from doubt. When love of God is in full flood, it is transposed into contemplation of the uncreated Light, which removes passion and brings the unutterable delight of liberty of spirit, since man now dwells beyond death and fear.

The experience of this state of freedom from the passions is given to us sometimes for longer, sometimes for shorter periods. In essence it is first and foremost love that 'casteth out fear' [cf. I John 4:18] of death, filling the soul with inspired contemplation of our likeness to God. But at the same time this very love plunges her into a sea of suffering. Indeed, 'the greater the love, the greater the suffering of the soul', as Saint Silouan noted.

Heavenly Light is not subject to physical control. Different, elusive by nature, it comes in a way that we cannot define. Reality of other dimensions tears through the screen of our earthly body, penetrating our feeble, created nature. Perception of supernatural Being is communicated to us, not through visual means but by spiritual visions. These visions are variously described, depending on the recipient's character or ability to express himself. But whoever has experienced visitations from on High will recognise the reality behind the words.

Proceeding from One Being, this Light leads to integral cognition of the God of love. There is no disparity in the after-effects of the manifestation of the genuine uncreated Light of the Holy Trinity – the visionary abandons all that he has to follow Christ [cf. Matt. 19:21].

When he judges good and evil, not according to the frequency of their occurrence but by the spiritual quality of his thoughts and reactions, the ascetic striver does indeed see himself as the worst of men. At the same time he feels overwhelmed, despite his vileness, with measureless blessing from God [cf. John 3:34 – 'for God giveth not the Spirit by measure']. He is at a loss to understand why so many others, better endowed than he, remain outside the Light.

The Fall of man was grievous but withal not absolute: there was still the possibility of repentance and salvation. It is written, 'That was the true Light, which lighteth every man that cometh into the world'. It follows that not a single one of us is completely outside this light. I label 'better endowed' those who remained content with themselves, and so 'knew him not' and 'received him not' [cf. John 1:9,11,16]. On the 'poor in spirit' [Matt. 5:3] 'grace did much more abound' because of their burning repentance [cf. Rom. 5:20; Luke 5:32; I Tim. 1:15].

Following the example of St. Paul, I, too, would beg anyone disposed to read what I write to pray God to inspire me, inarticulate as I am, worthily to expound the mystery of Christ [cf. Col. 4:3]. It is well known that he who speaks fittingly of God receives grace, while he who preaches falsehood will be cast into the bottomless pit. When we speak of spiritual matters before the face of the Spirit of Truth, we are the first to be judged against the words we utter – a judgment fearful to all those who hold dear the advent of the Saviour of the world.

In the climate of our times it is no easy matter to talk of gifts that depend on belief in Christ. My aim is to describe as honestly as possible my own experience, and to do so without concealing the impulses of my heart. Our God is the King of humble love. He calls on us to learn humility of Him, for He is 'meek and lowly' [Matt. 11:29]. His first words were, 'Repent ye'. And the age-old experience of Christianity has shown that no sooner does one realise with bitterness and sorrow the vileness of one's demoniac pretensions to excel – no sooner does one begin to loathe the dark spirit within – than the heart is led into the hitherto-unknown sphere of freedom, where the Divine Light dazzles and all is contemplation of the goodness of God. Within – silence: the mind can no longer think, nor the heart breathe a sigh of thanksgiving.

Oh, who will give me true understanding and the right words to speak of the Light of Divinity? I am filled with shame when I would bare my soul and uncover all that I have tried to keep hidden. Am I not mistaken in thinking I am prompted by Christ's love? . . . The fear that overwhelms me as I set out to make my confession – perhaps to many – will not let me draw back. And so, I beseech you, pray for me, wherever I be.

Christ is the measure of all things, divine and human. He is the spiritual sun illuminating all creation. In the light of His commandments we see the way. Through Him we 'have access unto the Father' [Eph. 2:18].

Man, as the image of the Absolute, is naturally drawn to the Principle of all principles, to the Primordial. This progression, however, begins with our descent into the abyss of hell. St. Paul says of Christ, 'Now that he ascended, what is it that he also descended first into the lower parts of the earth? He that descended is the same also that ascended up far above all heavens, that he might fill all things' [Eph. 4:9–10]. And this *is* precisely our itinerary after the Fall: there is no other. We descend in the act of self-condemnation into the dark abyss, because from the moment that in Christ and through Him the image of the eternal *man* is revealed to us, as he is in the creative mind of God, we apprehend the appalling extent of our blindness. After flashes of lightning the night seems darker than ever. In the same way the Divine Light shows up the blackness within us and we are disgusted with the evil we see. The vision fills us with grief at every level of our being. Our spirit knows suffering that is outside time, greater than any physical pain. We are drowned in tears. Slaves of passion, we suddenly see ourselves torn from God, wounded by the arrows of His love. 'Out of the depths' we cry unto Him [Ps. 130].

'Come, O Thou Who alone art holy,
And sanctify and cleanse me from all that defiles.
Come, O Thou Who only art in truth the Living One,
And restore me from the death with which I am stricken.
Come, Thou true Light, and abide in me for ever.'

Thus is repentance born in us. In the early stages it is accompanied by a profound sadness. Subsequently, there are changes in tension and form but repentance will remain with us constantly. There is no end to repentance on this earth – an end would indicate the fulness of our deification through perfect assimilation to the risen Christ.

Sometimes the upsurge of repentance is overpowering. To the exclusion of aught else mind and heart are filled with the agonising sensation of being held fast in evil darkness. And then, unforeseen, the Light of the uncreated Sun penetrates the dungeon of the soul: the Light which fills the whole cosmic expanse. It lovingly embraces us. We see Him and dwell in

Him, though we are not yet able to believe in this marvel of the Goodness of our Father. 'And when they saw him, they worshipped him: but some doubted' [Matt. 28:17]. They doubted, unable to take in what had happened. (Wretched and abominable as I am – can this really have happened to me?)

II.

I would look up at the clear blue sky, sometimes staring fixedly in one direction, at others letting my eyes sweep from one edge to the other. When my gaze reached the horizon, I would travel further and mentally embrace our whole planet. I would peer into the depths, trying to penetrate its boundaries; but the longer I stayed my attention on the marvellous scene – the more eagerly I studied the heavenly sphere, full of light – the more the mystery fascinated me. And when, by a gift from on High, it was vouchsafed to me to behold the Uncreated Light of Divinity, I saw the blue sky of our planet as a symbol of the radiance of heavenly glory. This radiance is everywhere – filling all the depths of the universe, ever intangible, *other*-worldly for the created world. Azure-blue is the colour of transcendency. Many human beings have been given the blessing of beholding this marvellous Light. Most of them cherished the blessing as the most precious secret of their life and, captivated by this wonder, departed to the other world. But others were bidden to bear witness to near and distant brethren of this lofty reality.

The soul feels apprehensive at approaching the subject of the Light which visits the man who craves to behold the Face of the Eternal. Its nature is mysterious – in what terms can it be described? Incomprehensible, invisible, yet it may sometimes be seen by the physical eye. Quiet and gentle, it draws heart and mind to itself, until the earth is forgotten, one's spirit caught up into another sphere. It can happen in broad daylight as in the blackness of night. It is a soft Light, yet more powerful than all around. In strange fashion it embraces from without.

You see it, but your attention is drawn deep within the inner man, into the heart burning with a love now compassionate, now grateful. It may happen that one is not aware of the material world, of external circumstances, and one sees oneself as light. Aches and pains disappear. Earthly cares fade away. Anxieties are absorbed into a sweet peace. The Light used at first to appear like a thin flame, healing and cleansing, consuming both within and without everything not in harmony with it, but calmly, hardly making itself felt.

This holy Light, coming in strength, brings humble love, banishes all doubt and fear, obliterates every earthly consideration – the whole pyramid of secular grades and hierarchies. The repentant man becomes a nobody, as it were: he no longer stands in the way of his brothers, seeks no place for himself in the world. This Light is in itself life imperishable, suffused by the peace of love. It brings to our spirit knowlege of another, indescribable Being. The mind is stayed, above reflection by the very fact of its entry into a new form of life. Weightless, more finely attuned than anything the earth knows, the Light conveys to the soul invulnerability, making her safe from everything that hitherto weighed her down. Death flees from this Light, and the prayer, 'O holy God, holy and strong, holy and immortal' in marvellous fashion is conjoined with it.

Our spirit exults: this Light is God – God Almighty and at the same time indescribably gentle. Oh, how discreet its approach! It will heal the heart broken by despair. The soul bruised by sin, it will inspire with the hope of victory.

The strength that is salvation lies in a firm belief in the Christ-God. He is the *supreme fact of Unoriginate Being*. He is the *Beginning* and the *End* – *Alpha and Omega*. On the foundation-stone of this faith true repentance becomes possible even for us, and further spiritual experience like the experience of the Apostles, the Fathers of the Church, ascetics of every generation. By the kind of gifts which follow on true repentance we can recognise their celestial origin. The Apostles Peter, James and John on Mount Tabor were caught up in Uncreated Light, and in its radiance heard the incorporeal voice of the Father testifying to Christ as His beloved Son. St. Paul on the road to Damascus saw the same Light, and in its manifestation realised the Divinity of Jesus. The same gift has been vouchsafed through the centuries to many hierarchs, anchorites, martyrs and righteous men. And even to our day this grace still continues to flow down on the faithful.

The vision of Light is preceded by the austere repentance that cleanses us from the passions. This is an exceedingly painful battle but sweet to heart and mind is the vision of Light. This Light is love of a quite especial kind, the blessedness of which may increase so long as one's strength can bear the heavenly flame.

This Light, which 'cometh down from the Father of lights' [Jas. 1:17], regenerates and even re-creates us. There is a radical change in the focus of our attention – before, it was centred on the material and temporary. Grace causes it to turn inwards and thence rise to the spiritual sphere of the 'unseen and eternal' [cf. II Cor. 4:18]. Temporal things that earlier seemed important, maybe of great moment, our spirit now finds insignificant. Riches, power, fame and the like lose their attraction. Even science, which does not bring us really vital knowledge – knowledge of God – like philosophical speculation, which is not life in the true sense, ceases to have anything but transitory value.

When this inviolable and nameless Light embraces us and penetrates within to our soul, we stand, as it were, outside time. This Light that proceeds from God is the light of love and knowledge; but love and knowledge of an especial kind, both merging into one – indeed, they are one in eternity. Love unites us in very Being, with very Being. And lo, we abide in it, this Being, and know it through our fusion with it. But there is no expressing this in words. Love draws us so powerfully that the spirit does not dwell on anything that is happening to us, although it is caught up in this happening. There is no movement towards oneself: our spirit is intent on feeling the Intangible, on clasping to itself that which cannot be clasped, on reaching that which cannot be reached – on being in Him alone, aware of naught else.

The Light manifests itself in different ways. What happens? I am not aware of how it is with others but if in my madness I may make bold to speak of what I do know I will say this.

The Lord gave me the *blessing of despair*. He gave me even more: a *sanctified loathing* of myself, steeped in sin. No one can find healing through his own efforts. In utter despair over myself, as I am, the only remedy is to appeal to God's mercy in hopeless hope. The step may be total, irreversible – I am afraid to turn back. I have not the strength to resist sin, to sustain a new, spotless life. The Lord, however, does not always take to Himself the soul in this state. 'Now the man out of whom the devils were departed' (fearful of leaving Christ) 'besought him that he might be with him: but Jesus sent him away, saying, Return to thine own house, and shew how great things God hath done unto thee' [Luke 8:38–39]. ('Believe that now not one of the unclean spirits that were entered into thee shall have power over thee.') Even if their case only relatively resembles the Gadarenes', the 'possessed', aware of their inability to resist the devil within, fear being parted from the one who delivered them from the alien power.

The life of the soul that experienced the blessing of the love of Christ is now harassed with affliction. 'In the world ye shall have tribulation: but be of good cheer . . .' [John 16:33]. To 'shew' – to bear witness to the Light of Divine love – in some strange fashion provokes antagonism in a great many. We must learn to sorrow with Jesus. Such sorrow will help us penetrate more deeply into His earthly life. 'O faithless and perverse generation, how long shall I be with you? how long shall I suffer you?' [Matt. 17:17].

God rejoiced that man was born into the world [cf. John 16:21]. The fallen world rejoiced when God appeared on earth. 'And the angel said, Fear not: for, behold, I bring you good tidings of great joy, which shall be to all people. For unto you is born this day . . . a Saviour, which is Christ the Lord' [Luke 2:10–11]. This Saviour brought us the gift of knowledge of the Heavenly Father. He made manifest to us 'the mystery which hath been hid from ages and from generations' [Col. 1:26]. He gave us the word which proceeds from the Father [cf. John 17:14]. He also gives us the pre-eternal glory which He Himself has from the Father [John 17:22]. In the world to come He wants to see us *there*, where He Himself is – on the right hand of the Father.

At first there is no sense of mystery, no questioning, about the vision of Light. Everything within and without is illumined: only the Light is seen. Mind and heart are silent, filled with blessed wonder before God. 'I will see you . . . and your heart shall rejoice . . . And in that day ye shall ask me nothing' [John 16: 22–23].

The Incarnation made it possible for mankind to set foot on the path to the Father by persevering in the spirit of Christ's commandments in every circumstance of earthly life. The love for Christ that comes from the keeping of these commandments renders prayer intense, ardent, leading to such thirsting for the Lord that the spirit travels beyond the confines of this world, to be absorbed in the One God. This kind of prayer makes the soul kin with the Spirit of Truth, and when she knows this Spirit she will recognise Him 'by His savour', as St. Silouan expressed it, and surrender herself to Him. And conversely, the soul will spontaneously, intuitively reject numerous phantom truths capable of attracting the inexperienced mind and the unenlightened heart. Divine *Light* reveals the true nature of tempting spirits and so delivers us from the foolish attractions of the 'opposition'.

The Light which appears to man when he believes in Christ testifies to His Divinity. Our spirit accepts the Lord Jesus as immutable Truth, authentically Holy. And this eternal Light begets testimony within us identical with the teaching of Christ.

In this Light we contemplate the Father. We apprehend this Light as the Holy Spirit. In it we see Christ as the only-begotten Son of the Father. In it we perceive the One-ness of the Three. Praying to this God, we live the *One Being* of the Three Persons. But we apprehend and relate to this One-ness variously: I approach the Father in one fashion; I pray otherwise to the Holy Spirit; I turn to Christ in a different manner. An especial spiritual feeling is associated with Each that in no way detracts from their One-ness of Being. With each Hypostasis of the Holy Trinity we have to a certain extent a differing relationship. Closest of all we know the Lord Jesus through His incarnation, His becoming man, and through Him we are led to First-Being, which is true God – the TRINITY, *one substance and undivided.*

Sometimes contemplation of Divine Light makes one totally oblivious to anything physical. In prayer the spirit enters the sphere of mental light and one loses all sense of both the outside world and one's own body. The spirit melts into such tenderness, in this vision, that it cannot tell what is happening to it. And afterwards one does not know whether one was in the body or out of the body.

More frequently, however, one continues to be aware of one's material surroundings and then, eyes open, may see *two lights* – the physical and the Divine. This is what the Fathers mean when they speak of beholding the Uncreated Light with the natural eye. Yes, *two* lights are seen but not in the same manner. The Uncreated Light differs from natural light which acts on the optic nerves and sets off the psycho-physiological process of vision, without affecting us spiritually. The opposite happens with Divine Light, which always communicates an especial feeling of grace, of which heart and mind, even the body, are conscious. By nature invisible, inexplicably it becomes visible. This manifestation, however, is less usual than spiritual states of grace, possibly intense, unaccompanied by any vision of Light.

The first of the modes of contemplation here described is

superior to the second, since participation in the Divine life, contact with Unoriginate Being, is experienced more profoundly (than in the second). But how is it explained that during the actual vision one can discern no activity in the mind – no notions, no images? And yet on emerging from this state both mind and heart are conscious of being filled with new knowledge. The heart, through the action in it of the grace of Divine love, more nearly apprehends the mysteries which excel any intellectual perception. Are we to call this the resurrection of the soul? Or the breath of Eternity embracing us? Maybe it is both.

In our earthly existence, before we 'taste of death' [Matt. 16:28], our closest contact with the Divine occurs through the shining on us of the Uncreated Light. When this Light comes 'in strength' we cannot help recognising that it is the Lord, the Almighty, the Creator of all that exists. At the moment of the vision man is enlightened by the Holy Spirit. As St. Silouan said, 'In the Holy Spirit is the Lord made known, and the Holy Spirit pervades the whole being – soul, mind and body'. The action of this Light cannot pass unnoticed, unrecognised. Being the eternal energy of God, this Light penetrates us with His power, and we become 'without beginning' – not through our origin but by the gift of grace: life without beginning is communicated to us. And there is no limit to the outpouring of the Father's love: man becomes identical with God – the same by content, not by primordial Self-Being. God will eternally be GOD for the reasonable being. Christ after His resurrection said to Mary Magdalen, 'Go to my *brethren*, and say unto them, I ascend unto my Father, and your Father; and to my God, and your God' [John 20:17]. St. Gregory the Theologian offers a masterly interpretation of the Lord's words. 'To my Father' by essence, before all time: 'To your Father' by the gift of the Father's love. 'To my God' through the humanity that I took upon Me, not in the literal sense. And this is the *eternal* situation. For the Man-Christ the Father continues to be God; for us likewise. But as the plenitude of Divine life is communicated to the Man-Christ, so is the same *plenitude* communicated to those who are saved in Christ. This follows from the prayer prayed by the Lord: 'They are not of the world, even as I am not of the world. Sanctify them through thy truth: thy word is truth . . . Neither pray I for these alone, but for them also which shall believe on me through their word; That they all may be one; as thou, Father, art in me, and I in thee, that they also *may be one in us:* that the world may believe that thou hast sent me. And the glory which thou gavest me I have given them; *that they may be one, even as we are one:* I in them, and thou in me, that they may be made perfect *in one;* and that the world may know that thou hast sent me, and *hast loved them, as thou hast loved me.* Father, I will that they also, whom thou hast given me, *be with me where I am; that they may behold my glory,* which thou hast given me' [John 17:16–17, 20–24]. And, 'All mine are thine, and thine are mine; and I am glorified in them' [John 17:10].

The Light proceeding from the Father of lights relates these words to us, makes them belong to us, makes them ours within us. The Light places them in the very core of our being. In this Light is our communion with Him, our 'personal' communion, face to Face, person to Person.

The initial action of a small degree of this Light – if one may measure a Divine gift – is recognised by a profound sensation of the Living God in our heart and mind; but it is not yet like the coming of the Kingdom in strength, not like manifest 'personal' contact with Him. It is essential to emphasise that Divine Light is *always and without fail* linked with a sense of grace of which our whole being is aware. In this connection Blessed St. Silouan both said and wrote: 'If thou seest light, and that is all' – to wit, feel no sense of grace – 'then it comes from the "enemy" and must be rejected'.

Intellection of the inscrutability of the Divine Self-Being does not necessarily require a high degree of spiritual knowledge. Many while still lacking experience of the Uncreated Light –

'that which may be known of God' existentially [cf. Rom. 1:19] – have perceived the unfathomableness of the Divinity through the normal process of philosophical contemplation. Philosophical contemplation cannot be equated with the experience accorded to Moses. 'And Moses drew near unto the thick darkness where God was' [Exod. 20:21]. Ontologically, it rates much lower, although it does denote the intellect's potential for genuine contemplation – but not in isolation from the heart, the centre of man's personalism.

I have already pointed out more than once that after intense concentration the intellect may perceive itself as light – faint, but light. And if the intellect regards itself as the highest manifestation of man, and without the love of the heart devotes itself to its abstract ascent to Absolute Being, in certain cases it arrives at Luciferism with its deadly 'cold light' and merciless contempt for the sufferings of millions.

Our *mind* is created in the image and after the likeness of the *First Mind* – God. Light is natural to it since it was made in the image of Him Who is Light unoriginate. When, in its ascetic contemplation of the mysteries of Unoriginate Being, the mind crosses the threshold of time and space, and for us ourselves becomes like light, then man stands in danger of mistaking this natural light of the created mind for the Uncreated, the Divine. In such states of aberration the human mind forges mystical theories which, however, lead not to genuine eternity but to that attainable by man as a created being.

Supernatural communion with God is quite a different matter. God is not the world of pure abstract ideas. He is Living. He is most concrete *Personal Being*. This feature of the *Personal Absolute* is the most important for many who find themselves halted by the insoluble contradictions between artificially-constructed hypothetical doctrines. Every dilemma is resolved by following Christ *in toto* – Christ, the God-man. This is the only way to arrive at true knowledge of genuine Being, when our enlightened mind is stilled in blissful awe, contemplating the creation of gods identical with the Unoriginate Himself.

The Christian dwelling existentially in the sphere of Uncreated Light may still not understand *what* this Light is. To the ignorant, speculation on its nature may seem superfluous, academic, lacking any real significance for our salvation. Not so with ascetic strivers who concentrate all their efforts on repentance. And how could anyone seeking true knowledge of God evade the question: *what* is it or *Who* is it that appears to him? Knowledge of God, existential knowledge, is inevitably united to the coming of God within man – an event by its nature indescribably grandiose. The heart has no doubts. Nevertheless, the manifestation in strength of Light so far transcends our fallen nature that no believer in Christ must trust himself without confirmation either from the Scriptures or the works of the Holy Fathers. And moreover, even the Scriptures, are not enough for a conclusive judgment, since almost everyone interprets them variously. It is absolutely necessary to have confirmation from someone of the same faith as ours who has been found worthy of Divine visitation before us. Therefore we need these three factors: 1) the New Testament; 2) the writings of the holy Ascetics of our Church; and 3) a 'live' witness. If there is no fellow witness, the virtuous soul cries to God, 'Have mercy upon me. Corrupt in soul and body, let me not fall away from Thy Truth to set foot on another, alien path'. 'Tempt me not to vainglory,' in the words that the canticle puts into the mouth of the most holy Virgin when the Archangel Gabriel announces to her that she shall give birth to the Son of God.

The appearance of uncreated Light is less rare than one might suppose. Many ascetics in a transport of repentance were found worthy of this gift without having had the temerity to let their mind dwell on it and perceive 'Who this is'. They are content with the action of Light on the soul – reconciliation with God, priceless comfort, a sense of eternity, the vanquishing of death.

Not all even among the greatest are capable of expressing with equal force what has happened to them. St. Peter, for instance, who was consumed with a burning love of Christ and worked miracles like the Lord Himself, is less eloquent in his Epistles than the Apostles John and Paul. Peter, who witnessed the Transfiguration on Mount Tabor, *knew* that through Christ, in Christ, he was united with God in eternity, that 'exceeding great and precious promises are given unto us: that by these we might be partakers of the divine nature . . .' [cf. II Pet. 1:4]; that 'there is none other name under heaven given among men, whereby we must be saved' [Acts 4:12]. Peter has many other splendid sayings but it is John and Paul, though they performed fewer visible miracles, who have given us richer material in their teaching, opening up for us limitless horizons of knowledge of God. St. Paul was better equipped (learning is often an advantage here) than the other Apostles to describe the experiences accorded to him, and found a whole range of profound words in which to speak of the mysteries revealed to him.

My thoughts naturally often return to my father in God, the Blessed St. Silouan. Existentially this humble man lived in a state which only very few throughout the whole history of the Church were found worthy of, but in his writing it is obvious that he lacks words to describe the great blessings poured down on him. The Church, however, reveres alike both those who in few words but an abundance of miracles and nobility of spirit founded her, and those who served the same ideal with the gift of teaching.

When He Who is God – ὁ ὄντως Ὤν – manifests Himself in the phenomenon of uncreated Light, man intuitively loses all desire to philosophise about the trans-personal Absolute. Existential – not abstract – knowledge of God is in no way confined to the intellect alone: a fusion – a communion – of the whole man with the Act of Divine Being is imperative. This is achieved in love. When Jesus asked 'a certain lawyer' how he interpreted the law, the answer came, 'Thou shalt love the Lord thy God with all thy heart, and with all thy soul, and with all thy strength, and with all thy mind' [Luke 10:27]. This is our gnoseology.

The commandment calls upon us to 'love'. It follows, therefore, that love is not something already given to us. Love must be acquired by the ascetic act of our free will. The Lord's appeal is first of all to the heart, the spiritual centre of the *persona*. The mind-reason is one of the energies of the human personality. Love is born in the heart through faith and the mind is thus confronted with a new inner factor. The flame of this love draws the mind wholly into the heart, where it merges into one with the heart and contemplates Being in the Light of Divine Love. We become 'whole' – we are healed.

There is no more difficult, more painful spiritual endeavour than the struggle for the triumph of the love of Christ, first in ourselves, then in the whole world. In point of fact this love is not of the earth but of Heaven. In it lies the meaning of the Being of God Himself, Who is Love; Who gave us the commandment to love. The spiritual ascent into the Kingdom of uncreated Divine Love demands prolonged ascetic striving – which may be likened to trying to climb a steep mountain, or the agonising struggle of gifted artists in all branches of art, or the long years of weary effort to acquire scientific knowledge. And so on. And since in most instances people willingly accept every possible sacrifice for the sake of obtaining short-lived material benefits or privileged social status, we should not be surprised at the still greater efforts required to achieve the eternal treasures of the Kingdom of God. As Christ said, 'The kingdom of heaven *suffereth violence*, and the violent take it by force' [Matt. 11:12].

III.

At this juncture I want to discuss what the Lord granted me after I turned to Him as an adult, when the visitation was bound up with profound prayer of repentance. At the beginning of this period Light appeared rather in the guise of Fire that consumed both in my body and in my soul something that I took, during the burning, to be foreign to God. Oh – then I knew and understood nothing of what was happening to me! I had no thought to explore the nature of this Fire, of this Light. My whole being was tortured by repentance; but I knew that my spirit had come to life. Mighty waves of both feeling and thought swept through me during those years. Sometimes there would be a sudden spurt, at others a gradual flow. Everything was jumbled together like a midnight thunderstorm. To describe what I experienced in chronological order is impossible now. What I remember for certain is my all-embracing reaching up to God in my terrible longing for Him. I would pour out this longing with such concentration that even if Fire descended, or Light, my attention was so stayed on God that I hardly noticed. And lo, on Easter Saturday, in 1924 perhaps, the Light visited me after I had taken communion, and I felt it like the touch of Divine Eternity on my spirit. Gentle, full of peace and love, the Light remained with me for three days. It drove away the darkness of non-existence that had engulfed me. I was resurrected, and in me and with me the whole world was resurrected. The words of St. John Chrysostom at the end of the Easter Liturgy struck me with overwhelming force: 'Christ is risen and there are no dead in the grave'. Tormented hitherto by the spectre of universal death, I now felt that my soul, too, was resurrected and there were no more dead . . . If this is God, then quickly let me abandon everything and seek only union with Him.

Now at the close of my life I have decided to talk to my brethren of things I would not have ventured to utter earlier, counting it unseemly. However insignificant I may be in every respect, fact remains fact: God the Father was good to me, as He generally is to every contrite heart [cf. Ps. 51:17]. He, the Father, drew me to His beloved Son, and the Son raised me up after my wretched fall [cf. John 6:37–40; 44–47]. The Holy

Spirit, proceeding from the Father, gave me to live 'the great mystery of godliness: God was manifest in the flesh, justified in the Spirit' [I Tim. 3:16].

Now I am certain that without such faith the states that I knew would have been ruled out. Even to someone still lacking experience faith can be given which will go on growing by virtue of the grace vouchsafed. I can bear witness that when one feels extreme loathing for oneself, as one is, and one's whole being is converted into prayer to Christ which wrenches the spirit from the vice-like grip of the passions and things material, then perception of Divine eternity is so keen that no logic or psycho-analysis can shake the obvious. Why do I mention logic and psycho-analysis? Logic, because it does not allow one to believe that the historical man, who can be seen and handled [cf. I John 1:1], who can be killed – hanged on the cross like a thief – is the Creator of the whole boundless cosmos. Psycho-analysis, because it convinces us of the necessity to discredit what we experience. No, as St. Silouan said, '*Such* light, *such* love, *such* life-giving Force and Wisdom can proceed only from the true source of all that exists'. St. Silouan was an extraordinarily gifted man but I, too, a poor wretch on all counts, am somehow able to judge the things that are intelligible to the human spirit, and even to the mind and psyche.

St. Paul secluded himself in the Arabian desert soon after Christ's appearance to him [cf. Gal. 1:16], and there in a transport of all-consuming repentance for his past was found worthy of many mighty revelations, including the confirmation that Jesus Christ is God. I do not seek logical proofs here below; but in my penitential weeping that exceeded my strength, that consumed me with fire, I too was convinced that He, Christ, is the loftiest eternal *Fact of Being*. The nature of my repentance precluded any possibility of 'imagining' that the Unoriginate God might be with me, so closely, so effectively. There were moments when I understood the manner of revelation of the heavenly mysteries to the Prophets, Apostles and Fathers of the Church. The Light that visited me is the Light of the Kingdom that is 'not of this world' [John 18:36], as King of which Christ named Himself.

What in fact happens? How explain such incidents? Our spirit is introduced by the Divine Spirit into the sphere of the Kingdom. When this happens all discursive thought ceases – we live a form of being new to us. We are given the experience of 'being' – I am. St. Paul and the other Apostles Peter and John and all the subsequent theologians of the Church relate *facts of being*.

I feel shame to the point of pain to utter such things which may seem over-prideful and repellent. But here lies a paradox – a two-fold consciousness in me, of my own nothingness, which I find abhorrent, and, on the other hand, of the compassionate condescendence of God. I argue to myself that God's gifts are given *without fail* to each of us [cf. Matt. 7:7–11] but according to the measure of our thirst and faithfulness to the Bestower: to some more, to others less abundantly. I know myself, I am indeed an insignificant individual – that goes without saying. But the experience that God saw fit to grant me is somewhat analogous to that of the Apostles, the Fathers and my preceptors. By virtue of this analogy I can express what was given to me in the same words that we find in the New Testament and the writings of the Fathers of the Church. There is no doubt about the colossal distance separating the Old Testament and the Testament of Christ [cf. Matt. 5:17–48]. And yet even within the bounds of the law of Moses the prophets sometimes spoke with the temerity of the Apostles. So it is in my case. Both in the monastery and in the desert it was given to me to experience the spiritual states that I am describing. I have not retained them in their full strength. Over the years since my return to the world I have gradually lost a great deal – but I do *remember*. The grace that I was granted freed me spiritually from the power of other people's opinions but fear of the Divine judgment never ceases to terrify me – which means that I never lose sight of my infirmities.

This is what St. Silouan wrote: 'There are some who say that all this belonged to bygone times and is not for our day. But with the Lord no word is ever diminished. It is we who alter, go to the bad and so lose grace. But to him who asks, the Lord gives all things, not because we are worthy but in that the Lord is merciful and loves us'.

Various circumstances obliged me to leave the Holy Mountain. In Europe little by little I found myself bereft of much that had filled my life on Athos. Helping people, as experience shows, means entering into their sorrows, their sufferings, their struggle against the passions, and their often primitive needs. Unfortunately, this does not assist one to continue in contemplation and hesychastic prayer. The course of events shows conclusively that my return to the world was the will of God. But even so I never cease to grieve over the loss of the gifts with which the Lord loaded me beyond all my expectations.

The action on man's spirit of the Light of which I write bears witness to its Divine Nature. It is uncreated, unnameable. It is mysterious, imponderable, inviolable. I do not know how to describe it. By nature it is otherworldly, supranatural. Its coming down on us is no less than the manifestation of God to man, the revelation of heavenly mysteries. By the gift of this Light at the Transfiguration on Mount Tabor was knowledge of God confirmed. From the moment it shone there on the three Apostles it entered into the history of our world, to become the inalienable inheritance of generation after generation of those who believe in Christ-God. Without this Light the earth would have for ever lacked true knowledge of God. Judging by my own experience I would call it the Light of resurrection. Its coming introduces the spirit into the sphere where there is no death. Without its irradiation it is impossible duly to apprehend the ways of salvation. The world – people – would remain in the darkness of ignorance. Even the most exquisite abstract theological formation does not mean salvation since it merely provides intellectual understanding without lifting one to the realm of Divine Being.

Sometimes this Light can be likened to a mountain-cloud over the heights where you stand. The cloud itself is saturated with light but you cannot see anything but cloud – all the rest of the world has disappeared. Thus the Divine Light, bringing a new image of spiritual being, screens from our eyes the sight of the material world. This Light is steady, entire. It is full of profound peace. In it the soul contemplates Divine Love and Goodness. In its rich outpouring man ceases to be aware of his surroundings, even of his own body. Furthermore, he sees himself as light. This Light approaches softly, tenderly, so that one does not notice its embrace. Such a condition is like the gentle falling asleep of an ordinarily healthy person; but, of course, it is by no means sleep but fulness of life.

With the departure of this Light, as quiet as its advent, the soul slowly returns to her usual awareness of the everyday world. In the softened heart there is a deep peace. The spirit continues to dwell at one and the same time on the divine plane and the earthly. The former, however, gradually recedes and a certain sadness invades the soul – a feeling of regret that with return of physical sensibility the inexpressibly benign touch of the Divine Spirit is fading away. The fragrancy of the vision fades but does not altogether disappear. However, the very fading away begets a gentle longing for God; but prayer flows peacefully and from the whole being. Dwelling with the Lord destroys the passions – there is no more hankering after renown, riches, power or anything else of this world, all of which are connected with the passions, marked with tragedy and of short duration.

Repeated visits of grace start one considering the similarities between the state of contemplation and the effects produced by the Gospel word. The Gospel teaching is now apprehended as Light, as life-giving power, as a fresh act of creation – not in the form of 'Let there be . . .' but as an appeal to the reasonable creature as the child of the Heavenly Father, silently calling him to a wondrous ascension into the Kingdom of the Father's love, where there is neither death, nor beginning, nor end. The spirit discerns that Christ's word does indeed proceed 'from the Father of lights' Who 'of his own will begat us with the word of truth' [James 1:17–18]. In Christ's word is Divine life, and he who opens wide his heart to it becomes God-like.

At the beginning of my monastic life on Mt. Athos the Lord granted me unceasing prayer which, without diminishing in strength, would switch every now and then from one subject to another. I will relate what I remember well enough, since we are talking of the prayers which marked me indelibly.

This is how it often used to be – towards evening, at sunset, I would shut the window and draw three curtains over it to make my cell as quiet and dark as possible. With my forehead bent to the floor I would slowly repeat words of prayer, one after the other. I had no feeling of being cooped up, and my mind, oblivious of the body, lived in the light of the Gospel word. Concentrated on the fathomless wisdom of Christ's word, my spirit, freed from all material concerns, would feel flooded, as it were, with light from the Celestial Sun. At the same time a gentle peace would fill my soul, unconscious of all the needs and cares of this earth.

How explain that with the descent on us of the Light of Christ His brief commandments, now inscribed on our hearts and minds, could make all other laws, including the law of Moses, superflous? His bidding, 'Thou shalt love the Lord thy God with all thy heart, and with all thy soul, and with all thy mind . . . and thy neighbour as thyself' [Matt. 22:37,39] is utterly persuasive. The Lord gave me to live this state, and my spirit yearned to cling to His feet in gratitude for this gift.

The same experience was repeated at intervals for months, perhaps years.

Under the influence of this Light prayer for mankind in travail possessed my whole being. It was clear that the inescapable, countless sufferings of the entire universe are the consequence of man's falling away from God, our Creator, Who revealed Himself to us. If the world loved Christ and His commandments, everything would be radically transformed and the earth would become a wonderful paradise. The first paradise, as described in the Bible, became a tangible reality for me in my vision. The thousands of years that have elapsed since then on the plane of the eternal spirit became a contemplation, outside time, without duration.

'And the Lord God took man, and put him into the garden of Eden to dress it and keep it' [Gen. 2:15]. What an inspiring exercise – man brought into collaboration with God Himself in the creation of the world! Freedom to pray in the stillness of the night on the Holy Mountain seemed to me to be an anticipation of the Kingdom. This sojourn with the beloved God gave me to understand the meaning of the words, 'God's paradise'. From Him, from the Holy of Holies, came the Gospel words which bear the absolute stamp of Divine omniscience.

When my prayer drew to an end I would find myself repeating the words of the Psalm, 'The darkness hideth not from thee; but the night shineth as the day' [Ps. 139:12].

Early in the 1930's – I was a deacon then – for two weeks God's tender mercy rested on me. At dusk, when the sun was sinking behind the mountains of Olympus, I would sit on the balcony near my cell, face turned to the dying light. In those days I contemplated the evening light of the sun and at the same time another Light which softly enveloped me and gently invaded my heart, in some curious fashion making me feel compassionate and loving towards people who treated me harshly. I would also feel a quiet sympathy for all creatures in general. When the sun had set I would retire to my cell as usual to perform the devotions preparatory to celebrating the Liturgy, and the Light did not leave me while I prayed.

One evening a monk from a cell near mine came to me and said, 'I have just been reading the hymns of St. Simeon the New

Theologian. Tell me – what do you make of his description of his vision of the Uncreated Light?' Up to that moment I had lived with grateful heart the Lord's blessing upon me but had not posed any question about the occurrence – my thoughts were fixed upon God to the exclusion of self. In order to answer Father Juvenaly I reflected on what was happening to me at the time. Trying to cover up, I answered evasively, 'It is not for me to pronounce upon St. Simeon's experience . . . But perhaps when grace was with him he was conscious of it as Light. I don't know.' I had the impression that Father Juvenaly retired to his cell without suspecting anything more than I had said. But soon after this brief exchange I began to pray as usual. Light and love were no longer with me.

Thus over and over again I learned from bitter experience that pure prayer happens only when the spirit is completely absorbed in God without any reverting to self. It is curious – when I was talking to Father Juvenaly I was not aware of conceit stirring in me . . . And yet . . . But could I not have foreseen that my continuing vision of Light in the evenings and at night at that time (the beginning of my priesthood) might lead to pride? If such a misfortune lay on my path the Lord found an excellent way of humbling me by taking away the gift. Glory be to Him for ever and ever.

God Himself, Light inaccessible and Life eternal, came into the world, dwelt with us in our tangible flesh, and the world knew Him not, accepted Him not. But those who cherish His coming know that through the Only-begotten Son they, too, 'receive the adoption of sons' [Gal. 4:5] to God the Father Almighty. Ineffably He is cognized in the manifestation of the Light of grace, delicate, consoling and quickening. The physical sun is a splendid image of the Sun of love and truth. Without the rays of the visible sun life on our planet would be impossible. We all feel the beneficial action of its rays. Formerly I had thought of the sun as im-material but following contemplation of the uncreated Light of Divinity the natural light of the sun seemed crude, at times aggressive. The sun illumines nature but does not enable our spirit to penetrate directly the mysteries of Divine Being. It is the contrary with the Light of Divinity which first and foremost affords revelation of the Kingdom of the Heavenly Father.

After His resurrection Christ appeared exclusively to those who were capable of apprehending Him in His now divinized and translucent flesh, and remained invisible to everyone else. Thus the uncreated Light stays unseen for those who do not seek to know God with all their being. And again, another curious analogy with physical light – it, too, is invisible without an object to catch and reflect it. Nature in the light of the earthly sun is a splendid sight for the eye. But the Divine Light, when it irradiates man, in a marvellous way transfigures him. The most ordinary individual, apparently disfigured by sin, in his prayer of repentance is illumined by Light and looks young and even beauteous.

Over and over again my heart would sing praises to Christ-God Who manifests Himself in Uncreated Light. Thus incalculably powerful, beyond all bounds, He descends to us. The inviolable, searchless Light of His Divinity quickens and embraces all that exists. Notions of place, of volume, do not apply, and yet non-spatially His Light is everywhere. To be illumined by this Light brings an experience of resurrection, a foretaste of bliss to come. Wordlessly the Light tells our spirit that, 'made in His image' [cf. Gen. 1:26], in his final consummation man will appear as the bearer of the fulness of God-man life, will be perfected after the likeness of Christ, God-and-man. Through the action of this Light within the repentant sinner a wondrous flower blossoms – the *persona*, the hypostasis. And we perceive that it is natural for this hypostatic principle in us through love to comprise in eternity inexpressibly grandiose and holy life.

Christ's Light is Divine energy, the uncreated, unoriginate life of God the Trinity. It is energy-action proper both to the

Father and the Holy Spirit. In this Light we know the Father and the Holy Spirit and the only-begotten Son. When this Light by God's providence shines on us the hypostatic principle in us ceases to be a potential – it becomes actualized and we can 'see' God [cf. Matt. 5:8]. We can apprehend His existential strength, the abundant life of God Himself. Here on earth man cannot contain this absolute perfection of Divinity but with the action in him of the Holy Spirit he realises that he is rooted in Him Who is verily the Creator of all life, the true Kernel of all that exists.

Time and again I return to my theme of the Light of life which the darkness of non-being cannot engulf [cf. John 1:5]. I do not live of myself. I am fully stretched towards Him Whom I love. He gave me life. It is He Who is my life.

Man is great when he is in God Who is great. With the strength of Divine love man embraces the whole world, and in a certain sense is a centre of the world. This idea occurred to me for the first time when God granted me 'the grace of mindfulness of death'. This rather negative experience at its most intense made me interpret my departure into non-being as the annihilation in me of the whole cosmos. In me, with my death, the whole human race would die, with all its sufferings and joys, aspirations and knowledge. Further – God Himself, still known only imperfectly, yet known, would die in me and for me. All created and all uncreated being would vanish in the black obscurity of oblivion. This in effect was contemplation of the 'absoluteness' (*qua* reflection of the Absolute) in our hypostatic principle, but under a minus sign.

When, though, the uncreated Light approached, bearing witness to my spirit that I was outside the power of death, everything that was hitherto dying in me was revived through the action of this Light.

The alarming darkness of death, the painful self-loathing because of our sinfulness which wrenches us away from the God of love, bitter hopelessness over ourselves and indignation at the absurdity of life in general as we had perceived it before

– all this is radically transformed with the growth of repentance in us, until it becomes a kind of Christ-like 'self-emptying'. Like unto Him now in our death, through the Holy Spirit we are raised and lifted up to everlasting glory like unto His [cf. Phil. 2:7–8; 3:9–11; Rom. 6:5]. Thus is Jesus Christ made known both in His eternal sovereignty and His inscrutable depletion 'for us men and for our salvation'.

Christ 'overcame the world' [cf. John 16:33]. And now there is no one and nothing that could set limits to His Sovereignty. In much suffering we free ourselves from the power of our past. Enriched by the experience of victory through repentance, we become kin to the only-begotten Son in His Lordship. Hell no longer has dominion over us – our old dread has gone.

I do not insist that it was exactly like this that the Lord Jesus Himself lived His 'Self-emptying' in the Garden of Gethsemane and on Golgotha. But in my repentance before Him for all my spiritual trespasses I was given to understand it so. Why should *such a Man* pray, 'My soul is exceeding sorrowful, even unto death . . . O my Father, if it be possible, let this cup pass from me . . . And his sweat was as it were great drops of blood falling down to the ground' [Matt. 26:38–39; Luke 22:44]?

In my utter worthlessness what was of great moment then continues so to this day, increasing all the time. With reverent awe I wonder to myself, 'What could He, my Lord, have seen that He should pray like that? He Who is infinite in His Divinity, Who is searchless in His humbling of Himself, immense in His love 'unto the end' [John 13:1], inaccessible in His glory?

His agony certainly had to be more acute than that of the whole of the rest of mankind if He were to be 'the Saviour of all men'.

Truly He is the Light come into the world, that whosoever believeth on Him should not abide in darkness [cf. John 12:46].

Manifestations of Light, Which is unique in its eternal nature, differ both in degree of energy and mode. Rarely in the history of the Church have visions of Light attained such fulness that the visionary is also vouchsafed a personal revelation. This did happen on Mount Tabor when Peter, James and John heard the Father's 'voice out of the cloud' bearing witness to His beloved Son. So it was with the Apostle Paul on the road to Damascus – 'And suddenly there shined round him a light from heaven', followed by personal converse with Christ, Who assured Paul that He was the God Whom he revered, Who had manifest Himself to Moses on Sinai. 'I am Jesus whom thou persecutest' [Acts 9:5].

Far more often the Light will embrace man when he is immersed in penitent prayer on the borderline of despair. In the early days of repentance for one's sins this holy Light tells of Divine mercy and love but there is still no encounter face to Face. This only happens when man is really in God and God in him; when the prayerful spirit knows that He Who has appeared to him is indeed the Eternal Master of all that is, the First and the Last; searchless and so near; invisible and at the same time tangible, even physically; filling the heart with the fire of love, illumining the mind with the light of understanding – the Light of knowledge inexpressible in words. Incidentally, He Himself proclaimed, 'I AM THAT I AM'. Each of us interprets these most sacred of words according to the measure of his actual experience. And no mortal can say that he has learned 'to the end' the Being hidden behind the revelation. But the hope, however, is given to us that the *eternal day* will come when He will be 'all in all' [I Cor. 15:28].

13

The Hypostatic Principle in the Godhead and in the Human Being

The incarnation of the Logos of the Father – Jesus Christ – furnishes a solid foundation for our knowledge of God. Actuated by love for Him, we undergo a profound transformation of our whole being. Christ's infinite life is transmitted to us. Our spirit finds itself on opposite poles – in both the black depths of hell and the Kingdom of God illumined by the Sun that never sets. The content of our being expands ineffably. In urgent prayer the soul aspires to this wondrous God but it is a long time before we apprehend that He Himself is praying in us. Through this God-given prayer we are united existentially with Christ – at first in His searchless Self-emptying and descent even into hell, and then in His Divinity. 'And this is life eternal, that they might know thee the only true God, and Jesus Christ, whom thou hast sent' [John 17:3].

The *Persona*-Hypostasis in Divine Being cannot be a limiting principle. And in our creaturehood the hypostasis is the principle that assumes infinity into itself. When his spirit enters into the world of Divine eternity man is struck by the majesty of the vision opening before him. At the same time the universe undergoes a certain alteration in its destinies: 'A man is born into the world' [John 16:21] – an event that communicates to all creation a new unfading value. Man as hypostatic spirit belongs to eternal ontology. Those who are saved in Christ – the saints – receive Divine eternity as their imprescriptible possession though they immutably remain created beings.

Two currents, of which one is negative, can be observed in

mankind's spiritual world. The ever-growing dynamic of the Fall – banal nihilism and moral disintegration – demonstrates the crude form of the negative current. The Book of Genesis [cf. ch. 3: v. 5] acquaints us with its sublimated, Luciferian form where the creature endowed with the freedom of self-determination rejects God's commandments. He considers them to be a kind of limitation imposed from without, whereas he is striving for absolute self-affirmation, self-divinization.

The other current is positive, upward. It manifests itself as love drawing us to infinite union with the Father, 'Which is in heaven'.

Parallel to these, we note the presence of two opposite tendencies, where we find those who aspire to divest themselves of their earthly mode of existence – they are fascinated by the profound quiet of some mysterious, all-transcending Non-being – and others who, accepting Christ's word, 'The kingdom of heaven suffereth violence, and the violent take it by force' [Matt. 11:12], engage on the painful battle to overcome our mortality. 'Not for that we would be unclothed, but clothed upon, that mortality might be swallowed up of life' [II Cor. 5:4].

It is characteristic of the former to think of the First-Absolute as trans-personal. For them personeity at its best is the initial stage of the degradation, the self-restriction of the Absolute. For the others it is precisely the *Persona* that lies at the root of all that exists [cf. John 1:3]. And this is how we Christians see God and the world. To us has been revealed the Hypostatic God, 'Maker of heaven and earth, And of all things visible and invisible' [*Nicaean Creed*]. He is Self-Being. He is the First and the Last. There is no one and nothing before or after Him. This is the God of Love imperishable, eternal. Those who love Him are promised the fulness of adoption through the only-begotten Son of the Father, Jesus Christ, Who said: 'Because I live, ye shall live also' [John 14:19].

The Hypostasis-*Persona* is the inmost principle of Absolute Being – its first and last dimension. 'I am Alpha and Omega, the beginning and the ending, saith the Lord, which is, and which was, and which is to come, the Almighty' [Rev. 1:8].

The Hypostasity of God escapes definition because it cannot be subject to any kind of determination. Not to be known rationally, it can be apprehended existentially and only in so far as God reveals Himself to man [cf. Matt. 11:27; Luke 10:22; John 17:26].

In man, too, image of the Personal God, the principle of the person is 'the hidden man of the heart, in that which is not corruptible . . . which is in the sight of God of great price' [I Pet. 3:4]. The created person is also beyond definition. Scientific and philosophical cognition can be expressed in concepts and definitions but the person is being, not subject to philosophical or scientific forms of cognition. Like God the *persona*-hypostasis cannot be throughly known from outside unless he reveals himself to another person.

God is a hidden God, and man has depths within him kept secret from alien eyes. God, not man, is the Origin of Being; but man is created with the potential of receiving and eternally bearing within himself the non-created Life of Divinity.

Christ, 'being in the form of God' – that is, being God without beginning – in the act of incarnation took into His Hypostasis the form of our earthly existence [cf. Phil. 2:6–7]. But the human hypostasis receives divinization through grace, wherefore the fulness of the Divine image is actualized in him. The personal principle in man contains, first and foremost, his likeness to Him Who revealed himself to us under the Name *I AM*. In the act of divinization grace exalts man from the dimensions and patterns of the earth to the dimensions and patterns of Divine Life. In other words, man hypostatizes divine attributes such as eternity, love, light, wisdom, truth. Becoming a god by the content of his being, the created hypostasis, however, in no wise becomes God for his fellows.

Various Fathers and preceptors of the Church down the ages have preached the revelation of our likeness to God, though not always with the same emphasis. This is partly because not all of them possessed equal knowledge of God and humankind.

To speak of likeness to the point of identity troubled those who interpreted this as a complete fusion with God. There is, and always will be, an ontological distance between God, Who is unconditioned Primordial Being, and man, who is His creation. But in the Act of creation 'in His image, after His likeness', our Creator in effect repeats Himself, and in this sense is our Father. Was it not this fact that the Lord had in mind when He taught us the prayer, 'Our Father'? Through His incarnation the everlasting Logos of the Father gives us to partake of His Blood and His Flesh in order thereby to pour into our veins His eternal Life, that we may become His children, flesh of His Flesh, bone of His Bone [cf. John 6: 53–57].

Christ manifested the perfection of the Divine image in man and the possibility for our nature of assimilating the fulness of divinization to the very extent that, after His ascension, He placed our nature 'on the right hand of the Father'. But even in Him our nature did not become one with the Essence of the Uncreated God. In Christ, incarnate Son of the Father, we contemplate God's pre-eternal idea of man.

The revelation 'I AM THAT I AM' shows the hypostatic dimension in the Divinity to be of fundamental significance. The principle of the *Persona* in God is not an abstract conception but essential reality possessing its own nature and energy of life. The essence is not of primary or even pre-eminent importance in defining Persons-Hypostases in their reciprocal relations. Divine Being contains nothing that could be external to the hypostatic principle. The profundity of the mystery of the Divine Persons is unfathomable. Their Self-determination in eternity is a *fact* having no beginning – there was no moment when the Father would not have had the Son and would not have breathed forth the Holy Spirit. The beginning of all things is the Father, Who in the pre-eternal begetting of the Son communicates to Him all the plenitude of His Nature, of His Essence. The same happens with the procession of the Holy Spirit. Hence the affirmation that the Son and the Holy Spirit are absolutely equal with the Father.

The incarnate Logos of the Father – Christ-man – is made

more intelligible to us by 'the words which He hath from the Father and which He hath given to us' [cf. John 17:8]. We know His earthly life through the gospel good tidings, through spiritual tradition concerning Him. In Himself He showed us 'His Father, and our Father' [cf. John 20:17].

Cognizance of the Holy Spirit as Person comes more slowly. The Holy Spirit continually quickens not only the Church and her children but the whole world, all creation, too. The Holy Spirit heals us from the consequences of the Fall, regenerates and hallows us. But all this He accomplishes in an invisible manner, like some diffident marvellous Friend Who does not want to burden us with gratitude to Him, for He knows that in our present state a proper feeling of gratitude may be burdensome. The great blessedness of knowing Him comes gradually, in proportion as, with His help, the hypostatic principle unfolds in us, by virtue of which we begin to apprehend all things – both Divine First-Being and cosmic being – after a different fashion, a fashion peculiar to man as *persona*, the actualized image of Him who revealed himself to us with the name, I AM.

The Person is He Who alone and genuinely lives. Aside from this vital principle nothing can exist: 'In him was life; and the life was the light of men' [John 1:4]. The fundamental content of this life is love: 'God is love' [I John 4:8]. The personal being realises himself through loving contact with another person or persons.

Proceeding from the marvellous revelation I AM THAT I AM, we experience and live man, created 'in the image, after the likeness', first and foremost as *persona*. It is precisely to this principle in us that eternity relates. Only as a personal being can man recognise his Prototype – the Living God. Man is more than a microcosm – he is a microtheos. Being created, he received the commandment to become a god [*vide* Basil the Great]. If the Creator in all was made like unto man [cf. Heb. 2:17], it follows that man was created with the possibility of being like unto God in all things: 'We shall be like him; for we shall see him as he is' [I John 3:2].

In the utmost intensity of prayer that our nature is capable of, when God Himself prays in us, man receives a vision of God that is beyond any image whatsoever. Then it is that man *qua persona* really prays 'face to Face' with the Eternal God. In this encounter with the Hypostatic God the *hypostasis*, that at first was only potential, is actualized in us.

Drawn by the Spirit of God to prayer for the whole world, to share in the Lord's prayer in Gethsemane, we suddenly behold in ourselves a divine miracle – a spiritual sun rises in us, the name of which is *persona*. It is the beginning in us of a new form of being, already immortal. At the same time we apprehend, not superficially, not with our reason, but in our very depths, the revelation of the Hypostatic Principle in the Holy Trinity. We behold in Light the sublime mystery of Unoriginate Being – the *Living* God: One in Three Persons; the only true God of love.

I am writing the story of my soul. I paid dearly for the deluded ideas which once fascinated me for some seven or eight years. Arguing in the ordinary way, I could not of my own strength have extracted myself from the bottomless pit of the transcendentalism of the East – the vision of the Supra-personal Absolute. When I was immature in body and mind this philosophy seemed far superior to the Christian emotionalism of 'Love God and thy neighbour'. At that time the very word *persona* was identical in my understanding with the conception of the individual. Would it not be absurd to apply this dimension to Absolute Being? was how I reasoned.

However, when by a gift from on High it was granted to me to comprehend the ontological place of the principle of the *persona* in Divine Being, everything naturally changed round and appeared in the opposite perspective: we are created beings; as *personae* we are beings created potentially, not actually. I am not First-Being but a created image of Him. By the Gospel commandments I am summoned to actualize, to realise in myself, my personal likeness to God; as *persona*, to overcome the limitation of the individual, which can in no wise inherit the Divine form of being.

Our God is omniscient, omnipresent Spirit: 'There is nothing covered, that shall not be revealed; and hid, that shall not be known . . . one sparrow shall not fall on the ground without your Father. The very hairs of your head are all numbered' [cf. Matt. 10:26–30]. 'Neither is there any creature that is not manifest in his sight: but all things are naked and opened unto the eyes of him with whom we have to do' [Heb. 4:13]. We do not comprehend this form of knowledge, immediate, non-sequential, total. But we believe in God's good providence for us. In the course of years of diligent striving to live according to His will we shall marvel many a time at the mathematical precision of God's care for us.

If God were not Personal Being, then neither could we, His image, enter into the hypostatic form of being. Moreover, our personal character would be no more than an epiphenomenon. But by virtue of the fact that the *persona* in us is born in supernatural prayer face to Face with the Living God, it, the *persona*, is not subject to the natural elements: it transcends earthly bounds and moves in a sphere of other dimensions. One and only, unique and irreducible, it cannot be accounted for arithmetically.

Absolute First-Being is Hypostatic; and man, the likeness of the Absolute, is hypostasis. God is Spirit; and man-hypostasis is spirit. And this spirit is not abstract, separate, since it possesses its own nature. On the earthly plane it is given concrete expression by the flesh which brings the first experience of existence. God-the-Word assumed human flesh [cf. John 1:14] and thereby proved that He is not a fabrication of our reason or the fruit of our imagination incited by mystic awe before unaccountable hostile forces. God is First essential Reality; and the human personality likewise is essential life.

The attitude of love is natural for the *persona* made in the image of the God of love. He does not determine himself oppositively, by contraposing himself over against the 'not I'.

Love is the most intrinsic content of his essence. Embracing the whole world in prayerful love, the *persona* achieves *ad intra* the unity of all that exists. In the creative act of his becoming, he aspires to universal unity *ad extra* also. In love lies his likeness to God Who is love [cf. I John 4:16].

The Creator of the world, the Lord, holds all that exists in the palm of His hand; and man as hypostasis is a kind of centre capable of containing in himself not only the plurality of cosmic realities but the whole fulness of Divine and human being. In himself the *persona* is a permanent value, of greater importance than all the rest of the cosmos. In his joy at finding the freedom of immortality he contemplates a new form of being.

Engendered by God in prayer, man is never alone. The hypostasis does not know loneliness: he is always in the presence of God the Omnipresent. Until the *persona* is completed he sometimes 'endures' Him with great difficulty, like Moses, who 'endured, as seeing him who is invisible' [cf. Heb. 11:27]. At other times he will be filled with a gentle, peaceful joy, knowing himself in the hands of the Holy Guardian.

Man-hypostasis is also not aware of loneliness because, however isolated he may be, he prays for the whole world, whether the world be suffering or content.

Even if only 'in part' [cf. I Cor. 13:9], nevertheless, for the sake of the prayers of my father St. Silouan, the Lord revealed to me the mystery of the *persona*. Year after year I prayed prayers of despair. The Lord did not despise me, and descended in mercy even unto me. At first it was His gospel word that acted on me. This word, that proceedeth from the Father [cf. John 7:16–17; 17:14, 17], took root in my hardened heart. My new life was born in suffering. To begin with, I was as it were suspended in the air, alone, outside the Church. I was completely ignorant then but an invisible fire consumed me, and my soul in agony reached up to the Almighty to save me. Somewhere inside me a ray of hope appeared that overcame my dread of starting out on the painful path. This pain that I am trying to speak of is sacred for me. A strange miracle – the dolour in my heart brought moments of rapture to my spirit. I marvelled how God had created my nature able to endure suffering through which hitherto-unknown depths of prayer were disclosed to me. There were times when, gripped by pain, in a whisper that yet cried aloud in wonder I would exclaim, 'Glory to Thee, all-wise Creator'. Prayer delivered me from the cramped prison of the world, and my spirit lived in the freedom of the infinity of my God. Without this suffering I could never have understood the love that the Lord spake of when He said, 'The prince of this world cometh, and hath nothing in me. But that the world may know that I love the Father; and as the Father gave me commandment, even so I do' [John 14:30–31].

If the love commanded of us in the Gospel were natural to us in our fallen state, it would have been unnecessary to bid us 'Love the Lord thy God with all thy heart, and with all thy soul, and with all thy mind . . . Thou shalt love thy neighbour as thyself' [Matt. 22:37–39]. When that love touches the heart, our spirit in Light beholds God, and lives by Him and in Him. He surpasses all human thought. Not a single one of our abstract conceptions is applicable to Him. He – lives. His might is incalculable, His love inscrutable. To dwell with him is ineffable riches. When I was a painter I never achieved satisfaction because the means at my disposal were impotent to portray the beauty of creation. And now all the words that I can find to express my wonder before God are quite futile.

To be blind is a great deprivation. But there is no greater affliction, no more bitter pain, than not to know God.

Mankind, multi-hypostatic, manifests the image of the Holy Trinity: one nature in a plurality of *personae*. But each of us individually bears within himself the image of the only-begotten Son, and our salvation lies in receiving 'the adoption of sons' [cf. Gal. 4:5] to the Father. To become like Jesus Christ it is essential to meet Him as *Persona*, to keep the commandments that He gave us; for no one can become a person-hypostasis, the bearer of Divine eternity, except through the Son 'beloved' of the Father. And to Him we sing praises daily, together with His eternal Father and the Holy Spirit proceeding from the Father.

I is a magnificent word. It signifies *persona*. Its principal ingredient is love, that opens out, first and foremost, to God. This *I* does not live in a convulsion of egoistic concentration on self. Created by the will of God the Creator from 'nothing', if wrapped up in self it will continue in its nothingness. The love towards God commanded of us by Christ, which entails hating oneself and renouncing all emotional and fleshly ties, draws the spirit of man into the expanses of Divine eternity [cf. Luke 14: 26–27 and 33; John 12:25; Matt. 16:25]. This kind of love is an attribute of Divinity. When the force of it touches the human heart, it opens the heart to infinity, bestows the joy of lovingly embracing all creation, the whole world. The fulness of imperishable love for God and our neighbour is connected in some marvellous fashion with a feeling of repulsion for oneself amounting to hatred. But this is a sacred hatred, God's gift to us. Through it we overcome our death, caused by the fall of Adam. Through it we are effectively introduced into eternity, since this love is only possible if God Himself unites with us and becomes our life.

Had the Lord Jesus not revealed this astonishing mystery to us, no mortal could have invented such a paradox – detest yourself because of love for God, and you will embrace all that exists with your love! And God, and all the riches of being created by Him, will become the content of your life! The *I* is forgotten in the transport of love for the God of love but nevertheless it is this *I* that blissfully contains in itself all heaven and earth.

It is both joy and torture to me to speak of this love, the grace of which I have lost. It has occurred more than once in my life in God that so soon as I began to perceive with my reason (my 'left hand') what was happening to me after God had condescended to me, the Light forsook me. This calamity befell me particularly after I was appointed spiritual confessor on Mt. Athos. But before that time, too, I suffered the state of being abandoned by God at the approach of vainglory. But then it was less difficult to rehabilitate myself through repentance. Now to tell others, on the market-place, as it were, of God's gift is much more perilous.

The Lord wants us to be *there*, where He is [cf. John 12:26; 14:3; 17:24]. Oh, if only we could see the world Christ lives in! Then we would appreciate His commandment – to become like Him in all things – as an inexpressibly great honour.

'In those days', when the time of His sufferings in Gethsemane and on Golgotha was drawing nigh, He began to concentrate on the act of self-emptying that lay before Him as man. 'Father, if thou be willing, remove this cup from me: nevertheless not my will, but thine, be done . . . and his sweat was as it were great drops of blood falling to the ground' [Luke 22:42–44]. When we are confronted with the commandment to love Christ to the point of hating ourselves [cf. Luke 14:26–27 and 33] and everything we have in the world, we sometimes come near to the danger of exclaiming like some of His disciples, 'This is an hard saying; who can hear it?'. To which the Lord made answer, 'No man can come unto me, except it were given unto him of my Father' . . . And, 'from that time many of his disciples went back, and walked no more with him'. But Peter felt the power of Christ's utterance – 'Thou hast the words of eternal life', he declared [cf. John 6:60–68].

'God is love . . . love made perfect that we may have boldness in the day of judgment: because AS HE IS, so are we in this world' [I John 4:16–17]. The 'hate' of which the Lord of love speaks, in its essence is the plenitude of God's kenotic love. Love, proceeding from the Father, draws us to follow Christ. Seeing ourselves held fast in the bonds of egoism and incapable of following Him, we hate ourselves. The pain of this hallowed loathing casts us beyond the bounds of time and space, until only the driving force of love remains – all else vanishes. In such prayer must the *persona* pray, as reflection and image of Christ praying in Gethsemane.

God is Love; and man-hypostasis is endowed with the ability to assume from God the flame of this love. 'God is light, and in him is no darkness at all' [I John 1:5] and we are called to shine forth in Divine eternity [cf. Matt. 13:43]. To God all things are open, all things are known; and man-hypostasis, contained in the Act of Divine Being, through God and in God becomes the bearer of omniscience. (The experience of centuries of prayer to the Mother of God and the Saints has shown this.) God 'filleth all in all' [Eph. 1:23]. He is present in all places, not as Essence, which in absolute fashion transcends all created things, but by His vital energy; and the sons of the Kingdom, in the Holy Spirit, become as it were present in all places. The Saints, who are focussed on the One God, in Him behold the whole world.

Man is a created hypostasis. Yet in his inner being as image of the Absolute God he is also a universal centre, great and wonderful in his final actualization through the Son, co-eternal with the Father. He partly apprehends this by the grace of what ascetics term 'mindfulness of death' – when death is lived (for him, in him) as a cosmic catastrophe extinguishing all things, even God Himself, Whom to a certain extent he has come to know. The negative character of this occurrence is transposed to a positive experience of the resurrection of the soul when the Uncreated Light shines down on him and begets profound prayer for all Adam.

The creature person-hypostasis is a godlike centrum: the Creator regards him not as His Act but as a kind of *fact* even for Himself. The hypostasis recognises no outside authority. By virtue of this there is no one and nothing in the whole universe that could force him to make one or another choice, whether in time or eternity. And God, Almighty and Creator of all that is, through His appearance in the flesh completed His revelation to us, by dying on the cross, of His limitless love, and thereby draws us to Himself – our Prototype [cf. John 6:44; 12:32].

If 'the man Christ Jesus' [I Tim. 2:5], Who of His own volition gave Himself for the redemption of all, prayed to the Father: 'O my Father, if this cup may not pass away from me, except I drink it, thy will be done' [Matt. 26:42], what may we, so faint-hearted, say of ourselves? 'This cup' – what cup? What did He see when He was praying that made Him so express Himself? We do not attain to the magnitude of His vision. The mystery of His perception is only partly revealed to the faithful when it is given to them to approach these indescribable frontiers. Men and women of exceptional courage, who went into the desert to live in loneliness far from the world, wept but not, of course, for the loss of some earthly benefit but because they were confronted by fearful abysses. Whoever has found himself in such circumstances knows that he has been brought to the final bounds accessible to man. And yet, this is still not the end: 'Yet once more I shake not the earth only, but also heaven. And this word, Yet once more, signifieth the removing of those things that are shaken, as of things that are made, that those things which cannot be shaken may remain' [Heb. 12:26–27] – as things divinized. When we think of this new trial of all that is created and able to be shaken, we cannot be at all confident of ourselves to the end. Recognition of our earthly frailty is with us always, except for the rare moments when the Light comes down on us and we anticipate the Kingdom of our Holy Father [cf. Matt. 16:28].

All our striving is concerned with acquiring the love commanded of us by Christ. When this spirit of Christ-like love enters within us our soul thirsts for the salvation of all people. We are appalled that by no means everyone wishes for himself what we ask for all in our prayers. Worse, we often meet with refusal, even hostility. How can people be saved when there is such perversion? We live in an age, the events of which make the tragedy of our fall more and more evident. To take my own life: for over half a century I have prayed, some-times weeping bitter tears, sometimes in wild despair, for the peace of the whole world and the salvation, if it be possible, of all. And what do you suppose? To this hour, in my old age, I see evil ever increasing in its dynamics. The close of mankind's earthly history is scientifically thinkable and may become technically realisable tomorrow. We are nonplussed by the utterly irrational character of the happenings of our time. We look to the Divine Word for enlightenment and (*inter alia*) come upon the following (in Ch. 21 of St. Luke's Gospel): '. . . ye shall hear of wars and commotions, be not terrified: for these things must first come to pass . . . there shall be great distress in the land . . . men's hearts failing them for fear, and for looking after these things which are coming on the earth: for the powers of heaven shall be shaken . . . And when these things begin to come to pass, then look up, and lift up your heads; for your redemption draweth nigh'. And again, 'Yet once more I shake not the earth only, but also heaven' [Heb. 12:26]. So in all things the Lord calls us to the grandiose battle for the Kingdom 'which cannot be shaken'. Clearly a Gospel such as this has come to us 'not after man . . . neither was it received of man' [*cf.* Gal. 1:11–12].

So what are we to do? Despair and reject the 'everlasting gospel' [Rev. 14:6]? And if we decide on rejection what else in the whole world is there to satisfy us? Positively nothing could separate us from Him, however bitter the trials that we must suffer [cf. Rom. 8:35–39]. He has opened our eyes to infinity, and now we cannot close them and prefer the blindness of newborn puppies. 'Be of good cheer; I have overcome the world,' said the Lord [John 16:33; cf. I Cor. 13:11]. And now we stand before the Living Absolute – which is exactly what, and only what, we are seeking.

Lively experience of the *Persona* is rarely given to people here below. It comes by praying like Christ for the whole world as for oneself. Led to such prayer by the workings of the Holy Spirit, man existentially lives the image of the Triune God. In this kind of prayer one experiences the consubstantiality of the human race. Such prayer reveals the ontological meaning of the second commandment, 'Thou shalt love thy neighbour as thyself'. All Adam becomes One Man – mankind.

Anything less than this is less than the Gospel commandment. Not without reason one may say that the reality contained in Christ's commandments, historic Christianity has not fully implemented. In its existential virtue Christianity ineffably surpasses the understanding of those who are too indolent to pursue knowledge of God, 'which is life eternal' [cf. John 17:3].

Men seek Truth. A great many love Christ but too often try to reduce the Gospel to the level of ethics. They overlook Christ's pronouncement that only those who 'do his will shall know of the doctrine, whether it be of man or of the Heavenly Father' [cf. John 7:17]. If we really want to fathom the deifying power of the Gospel tidings we must expend far more effort than it takes to acquire everyday practical or scientific knowledge. Neither the reading of a vast number of books nor familiarity with the history of Christianity, or the study of various other theological systems, et cetera, leads to the sought-for goal – salvation through knowledge of the 'only true God, and Jesus Christ whom he sent' [cf. John 17:3]. Age-old experience of academic theology has shown convincingly that it is possible to acquire wide erudition in the science of theology without having a lively faith – that is, in a condition of total ignorance of God. In such cases theology becomes an intellectual profession, like jurisprudence which differs in each country in the same way as theology differs in the multitude of confessions divided among themselves.

The Name of God is I AM THAT I AM. For man, the image of the All-Highest, this word *I* is one of the most precious of all, since it expresses the principle of the *persona* in us. Outside this principle there would be no meaning, nothing. Let each of us hold on to his personal worth, which alone contains the wealth and beauty of our being. In the conditions of our historical existence the struggle to actualize the lofty idea for us of our Creator and God is far from easy. The Lord was pleased to confer on us the light of the revelation of the *persona* but we were born and left to live among the unwieldy mass of individuals prone to selfishness and pride. But to the *persona* it is given to embrace all creation in the flame of Christlike love. We are tied to this world as it became after the Fall, and at the same time obliged to wrestle for our freedom in God. Contemporary civilization is individualistic by nature. Individualism is cultivated in all its impassioned aspects. This is particularly obvious in the realm of the arts. Geniuses are acclaimed – originators of one or another particular style. It is the originality, the individuality of the artist that is prized. This is the principle on which our social structure is based. But individuals *en masse* live in a state of decline and ineludible tragedy. The cult of decline leads to alienation from God – man is reduced when the Divine image is obscured in him. Contrariwise, an assembly of *personae* is 'the salt of the earth, the light of the world' [cf. Matt. 5:13–14]. This is realised in Christ's Church and with particular force in the liturgical act – precisely where the true image of the Holy Trinity is made manifest. The whole content of the Divine Liturgy calls upon the priest to bring to God the ministry proper to the *persona* in the spirit of Christ's prayer in Gethsemane.

The Hypostasis in the Divine Being we do not think of as static, self-contained principle. This might be possible in the perspective of the henotheism of Islam, and even within the bounds of the Old Testament, but can in no way apply to the Trinity, as revealed to us, the Triune totally dynamic Being. We have learned to see these dynamics in the love that is the most profound moment in the *fact* of eternal Self-determination of the Persons of the Holy Trinity. We do not say that love is the essence of Divinity but that it expresses Divinity more than aught else [cf. I John 4:8]. Essence cannot be imparted to the creature and therefore remains eternally unknowable. What cannot be communicated to reasoning beings cannot be known. But the Energy of Divine Love is poured down on us who are created 'in the image and after the likeness', and we are commanded to acquire love.

In the Divine Being the moment that denotes essence is termed Act – Energy. The imparting to us of this uncreated

Energy effects our likening to the Creator – our divinization. Love, being the pre-eternal and immutable life of the Triune God, when it comes to dwell in us makes us not only immortal, in the sense of living for evermore, but 'without beginning', too, since the love that is in the Trinity is pre-eternal. When the uncreated Light shines down on him man receives a living experience of this love. Its action overcomes the death with which we are stricken and we experience it as a resurrection from the dead into new life, already without beginning. At the same time we lose the sense of our earthly provenance.

This experience, however, is only a kind of foretaste of the divinization promised to us – a call to wage the ascetic battle, not the accomplished act of divinization. This gift of grace enriches us with knowledge of 'the things which God hath prepared for them that love him' [I Cor. 2:9] but which are not yet fully ours and can be taken away as 'unrighteous mammon' [cf. Luke 16:11–12]. Even the attentive ascetic-striver does not always continue in an equal state of grace. After abiding with us for a while, grace may lessen and we find ourselves in twilight again.

But the knowledge remains as memory in the soul.

Man-Hypostasis is made manifest for himself in the act of self-cognition, self-determination; in his ability to cognize not only the created world but Divine Being – that is, the Creator Himself – also. He finds himself more fully in the ardent love that unites him with his beloved God. Love uniting him with God, as love always unites, brings knowledge of God. God reveals Himself to the personal principle in us, in light and as Light; in fervent love and as Love. Illumined thus from on High, man sees the Gospel truth as a reflection of the life of the Unoriginate God Himself on the plane of our earth. In the appearance of uncreated Light the glory of Christ as the only-begotten of the Father is made known. This uncreated Light has appeared down the centuries to those who with profound and unshakeable faith accepted Christ as God. It is Divine Energy, and, as such, is the One Light of the Holy Trinity.

This Light proceeds from the Father. It is the Light of the Logos co-eternal with the Father. It is the action within us of the Holy Spirit. When this Light condescends to us, it is like a personal revelation to those who have been found worthy of the blessing. By virtue of this good will of the heavenly Father the New Testament Scriptures appear in their immutable actuality. They are not just sayings pronounced some time in the past. To the spiritual eye they contain eternity, embracing all time [cf. Matt. 24:35].

Personal revelation of heavenly Being can happen *of a sudden*, as it were, like a flash of lightning. But though received suddenly, it must still be absorbed gradually, in a long process of prayerful striving. At the first touch of light-bearing grace the essential content of the vision is clear inwardly – the soul requires no explanation in rational concepts of what has happened. She marvels at God's goodness and is filled with the presence of the Divine Spirit in her. But when the Light departs the quiet rapture turns to sadness and the longing naturally grows for a more perfect – that is, a lasting and imprescriptible – unity with the beloved God.

Absolute God first revealed Himself as *Persona* to Moses. But notwithstanding his exceptional genius Moses could not apprehend all the profundity of the I AM that appeared to him [cf. Exod. 33:23]. The history of the God-inspired religion of the Old Testament shows that not one of the prophets achieved the plenitude proper to the personal principle. The manner of this being was manifested to the world in all its power by Christ. But comparatively few have duly apprehended this. Even in the historic Christian Church only occasional individuals through the centuries have attained this form of being. These spiritual heroes are rare but their influence spreads to the vast multitude of members of the Church. The countless number of the faithful striving to follow in the steps of God's chosen are in the same perspective though they have not attained its heights. This is how I see myself. St. Silouan was an event of extreme importance on my journey through life. Thanks to him, year after year I was able to observe at close quarters a truly Christian life, and even become a disciple. I am incomparably more indebted to his prayers than to all my other preceptors, though among them were several outstanding representatives of our Church – grace-endowed ascetics in monasteries and hermitages, bishops and priests; likewise professors in theological schools.

The Lord appeared to St. Silouan at the outset of his monastic life. Only a few months after he entered the cloister the Lord was manifest to him in great Light (a happening that I tried to describe in my book about him). It was then that he knew God through the Holy Spirit; then that it was given to him to delight in Christ's indescribable humility; then that he began to pray for the whole world as for himself. It would be superfluous to point out that this spiritual grace goes far beyond the confines of human ethics; that to St. Silouan it was given to live in the sphere of this Light, to breathe the air of the upper world.

The process of my own growth was a slow one, compared with St. Silouan's. Nevertheless, what I received was undeservedly glorious for me. Later, 'in the desert', prayer brought me understanding of the ontological place of the personal principle in Divine Being and in human being.

Let it not seem a contradiction that it was in the solitude of the desert that I more profoundly perceived the Hypostatic Principle. I am convinced that this happened because of my striving to live all things in Christ, through His Hypostasis. Without Him I know neither God nor man. In the desert also, more than elsewhere, it was given to me, too, to pray for the whole world, for all mankind, all Adam. Through prayer 'all Adam' ceases to be the product of an effort of the imagination but becomes a concrete reality, the effective content of contemplation. The Second World War likewise promoted compassion for all mankind. I hope it is not insanity or inordinate presumption to think of my prayer as coming from God, like a faint echo of Christ's prayer in Gethsemane.

When the Living God – I AM THAT I AM – enters the heart, the joy thereof is full of Light. He is quiet. He is gentle. I can address Him as 'Thou' and in His 'I' and in my 'Thou' all Being is contained – both God and this world. He is self-existing; He is loving; He is humble. And at the same time He is infinitely powerful. His eyes see and penetrate all that is. 'Neither is there any creature that is not manifest in his sight: but all things are naked and opened unto the eyes of him' [Heb. 4:13]. Every moment of my life, my every heartbeat, are all permanently in His hands. My personal being, both temporal and eternal, is entirely from Him, down to the last detail; save for my sins, about which He knows but in which He has no part. When I am in Him, then 'I am', also. But apart from Him, I die. When His Spirit descends on me, I love Him with my whole being. I live this state as if it were my own, not as something existing outside me. But even from my experience I know that this life proceeds from Him. Through His coming within me, therefore through union with Him in the very Act of Being, I live as He does. He is my life: His life is mine. In the hours when He dwells with me, I know that He is Love. A strange, especial love, however, which could in no way come to the mind or heart of man if his reflecting springs from himself as he is now, in his fallen state.

God's love is kenotic. He revealed the secret of His Being when He commanded us to love God to the point of hating oneself [cf. Luke 14:26–27 and 33]. He reveals the secret to us not through abstract philosophy but *existentially* – that is, by so including us in His Being that it becomes ours. Thus, precisely, is how we live this gift.

A frequent occurrence on Mt. Athos is to see a monk entirely in God, in Light, and the Light in him. But he has no intellectual reaction – it seems to him a *natural* state to be in.

The mystery of Divine *kenosis* passes understanding for the created being: the infinite God, in all His unchanging omni-potence, making Himself of small account, 'unto the end' [cf. John 13:1]. And this is characteristic of the eternal life of God. The mystery is unthinkable for us since we see this self-emptying *kenosis* as death; and thus it will be until the Eternal God reaches down to us. No man can follow Christ unless the Father's strength be with him [cf. John 6:65]. Until he is born again from on High [cf. John 3:3] the natural man cannot apprehend the Gospel word as the good news of the *divinization of man* through the imparting to him of Divine eternity as an inalienable possession. Christ's commandments are nothing less than the *Self-revelation* of God as a projection of His Being on the earthly plane. But for some they 'are the savour of death unto death; and to [others] the savour of life unto life. And who is sufficient for these things?' [II Cor. 2:16]. Prayer is the approach to sufficiency – prayer if only partly akin to the prayer of Gethsemane.

'I am the way, the truth, and the life' [John 14:6]. Within the limits in which it is given to us to know Jesus Christ, praying in Gethsemane, dying on the cross, descending into hell, rising and ascending into heaven, sitting on the right hand of the Father, sending down the Holy Spirit proceeding from the Father in 'an inheritance not to be taken away from the faithful' – we know that there is none other that could excel Him in anything whatsoever [cf. Phil. 2:9–11; Eph. 1:10]. That was how I understood matters in those blessed days when the Lord was graciously pleased to regenerate me in His love. So it is to the present time, with the sole difference that as my experience deepens, so my vision grows clearer. Through faith I saw my future like an examination – the one important examination for every human being. Oh, how I dreaded, and continue to dread, failing this testing before the Face of the beloved God! Would it be inordinately bold of me, the sort of person that I am, to say that 'the Father drew me to His Son' [cf. John 6: 44,65; Gal. 1: 15–16]? No matter what direction my spirit took in Divine infinity, no matter the problem that confronted me, He, the only-begotten Son, was, and is, my guiding star. Through Him I came to know the Father. He taught me how to recognise the Holy Spirit. And the Holy Spirit made me aware with my whole being that I, too, had found Primordial Truth [cf. John 16:13–14; 14:26]. Thenceforth my one concern was to give effect to this wondrous Truth in my life. When I did not achieve this sacred aim I sank into indescribable anguish. Knowing my sinful past, I grieved bitterly over my unworthiness. For years on end I sorrowed. My chest hurt with my heart's unrestrainable groaning. And whence came this intensity? No one will understand who has not sinned like me. But it would be a mistake to think that I exaggerate. There is no greater misfortune than to offend against the love of the Holy of Holies. My heart would be like warm wax. But its pain was curiously vivifying. A sort of ugly death was washed away by scalding tears, in the same way as certain chemical detergents clean accumulated dirt from much-worn clothes.

On the threshold of physical maturity – when I was about seventeen or eighteen – the Lord forsook me and I fell like our forefather Adam. He did not go away from me altogether, as I can see now, but called me from the dark abyss and unfolded to me the spiritual essence of original sin. If one understands sin as a turning aside from our God and Father due to some aberration of the intellectual vision of Being, or because of an offence against His love, then Adam's sin – my sin – showed both these aspects.

A man who is conscious within himself of a reflection, an echo, of Absolute Being, risks arriving at an exaggerated conclusion about himself and trying to exact something beyond his measure. Entangled in an error like this, he struggles to become firmly established in his vision, mistakenly accepting it for the truth about himself. This is exactly what happened to Adam, and after him many of his descendants repeated and continue to repeat the same sin. Proud upsurges of insane freedom are not alien to mankind. It is vital that we know this truth about ourselves. But the fateful madness that has separated us from the Father's love can and must generate hallowed dread in us, and prayer with profound weeping. We are creatures. Absolute True Being bestowed being on us and promised to communicate His unoriginate and eternal Life to us. We rejected this promise and adopted paths to another, imagined Absolute, fusion with which necessitates our personal death.

Salvation from death comes by accepting Christ – the sort of acceptance that He Himself would have from us: ' . . . If ye believe not that I am he' (Who was made manifest to Moses on Mount Sinai) 'ye shall die in your sins' [John 8:24]. But when we believe in Him as Truth of indestructible Being, then the Heavenly Spirit will lift us into the realm of Divine Light.

Revelation through Christ means that the Absolute is Personal though not *One* Person – which is Islamic henotheism – but *Three* Persons, one in Substance, in their Kingdom, their Glory, their Action – which is Christian monotheism. Through faith in this God of Love, the Holy Trinity, we enter the eternal Kingdom, while preserving our personal being. Here we have a preliminary encounter with our Creator – the perfect union with Him that we seek lies beyond the bounds of our earthly existence [cf. I Cor. 13:12].

In the perspective of our revelation of the Absolute-*Persona*, with our contemporary experience it is possible to conjecture something of the 'psychology' of Adam's fall into sin – apprehension before the Face of the searchless God, God in no way determined and always completely free in His reactions to man's every movement. Having placed man before Him, the inscrutable God, in no way determined, expects from man the loftiest form of responsible cognition. On the one hand, there is the call to the imperishable glory of sonship; on the other, Christ-like self-emptying involving agonising prayer and 'sweat as it were great drops of blood falling down to the ground' [cf. Luke 22:44]. This God of ours continually attracts us to further ascent, constraining His sons to abandon previous stages travelled through so laboriously. He is all-good yet never seems to be satisfied with what we have achieved [cf. Luke 17:10]. And the pain we suffer in following after Him does not appear to inspire in Him the compassion that we expect. 'The Lord . . . scourgeth every son whom he receiveth' [Heb. 12: 1–11]. Without doubt we see this ordeal manifest to the extreme in the incarnation of the only-begotten Son: 'O my Father, if it be possible, let this cup pass from me . . . If this cup may not pass away from me, except I drink it, thy will be done' [Matt. 26: 39, 42].

It is natural for man to be attracted to the Divine form of being. Did not the 'temptation' described in the third chapter of the Book of Genesis mean exploiting man's natural aspiration to immutable eternity in order to instil in him the idea that his sought-for divinization might be achieved separately from this 'cruel' God? Not to walk the way of the crucifixion [cf. Gal. 5: 24–25] but to eat the sweet fruit of knowledge of good and evil? 'And when the woman saw that the tree was good for food, and that it was pleasant to the eyes, and a tree to be desired to make one wise, she took of the fruit thereof, and did eat, and gave also unto her husband; and he did eat' [Gen. 3:6]. In our day, too, it is not unusual to come across people prepared to turn aside from the Gospel way of the cross in favour of union with the Absolute by means of *knowledge – gnosis*.

Persuaded of the relativity, far removed from perfection, of the personal principle in himself, man logically accepts the idea that this principle cannot be applied to the Absolute. Hence the naturalistic intellect inevitably slithers to the notion of a Supra-personal Principle transcending all that is relative. In its progress towards this nameless Principle it is not without difficulty that man's mind manages to detach itself from the conception of Him as cosmic totality. But when he crosses over this imaginary threshold of cosmic realities he arrives at the idea of Pure Being.

This is how it was with me in my youth – I am writing my own story. My intellectual asceticism consisted in concentrating thought and will on divesting myself of the materiality of the physical body; next, to proceed towards all-transcending Pure Being by renouncing in myself the personal principle, the thinking process and other forms of cosmic being. Thus in those years did I serve the 'god of the philosophers', who does not really exist.

I paid for my delusions with many years of weeping. There is no more dreadful deprivation than to be ignorant of the True God. Not only illness and other suffering but joy and satisfaction and so on are blotted out in the darkness of ignorance. By contrast, there is no higher gift than to meet with the Living God. In the light of this acquaintance not only happy circumstances but all the troubles that beset us are full of profound meaning and so become bearable, warranted [cf. II Cor. 4: 6–11]. All our many-sided experience of life, the whole world-system that contributes to our cognition, must serve to prepare us for a personal encounter with Him, which by its nature appertains to meta-history, since it concerns our entry into eternity already actualized. Whoever is given the blessing of this encounter at the same time receives understanding of the manifestations of God as described in the Old and New Testaments.

Moses, that unique genius, could not grasp all the profundity of the 'I AM' that appeared to him: 'Thou shalt see my back parts: but my face shall not be seen' (by thee) [Exod. 33: 23; cf. Matt. 18:10]. The true content of the Sinaitic Revelation continued undiscovered for centuries, and the hidden God was contemplated in darkness [Exod. 20:21; cf. II Cor. 3: 14–16].

'No man hath seen God at any time; the only begotten Son, which is in the bosom of the Father, he hath declared him' [John 1:18]. The law given through Moses contained seeds which would mature to prepare people to accept the incarnation of God and enable them to recognise the Prophet Whom Moses foretold. This Prophet would communicate to the world knowledge of the True God as Light in whom there is 'no darkness at all' [I John 1:5] – no longer in the thick darkness of Sinai but the Light of Tabor [cf. Deut. 18: 15–19; John 1:45; 6:14; 4: 25–26; Matt. 11:3; Acts 3:22].

To all that was unfolded in the Old Testament the Lord gave new, eternal dimensions but intimations concerning their forthcoming fulfilment were absolutely necessary in the history of God's revelation [cf. Matt. 5:17 *et seq.*]. The Old Testament is a noble and sacred book for us when we interpret it as Christ Himself and His Apostles, and even Moses, taught it. Not one of them pronounced the Law to be absolute – to be final perfection requiring the rejection of any new additional revelation. And Moses himself bade his people wait for another Prophet who 'when He comes will make all things known to us' [cf. Matt. 5:17].

Christ spoke to the people in the simplest language that all could understand but the content of His talks was realities beyond the grasp of anyone on this planet, even the Apostles: 'Before Abraham was, I am.' 'I and my Father are one.' 'No man knoweth the Son, but the Father; neither knoweth any man the Father, save the Son, and he to whomsoever the Son will reveal him.' 'My Father will love him, and we will come unto him, and make our abode with him.' 'I will pray the Father, and he shall give you another Comforter, that he may abide with you for ever' [John 8:58; 10:30; Matt. 11:27; John 14:23; 14:16].

Here we have a Third Person. How are we to reconcile this with our profound feeling that *God is One?* Again, the Lord said: 'When the Spirit of truth is come, which proceedeth from the Father, he will guide you into all truth' [John 16:13; 15:26]. And He, the Holy Spirit, did come and really does guide us but, as we see, this guidance, too, turns out to be a slow process.

Christ revealed to us the Mystery of Primal Being; of Him Who was 'in the beginning': Three Persons, not to be amalgamated one into the other, are One Being, where, however, plurality of differentiation is no contradiction. Our discursive thinking does not tally with the facts of Revelation. And the Lord did not go to great lengths to explain this Mystery but pointed out the way to existential grasp of Eternal Being – the way of His commandments.

'Thou shalt love the Lord thy God with all thy heart, and

with all thy soul, and with all thy mind. This is the first and great commandment. And the second is like unto it, Thou shalt love thy neighbour as thyself. On these two commandments hang all the law and the prophets' [Matt. 22:37–40]. And when a gift from on High empowers man through prayer to enter into the real dimensions of the second commandment, new horizons open out before him – horizons unimaginable in his former state. In profound prayer for the whole world as for himself – making him like Christ Jesus praying in the Garden of Gethsemane – he really does live all humanity as *one life*, one nature in a plurality of persons. This form of acquaintance with multi-hypostatic unity leads to theologic assimilation of the dogma of the One-ness of the Holy Trinity. Christian mono-theism is not the same thing as the henotheism of Islam.

After experience of 'hypostatic' prayer we abandon the categ-ories of formal logic and move to those of existence itself. Truth is not the product of human philosophy. Truth is He Who *is* verily before all ages.

When we 'return' from pure prayer to the opaque flesh of this world we fall from the oneness of man that we have experi-enced, and in sorrow see again that people are not altogether transparent for each other. The border-lines between human *personae* do not disappear to the same extent as in the Divine Trinity, where each Hypostasis is totally unveiled to the others; where kenotic love is manifest as the basic trait of Divine Life because of which the *Unity* of the Trinity is complete and absolute – as expressed in the theological concept of 'reciprocal penetration' [*Gr. perichōrēsis*]. Mankind is called upon to become One Man after the likeness of the Oneness of the Trinity [cf. John 10:30; 17:21].

Gods invented by people are not real. But to know the Living God is an incomparable gift. It first comes through the manifes-tation of God to man, and thereafter lies at the foundation of his whole life. Being by its nature Divine action, every manifestation of God to man affects the destinies of the whole world – and in certain cases exerts immense influence on the course of all history. For instance, the Sinaitic Revelation became the source of strength and power for everything that Moses was to perform – although its ultimate profundity exceeded his understanding, just as it found no place in the consciousness of the Jewish people right up to the appearance of Christ. The Gospel Revelation to the Virgin Mary she accepted as indeed coming from God; but at the moment the sublimity of the Angel's message was too much for her to take in and she needed confirmation of the mystery – confirmation which came with Elisabeth's greeting, 'Blessed art thou among women . . . And whence is this to me, that the mother of my Lord should come to me?' . . . Then the Holy Virgin exclaimed, 'My soul doth magnify the Lord . . . He hath regarded the low estate of his handmaiden' [Luke 1:41–49]. And her whole life was transformed. And with her, and thanks to her, the history of the world stepped into a new orbit immeasurably more grandiose than ever before.

In seeking knowledge of the natural world experimental science uses the inductive method – working through the particular to the general. It is different with revelations coming to us from on High. The soul intuitively recognises 'whence' came that which she contemplates. Though still not able to grasp the fulness of the blessing poured down on her, she nevertheless begins to construct her future on the rock of the knowledge bestowed in such marvellous fashion. 'And let them make me a sanctuary; that I may dwell among them. According to all that I shew thee . . . shall ye make it' [Exod. 25:8–9]. 'And thou shalt rear up the tabernacle according to the fashion thereof which was shewed thee in the mount' [Exod. 26:30]. Likewise does the Christian, too, found his earthly and eternal life in accordance with the blessed vision that he has received.

When we talk about *existential* knowledge of the *Personal* God, we have in mind *community of being*, not crude intellectual interpretation of the problem. Man-*persona* lives by God and in God. This reality can be expressed in another way – God takes possession of the entire man, mind, heart and body. The cognizant *persona* and the God Who is cognized are conjoined. Neither the one nor the Other in any way becomes *materia circa quam* in this fusion. Reciprocal cognition – by God of man and by man of God – is a 'personal' matter which excludes 'objectivisation'. This alliance of love is a spiritual act through which the Beloved becomes our life. By its genus, virtue, majesty, harmony and power, Divine love surpasses all that the earth knows. This being so, it is a marvellous thing that such a state be apprehended as the only one natural for man. How wondrous that He is Other and at the same time mine!

Attainment of this love means, in essence, 'to acquire the grace of the Holy Spirit', of which St. Seraphim Sarovsky speaks. There are three stages to the process. Firstly, an initial union with God is possible as a gracious gift bestowed at a moment that God judges to be favourable – when man will receive the visitation with love. This is an act of Self-revelation on the part of God to a given person, when the Divine Light affords a genuine experience of Divine eternity. This, however, does not complete man's divinization. It may be looked on as the 'mammon of unrighteousness' – in other words, Divine grace has not yet so flowed into us that our nature and grace have become one for all eternity [cf. Luke 16:9–12].

The second stage is a long spell of varying degrees of being deserted by God. In its extreme extent this is a dreadful experience. The soul feels her fall from Light as a spiritual death. The Light that has appeared is not yet the inalienable attainment of the soul. God has wounded our heart with love and then departed. We are faced with the prospect of an austere struggle which may last for years – many, many years. Sometimes grace moves nearer, bringing hope, renewing inspiration, only to desert us again. This alternating state is an extremely important period in man's advance towards the possibility of self-determination in eternity. God leaves us so that we may show our liberty. And knowledge concerning the way to perfection we have inherited from the Fathers. It is noticeable that many who are unfamiliar with this feature in the spiritual growth of the Christian fall away from God when deprived of the grace that they have experienced. They tend to interpret their visitation from on High as some temporary psychological elation more especially peculiar to the approach of manhood. St. Silouan spoke of it thus: 'Everything that grace has ever taught one must be followed to the end of one's life . . . The Lord sometimes abandons the soul in order to test her, so that she may manifest her understanding and her free-will. But if one makes no effort and remains inert, grace is lost. On the contrary, where there is determination, grace smiles on one and will not desert one'.

'Grace will smile on one and not desert one' – thus the culmination of the ascetic struggle to acquire grace. This is the third and final stage. Its perfecting cannot be a protracted matter like the first, since the earthly body could not long stand up to the state of divinization through grace – the 'passage from death to life' must inevitably follow. And man himself has no wish to return to the wearisome old see-sawing. But if it please the Lord to prolong the ascetic's stay in this world, He will preserve him in the degree of grace which will allow him to continue functioning, and competent therefore to 'commit to faithful men, who shall be able to teach others also' [cf. II Tim. 2:2] what he himself received from the Fathers and directly from God.

Flawless life in the True God finds expression in the simple words of the Scriptures but the teaching can only be mastered by mighty and prolonged striving. Over and over again we go back to these same Gospel words yet scarcely even begin to grasp their eternal purport. We switch from one state to another – from good to evil, love to hostility, Light to the darkness of the passions. We compare their effects on the soul and struggle to take hold of the best. Subject to the most diverse ordeals, we thereby grow spiritually. We have to progress from childish thinking to the understanding of the 'perfect man, unto the measure of the stature of the fulness of Christ' [cf. I Cor. 13:11;

Ephes. 4:13] – progress until we are capable of deliberately opting for self-determination, thus fixing our whole destiny. Freedom without full understanding easily turns to evil.

Having manifested Himself to us in His Light, God then withdraws from us. In profound grief over her loss the soul surrenders to total repentance – repentance to the point of self-hatred. Otherwise, as descendant of our forefather Adam, man would hardly be able to rid himself of the traces of the Luciferine Fall. Yet this is the only way that we can enter the realm of the Light that never sets, 'which is within the veil, whither the forerunner is for us entered, even Jesus' [cf. Heb. 6:19–20]. This is our crowning divinization, precluding any new fall.

Tokens of 'stature of the fulness of Christ' here below are prayer, like Christ's prayer in Gethsemane, and death at Golgotha. This is the way for man to penetrate into Divine eternity – to 'enter into the joy of the Lord' [cf. Matt. 25:21].

In prayer like the Gethsemane prayer we are given existential experience of the hypostasis-*persona;* and self-emptying is the way to make our death like Christ's death. The more total our self-emptying, the more absolute is our spirit's ingress into the bright realm of Eternal Divinity. And whether man speaks or is silent about his real state, he lives it as existential cognition. Now in Christ he, too, may say, 'I am'.

14

Prayer wherein God is revealed as Truth

Every single human being, whoever he may be, wherever he lives, whatever position he holds, be he erudite or unlearned, rich or poor, famous or unknown, young, middle-aged or elderly, happy or wretched, to some extent or another ponders on the meaning of life and asks himself, '*What is truth?*' [John 18:38].

Nineteen centuries ago Pilate perfunctorily put this question to Christ. The content and spirit of the query may vary radically, though the formula be one and the same. In Pilate's case we sense the scepticism of the mediocre Roman philosopher: having posed the question, without waiting for Christ to reply he went out to the Jews, convinced that there was no satisfactory answer. I suspect that in our day, too, the overwhelming majority of people are no better than Pilate and base their everyday lives, not on the rock of faith but on denial of the possibility of an after-life.

What is Truth? Does it exist in general? Even before we come to know Truth our hearts tell us that if there were no Truth existence itself would be inconceivable. Truth cannot be proved by logic but we are certain of its existence for we have been given direct knowledge which anticipates our every thought. Without this recognition the very process of thinking, the purpose of which is always to arrive at a veritable conclusion, would be negated.

At what level do we start our inquiry? The various possibilities are countless. Let us ignore all the rest and start by considering our idea of man. Man by his nature cannot stop half-way: he must continue to the end. He envisages the Primordial Truth that lies at the root of all that exists.

What does this First and Last Truth, eternally immutable, universal, consist of? Here we have the one needful question [cf. Luke 10:42]. After we have suffered failures, defeats, the loss of people dear to us, carried off by death into unknown 'nothingness'; after we have survived the expiration of many of the idols of this world – science, philosophy, the arts, humanism, politics – then it is that a kind of hope or expectation (there is no exact word for it) grows in us of something immutable.

Convinced of the inadequacy of all human effort to attain our sought-for eternal Truth in such a way as to merge with it and make it mine, I turned to prayer – not Christian prayer, at first, but more the meditation-technique of the Far East. After some long while – about seven or eight years – I saw myself very definitely on the wrong path. He Who said, 'I am . . . the truth' [John 14:6] appeared to me in spirit. Oh, the radiant moment that extracted me from the hell of mortal ignorance! With my whole being I felt that I had stepped on the true path. But however splendid the way, it is at the same time strewn with much tribulation before we attain Him Whom we seek [cf. John 16:33].

When the fire of faith in Him thrust into my heart like a sharp sword I was filled to overflowing with buoyant inspiration. I had not yet attained the Living Truth but the inspiration itself was transmuted into an awareness, into presence within me [cf. Heb. 11:1] of Truth. I endeavoured so far as possible to accommodate my mental vision in order to see, in focus, as it were, and detect the outlines of the Sacred Truth manifest to me; but I soon realised that this was foolishness on my part – the more I peered, the more limitless it became.

It is not my intention to treat of some hitherto-unknown Truth. I am writing about how it was given to me to live my repentance. Our spirit hungers and thirsts to know Truth – Primeval Being, unconditioned by anyone or anything; absolute Self-Being of which the Old Testament Prophets spoke, to which the Apostles of the New Testament bore witness [cf. Exod. 3:14; Isa. 44:6; John 1:1–4; Rev. 22:13].

We do not imagine – we could not imagine – Him proceeding from ourselves. We do not create God 'in our image, after our likeness' [cf. Gen. 1:26]. In reverent prayer we look to Him to hear our cry and give us a 'sign'. In our affliction we open ourselves for a response – a revelation – coming from Him. We want to 'know' Him, the Author of our being, 'as He is'. He manifested Himself to our fathers and forefathers, and we treasure the witness that we receive from them. Trusting them, we trust the message they have bequeathed to us but at the same time, like Moses, we appeal to Him, 'Grant me to know Thee as Thou art in Thine eternity'. For 'faith by hearing' [Rom. 10:17] is one thing and 'to know Thee' quite another.

No sooner have we resolved to commit ourselves 'into the hands of the living God' [Heb. 10:31] than those hands hurl us into expanses we could never have suspected. We are appalled at the abyss that opens out before us. God seems cruel to us. And yet through the pain, by a process which is not explainable, the ability unfolds within us to contemplate Him 'as He is' . . . be it still only 'in part' [cf. I Cor. 13:12].

He is Light and Truth. And when this True Light [John 1:9] embraces us we live His love and Wisdom. We are joyous, and profound knowledge descends on us, not as thought but as *state* of spirit.

He is. In Him is no beginning, no end. He Himself is both the Principle of all that exists and the infinite conclusion of our every expectation. We recognise in our heart that He wants to see us perfect, even as He is perfect [cf. Matt. 5:48].

Exhausted by the tyranny of base passions, we naturally pray the Good Lord that His Spirit may rest in us – the Spirit of understanding of the ways of His salvation. And fortified by this Spirit we see that in tragic ordeals we rid ourselves of the consequences of the Fall; that through suffering our being expands and we are opened to other, sublime worlds. We over- come the cast-iron egoism of the primitive individual. We emerge from the half-savage condition of not knowing our Creator. Realising that for me, created from nothing, it was essential to go through fiery torture in order more profoundly to apprehend the 'man of sorrows' [cf. Isa. ch. 53], I accept the sacred pain with grateful love. It is brimful of meaning. It initiates me into the mysteries of being, not only created but Uncreated, also. Thanks to it, I become ruthful. Through it I behold in spirit all who suffer. Divine love descends into me, at first as compassion for every living thing, and in the world to come as the blessedness of beholding the redeemed in imperishable glory.

A small digression: What I have written above does not in the slightest mean that we cultivate '*douleur*' in the psychological sense. Not at all. But anyone who has gone through the metaphysics of spiritual suffering knows that this pain is something qualitatively different – an essential stage in our progress from earthly to cosmic, even eternal dimensions. Is not this what Christ's Good News – the Gospel – is all about?

When he begins to understand the place of the Cross in our life according to God, man 'bears his cross' [cf. Luke 14:27] differently. He understands the very cross differently, perceiving it as a call from the Heavenly Father on High [cf. John 6:44; 18:11]. In the cross, as in the Saviour's cup, my created being becomes linked with uncreated Divine Being.

We do not deny the reality of the transient. It is natural for Christians to live simultaneously on two planes, the temporal and the eternal. And time itself we apprehend as a wondrous process of the creation by God from nothing of gods like Himself. When the created being attains his crowning perfection, then we shall hear the 'angel swear by him that liveth for ever and ever . . . that there shall be time no longer' [cf. Rev. 10:5–6].

The Lord said of Himself, 'I am the truth' [cf. John 14:6] and He called the Father and the Holy Spirit to witness. To understand this aspect of Divine Being requires many years of repentant prayer. The more we follow after the Lord in the keeping of His commandments, the broader and more profound does our personal identity become. Thus when we ourselves grow near to the realisation in ourselves of the principle of the *persona* in which first and foremost the Divine image is expressed in us, our own experience tells us that to establish our identity we need to meet with another person, other persons, even. Such an encounter reflects not only a likeness to the Hypostatic Principle in Divinity but also the image of the life within the Trinity. It is given to us in prayer for the whole world to live all mankind as one man. Through such prayer we receive new, existential knowledge. By nature, structure and character the *persona* cannot live isolated in himself. He must look outside himself in love for others like himself. By the action of love he responds to the other and so attests to him.

Not only in the Godhead, in the Holy Trinity, do Father, Son and Holy Spirit bear witness One to Another – They bear witness, also, to us, men, One of Another. Further, the Lord charged the Apostles to testify of Him. 'But when the Comforter is come . . . the Spirit of truth, which proceedeth from the Father, he shall testify of me: And ye also shall bear witness, because ye have been with me from the beginning'.

Such is the relationship between people and between God and men – testimony, like true life in love, eternally advancing in all directions. [cf. John 1:7–8, 15,32,34; 5:31–39; 8:13,18; 12:28; 15:26–27; 17:1; Acts 1:8; 10:39–43.]

My spirit sighed after the Living Truth. 'And my groaning was not hid from Him' [cf. Ps. 38:9]. 'Out of the low dungeon, I called upon His name, and He heard my voice' [cf. Lam. 3:55–56]. His love reached out to my heart. The realm of Christian prayer was indescribably beautiful. Through it I was granted communion with the God of Truth and Life.

Now I testify to the truth, which our fathers and forefathers knew. I am setting forth how truth was disposed to appear to me in response to my long-drawn-out weeping of repentance which so exhausted me. I lived this truth as really immemorial, and in accordance with my belief so do I speak and write. St. Paul, too, wrote of it: 'Having the same spirit of faith, according as it is written, I believed, and therefore have I spoken; we also believe, and therefore speak . . .' [II Cor. 4:13].

I am aware that my knowledge is not absolute but that does not mean that there is some other truth. I believe that I came in contact with Truth unoriginate but I know, also, that I have not realised in the act of my life the experience taught to me by prayer. But where is the criterion that would confirm our trust in what is granted to us of God Who is Truth?

Imprescriptible is our urge towards Him, Who IS before all ages; Who penetrates all that exists and by His power preserves. It is difficult for us to believe that this infinite Master does not despise us 'little ones' [cf. Matt. 18:10]. Strange as it may be, when we turn to Him in real – that is, repentant – prayer, He hastens to meet us [cf. Luke 15:20] and lovingly embraces us. This phenomenon cannot be the fruit of imagination, since it surpasses one's capacity to imagine [cf. I Cor. 2:9].

I base my argument on the revelation that man was created 'in the image, and after the likeness of God' [cf. Gen. 1:26]. From this it follows that man is endowed with the potential to attain likeness to his Creator; that the idea of Absolute Being is implanted in his very nature, so that when Almighty God enters into communion with his spirit man can 'recognise' Him, since He is kin to him. Introduced into the sphere of the Mind of God the Creator, man's created spirit begins to see God 'as he is' in Himself [cf. I John 3:2]. (I use the term 'created spirit' instead of 'mind' in order to avoid any misunderstanding through confusing *mind* with *reason*.)

Our first step is towards Him Who was 'in the beginning'. Intellectually we are ready to accept Him as initial Truth, whether or no such Ontological Truth tallies with our preconception of Truth. And great is our joy when the new message [cf. I John 1:5; 4:13,16] confirms the vision given to us from on High – to wit, that we are created 'in the image of' God:

He manifests Himself to us as God of love and we live Him within us as absolute harmony, and begin to 'worship the Father in spirit and in truth' [John 4: 23–24].

'If we say that we have no sin, we deceive ourselves, and the truth is not in us' [I John 1:8]. Hence only repentant prayer is in keeping with the truth about us. At this point I persist in stressing that when we stand before the Heavenly Father aware of ourselves as sinners, we take our place on the plane of Divine Truth. The more profoundly we see our sin as something that brings death to us, the more fully do we surrender to God in prayer, and by His life-creating strength escape from the clutches of time and space. May the Lord forgive me, and my brothers not condemn me too severely, if I say that thus it was with me. And so, reading St. Paul's Epistles, I surmise – confidently, I make no secret of it – that he, too, was given 'visions and revelations of the Lord' [cf. II Cor. 12:1–6] in his repentance before Christ 'with strong crying and tears', and 'was heard in that he feared' [cf. Heb. 5:7].

In prayer of this kind our mind-spirit is included in the Mind of God and receives understanding, the nature of which our everyday language is not qualified to define. For instance, all things are created by His will, His thought. He conceives of the world and His creative thinking becomes created being. Not matter but the thinking of God the Creator is the initial factor. Thus we live this world not only through the prism of experimental knowledge but in the Spirit also behold it in another fashion [cf. Heb. 11:1–3].

'If ye love me, keep my commandments. And I will pray the Father, and he shall give you another Comforter, that he may abide with you for ever; Even the *Spirit of truth;* whom the world cannot receive, because it seeth him not, neither knoweth him: but ye know him; for he dwelleth with you, and shall be in you . . . Ye see me: because I live, ye shall live also. At that day ye shall know that I am in my Father, and ye in me, and I in you. He that hath my commandments, and keepeth them, he it is that loveth me: and he that loveth me shall be loved of my Father, and I will love him, and will manifest myself to him . . . If a man love me, he will keep my words: and my Father will love him, and we will come unto him, and make our abode with him . . . The word which ye hear is not mine, but the Father's which sent me . . . But the Comforter, which is the Holy Ghost, whom the Father will send in my name, he shall teach you all things, and bring all things to your remembrance, whatsoever I have said unto you' [John 14:15–26].

'The Comforter, the Holy Ghost . . . shall teach you all things.' He will 'teach us' to think as God Himself thinks. He will teach us to love as God loves. Do not be surprised at this – it is the purport of the Gospel summons. All the Epistles – of John, Paul, Peter and the others – say the same. So do the Fathers down the ages.

The question arises – how can we attain this blessing? Christ gave us the answer: 'Keep my commandments. And I will pray the Father, and he shall give you another Comforter, that he may abide with you for ever'. Thus, we 'know' the Holy Spirit through the sacred tradition of the Fathers of the Church, as also through our own experience of Him, the Spirit, acting in us. He 'brings all things to our remembrance'.

Furthermore, 'If a man love me, he will keep my words: and my Father will love him, and we will come unto him, and make our (eternal) abode with him'. What can this mean if not a promise that we shall inherit the fulness of Divine life, the fulness of knowledge and strength of love which is manifested to us by Uncreated Light in which is no darkness at all [cf. I John 1:5]?

Here is St. Paul's witness: 'Now we have received, not the spirit of the world, but the spirit which is of God; that we might know the things that are freely given to us of God'. And again, 'Who hath known the mind of the Lord, that he may instruct him? But we have the mind of Christ' [I Cor. 2:12,16]. School education introduced us to universal thinking and we became participants in experimental knowledge. Something similar happens to us in the realm of the Spirit: by living according to the Gospel commandments we enter into the closest affinity with the Divine Mind. The commandments are none other than the Self-revelation of God 'as He is'. When they become the one and only law of our whole being they communicate to us the 'image' of Divine Being that we seek. 'We know that the Son of God is come, and hath given us understanding, that we may know him that is true' [cf. I John 5:20].

God Who is Verity did not create anything false or contrary to truth. And every manifestation of energy proceeding from Him is truth. Christ showed us true man as conceived by the Creator: the Verity of God Himself is implanted in us, for we are made in His 'image', after His 'likeness'. Eternal truth is communicated to the hypostatic principle in us. And just as the *persona* in man starts as potentiality, so must the seed of Truth in us develop from the potential to the actual. In Adam's fall truth in us suffered distortion. Through the grace of repentance and loving obedience to the Father, truth in its primordial sanctity is imparted to us as the life of God Himself.

But what happens with the man who repents with tears? He lives the truth not as a result of his meditations but as the *state* of his spirit accorded to him by the Divine Spirit. 'State' is a fact of being which prompts our thought, operating after its own fashion, to understand truth. Such understanding is not achieved by demonstrative reasoning but through an intuitive penetration or an establishment of fact as knowledge of Divine Being descending to us from God.

Understanding of the Lord's ways does not come quickly. It was anguish to me to think how brief was our time here. My soul was filled with dread at the idea of going to the grave before God answered my cries to Him. But I was not finally left desolate: because of my prayer of positive belief in Christ-God His compassion for fallen mankind was gradually transmitted to me, too. My sense of being doomed caused me agony and this agony cracked the walls of my stony heart. As I was accustomed to apply my experiences to all mankind, I felt pity for all who, like me, were distanced from God. Thus humanity's sufferings became mine, and in the solitude of the desert prayer would come to me for the whole world as for myself. And in that prayer I sensed the eternal God as our Father. And this feeling was convincing witness to the everlasting Truth as conveyed to us by Christ.

In fear and trembling I recall the hours when the Lord gave me to live this lofty spiritual event. But now, alas, I do not find that sacred power in myself.

The theme about which I am so helplessly inarticulate is the difference between Living Truth and scientific or philosophical truths. The Truth that is made manifest to us goes immeasurably farther than intellectual speculation. It is not some abstract formula of our logical thinking; not some mathematical equation but *Persona*. First of all, it is that which was 'from the beginning' – Eternal God the Holy Trinity: Father, Son and Holy Spirit. But our rational mind is not capable of applying its concepts to the real Being of God. For instance, we live the Father as absolute Truth. And the Son, too, is absolute Truth. The Holy Spirit, likewise, is absolute Truth. But Truth is One and not three absolute truths. As One God He is also the Trinity of Persons. In his final actualization man, too, must become One Man in a plurality of hypostases.

Another paradox – the Person in God we live as the bearer of absolute fulness of Being; and at the same time the Person does not exist alone. In formal logic this is proof of the insufficiency of the Person by itself and consequently, the negation of absoluteness. But the Holy Trinity, God of perfect love, is precisely thus. Perfect love does not live locked in itself but in the other Person, in other Persons. The whole conjunction of Being obtains as the imprescriptible possession of each of the Three Hypostases. But the Hypostasis manifests itself thus in the act of perfect love which similarly implies complete self-emptying, the belittlement of self.

'Greater love hath no man than this, that a man lay down his life for his friends. Ye are my friends, if ye do whatsoever I command you' . . . 'Jesus . . . loved his own which were in the world, he loved them *unto the end*' . . . 'He that is greatest among you shall be your servant. And whosoever shall exalt himself shall be abased; and he that shall humble himself shall be exalted' [John 15:13–15; 13:1; Matt. 23:11–12]. From these sayings of Christ we see that the same kind of self-emptying love that was made manifest to us in the Holy Trinity is *commanded* of mankind: through the utmost self-emptying that we can manage in our act of repentance, we become capable of apprehending the fulness both of Divine love and love for our neighbour [cf. Matt. 22:37–40]. 'On these two commandments hang all the law and the prophets', and holy eternity is contained in their spirit.

Eternity and Truth – here we have our subject matter. And behold, when the power of this Divine love descends upon us, without the slightest doubt we come alive – we abide in Truth and Eternity.

Our dogmatic cognition can be summed up as follows: 'I AM THAT I AM', 'I am Being', 'I AM THE TRUTH'. The personal Principle in Divine Being is its *ontological kernel*. It is He Who verily lives. The First and the Last, Alpha and Omega. Thus do we interpret the Sinaitic revelation which was subsequently completed by the incarnation of the Logos of the Father and the descent of the Holy Spirit to the Church on the day of Pentecost.

This God in His eternal Essence is the absolute Truth that we seek. Existential knowledge of this Truth is possible only if His strength enters into us. Personal Truth is made known by the same personal principle implanted in us in the act of our creation 'in the image and after the likeness' of God. Just as this undetermined principle in us is not liable to any coercion from outside, so does our union with Truth depend not only on God Who bestows [cf. Matt. 11:27] but on man, too, who receives [cf. John 1:9–12; Acts 13:46].

By himself the created spirit – man – cannot attain this Truth, though as the image of God he is able to postulate Truth but no more. Existential knowledge of Truth is bestowed on us as a gift of love from the Creator to the reasonable being. In our personal relations with our Personal God nothing is effected by the will of one party only – consent and cooperation must always be present. There must always be the conjunction of two wills, God's and man's. In this is our life.

'All men are liars' [Ps. 116:11] in themselves because they spring from 'nothing'. Only by God Who is Truth taking up His abode in us can we, too, become true (truth-filled). The Living Truth transfigures us by His advent within us. Absolute, Truth is all-embracing, too, containing all things. To 'know' this Truth is, according to the word of Truth Himself [cf. John 8:32], to be made free of the power over us of sin, wherein lies death. Immortal, this Truth makes us, too, immortal. God-Who-is-Truth really makes us gods – 'gods' not over other men but by the form of being that is communicated to us and the content of such life.

Divinely universal, Truth cannot be contained in fulness by any creature here on earth. We know the Truth, like St. Paul, only 'in part' [I Cor. 13:12]. But this does not mean that Truth in itself is completely different from the way we understand it. It is one thing to *know Truth*, and another not to be able to accommodate it in its absolute plenitude – not to be equal to manifesting it in all its perfection in the act of everyday living. With the Apostle Philip we declare without hesitation, We have found the Truth, We know the Truth, He is CHRIST [cf. John 1:45].

So then, if we confess Christ as equal with the Father, Who is God and Truth, we must naturally, in order to attain Truth, follow after Him. And here a tragic factor emerges. He said, 'If any man come to me, and hate not his father, and mother, and wife, and children, and brethren, and sisters, yea, and his own life also, he cannot be my disciple'. Likewise, 'And whosoever doth not bear his cross, and come after me' . . . who 'forsaketh not all that he hath, cannot be my disciple' [Luke 14:26–27, 33].

This is what happened with me – having in spirit beheld Christ, Who loved us unto the end [cf. John 13:1], Who prayed in Gethsemane and then on Golgotha, 'resisting not evil' [Matt. 5:39], I hated myself, as I was, and in prayer engendered by this rightful hate I accepted Him as absolute Truth, as verily God Almighty. In this prayer it was given to me to go beyond the 'temporal things which are seen' to 'things not seen which are eternal' [cf. II Cor. 4:18].

'In the world ye shall have tribulation: but be of good cheer: I have overcome the world' [John 16:33]. And experience shows us that 'all that will live godly in Christ shall suffer persecution' [II Tim. 3:12] and be in conflict with the rest of the world [cf. Matt. 5:10–12]. Further, 'A woman when she is in travail hath sorrow . . . but as soon as she is delivered of the child, she remembereth no more the anguish, for joy that a man is born into the world. And ye now therefore have sorrow: but I will see you again, and your heart shall rejoice, and your joy no man taketh from you. And in that day ye shall ask me nothing' [John 16:21–23].

Why shall we ask Him nothing?

When the Holy Spirit gives us to see Christ, as He is, through love proceeding from the Holy Spirit, it will become plain to us that He, Christ, is *all things* – in Him is fulness of Divinity and fulness of man. He is Truth in its two aspects. (1) He is primordial *Fact* of Being; (2) By His 'ethical' character He is True. True, that is, Holy; Holy, that is, Good; Good, that is, 'Light in which is no darkness at all'.

We lose heart when it is given to us to see the supra-terrestrial character of the Gospel. We would like somehow to narrow its real dimensions, to approximate it more to our fragile consti-tution, but He will in no wise consent to any adulteration of His commandments. With our repentance stretched to its utmost we begin to discern that this Revelation is final because it is all-perfect. It is accorded for ever to all tribes and peoples to the end of time.

Blessed St. Silouan wrote, 'He who does not love his enemies has not yet come to know God as He should be known.'

'But I say unto you, Love your enemies, bless them that curse you, do good to them that hate you, and pray for them which despitefully use you, and persecute you; That ye may be the children of your Father which is in heaven . . . Be ye perfect, even as He is perfect' [cf. Matt. 5:44–45, 48]. To repeat, when the Holy Spirit communicates Christ's love to us – 'Love your enemies' – the mind-spirit delights in the Truth of this love. As certainly as our body can feel strong, or be aware of the warmth of the sun, so, directly with all our being, we *know* that this love is eternal Truth. Man then *knows* that he 'is passed from death unto life' [John 5:24].

This marvellous feeling of the coming of God within us is attended by complete concord between mind and heart. The Divine harmony of this spiritual *state* means rejoicing for the heart and light for the mind. The entire man – mind (spirit), heart and even the body – experiences the 'peace of God, which passeth all understanding' [Phil. 4:7]. Love and Light and peace come down from the All-Highest [cf. James 1:17].

It is a great good to 'know' the True God and 'know' Him with knowledge 'which shall not be taken away' [Luke 10:42]. All this is given to the world through the Incarnate Son of the Father, Christ Jesus, and the thankful soul is drawn to Him, Who of yore revealed Himself on Sinai with the Name 'I AM', and reiterated it more than once in His appearance in our flesh. He communicated to us this 'more abundant life' [cf. John 10:10]. And the soul knows what is happening to her and declares:

NOW, O MY CHRIST, IN THEE AND BY THEE . . .
Now – *I* am.

To him to whom it is given by faith in Christ-God if only partially to enter into the eternal stream of His prayer in Gethsemane and then, again only partially, arise and go forth to His deathless Golgotha, in some incontrovertible manner is revealed the 'great mystery of godliness: God manifest in the flesh, justified in the Spirit, seen of angels . . .' [I Tim. 3:16]. From that moment the believer does not 'know' Him by the flesh, that is, as a natural man, but as the Omnipresent Almighty come into the world to save sinners [cf. II Cor. 5:16; I Tim. 1:15].

Thus he that genuinely 'believeth on the Son of God hath the witness in himself' [I John 5:10].

Epilogue

At the beginning of this century the word of the Lord came to St. Silouan, 'Keep thy mind in hell, and despair not'. I never learned the exact date – it could have been in 1906. Just before then, perhaps a year earlier, in 1905, the world became acquainted with Einstein's Equation: $E = mc^2$. This equation laid the foundation for contemporary science and technology. It opened up colossal sources of vital energy yet, on the other hand, it was the first step in the preparation of apocalyptic fire to annihilate all life on earth [cf. II Pet. 3:7; II Thess. 1:8; Heb. 10:27; Luke 21:35]. But the matchless injunction given to Silouan appears to many faithful believers like a guiding light to the 'kingdom which cannot be moved' [Heb. 12:28]. In spirit it is akin to the teaching of the Egyptian fathers of old – Antony, Macarius, Sisoe, Pimen the Great; and others, less well known but no less great, maybe, in their living.

Christ's prescript – 'and despair not' through St. Silouan is directed to our times which are noted for the extraordinarily black despair that envelops the whole universe. People of our day, often against their will, become moral participants in endless local and even world-wide fratricide. As such – that is, as impenitent moral accomplices – they naturally lose the grace of the Holy Spirit and are no longer able to believe in their immortality through resurrection. Nor do they even seek to. In this self-condemnation to evanescence lies the spiritual essence of *despair*.

Silouan besought the Lord to teach him how to overcome deadly pride, the source of all evils. And Christ gave him the precept in which we can discern an analogy with *what He did*

Himself when He was in our flesh. Read the Gospel carefully and you will notice how Jesus, when praised for the miracles He had performed, thought of what lay before Him: the unjust trial before Caiphas and the Sanhedrin [cf. John 11:49–50; Matt. 26:57, 59], the infamous conduct of the Roman soldiers, His crucifixion and death on the cross; burial . . . but also the *resurrection* that would follow it all. There is a like sequence with St. Silouan: 'I started to do as the Lord bade me, and my mind was cleansed, and the Spirit bore witness of *salvation*' – that is, of the transition 'from death to life'.

'Verily, verily, I say unto you, He that heareth my word, and believeth on him that sent me, *hath everlasting life*, and shall not come into condemnation; but is (already) *passed from death unto life.*'

'Verily, verily, I say unto you, The hour is coming, and now is, when the dead shall hear the voice of the Son of God: and they that hear *shall live*' [John 5:24–25]. [Luke 21:28]

'And when these things begin to come to pass, then look up and lift up your heads; for your redemption draweth nigh.'

AMEN